Crossing Boundaries

Edited by
Geeti Sen

Orient Longman

ORIENT LONGMAN LIMITED

Registered Office
3-6-272, Himayatnagar Hyderabad 500 029 (A.P.) India

Other Offices
Bangalore/Bhopal/Bhubaneshwar/Calcutta
Chennai/Ernakulam/Guwahati/Hyderabad
Jaipur/Lucknow/Mumbai/New Delhi/Patna

By arrangement with India International Centre
New Delhi

First published in book form 1997

ISBN 81 250 1341 5

Typeset by
S.J.I. Services, New Delhi 110 024

Printed at
Pauls Press, New Delhi 110 020

Published by
Orient Longman Limited
1/24, Asaf Ali Road, New Delhi 110 002

ACKNOWLEDGEMENTS

In assembling a volume of this nature with contributions from three countries, we have received help from many who facilitated the process—although their names may not appear among the list of authors.

At the preparatory stage two advisory meetings were called at the IIC by Dr. Karan Singh and attended by Dr. Kapila Vatsyayan and distinguished experts from different disciplines, who asked for an update on cultural contacts between India, Pakistan and Bangladesh. Shri N.N. Vohra's support and enthusiasm on this project gave us the confidence to persist in our endeavours. In Delhi, Professor Muchkund Dubey, Mushirul Hasan, Sukrita Paul, Sumanta Banerjee and Rakshat Puri gave generously of their time in discussions, and in helping us locate authors.

Both the Indian High Commissions at Dhaka and at Islamabad have helped facilitate my visits to Dhaka and Lahore, and in maintaining contact with our authors in these respective countries. So also, the enthusiasm of Mr. Atiqur Rahman of the Bangladesh High Commission has opened up new channels of communication.

I am particularly grateful for the conversations held in Dhaka with Professor Anisuzzaman and in Lahore with I.A. Rehman, helping me gain insight into complex issues of cultural and political identity. Stimulating discussions were held with Syed Shamsul Haq, Kabir Chowdhury, Meghna Guhathakurta, and Dr. and Mrs. Enamul Haque. Mr. Noorul Quaider spared time to provide insights into the formative period of the Bangladesh government in exile, and has graciously provided pictures from his personal collection of works by Shahabuddin and Qamrul Hasan.

To my new-found friends, Siraj al Haque, Mrs. Haque, and Ghulam Moustafa who showed me around Chittagong, and to Ajaz Anwar, F.S. Aijazuddin and Shehnaz Aijazuddin, Samina Ahmed, Salima Hashmi and Madeeha Gauhar who enriched my experience of Lahore, I shall always remain indebted for their warmth and hospitality. These new contacts bear the promise of human friendship and the sharing of a sensibility which cuts across all boundaries—as indeed, has been attempted in this volume.

In designing this volume, we are grateful to Suhas Nimbalkar for his commitment and sensitivity. We cannot forget to thank Sujit Mukherjee for his encouragement in helping us to contact Orient Longman. Our negotiations with Shri Rameshwar Rao and Ms. Priya Adarkar of Orient Longman have provided us with warm support in this co-publishing venture. Now this volume of outstanding essays will be available not only as a journal but as a book that reaches out to interested readers.

CONTENTS

III. STREAMS IN MUSIC

IV. NATIONALISM AND ACTIVISM

V. IDENTITY: SELF AND THE OTHER

INTERVIEW

On Language and Identity

> The idea that the people across the border are a part of us can never be erased from our memories....
>
> Krishna Sobti, interview.

For a generation which grew up in the 1930s and '40s, the great schism of 1947 has remained a traumatic experience. Crossing the border becomes a metaphor for recalling this period in time, in writing, theatre and film. Thus Intizar Husain writes for the first time in this volume, his own journey across the border from Meerut to Lahore—a journey which was undertaken by thousands, in both directions. He confesses at the outset: "My personal memories are fading into collective memory, handed down to us from time immemorial..."

It is curious that in each of these memoirs assembled in the first section, the personal note is subsumed in a collective voice—of fear, anguish, hope and aspirations for the future. This becomes equally true of Zohra Segal's description of the heydeys of the IPTA movement and Prithvi Theatre, when the actors were inspired by a new agenda, an ideology of nation-building in the '50s. There were other cohesive forces in culture, such as the Progressive Writers' Movement and the Progressive Artists in Bombay. Their collective experience stood in strength, above individual voices from different communities—as a fleeting moment of unity, of true secular spirit in India.

In the fiftieth year of Independence we celebrate the occasion not by recovering India's achievements but by crossing the borders—to find common cause and shared experiences in identity with Pakistan and Bangladesh.

The Jama Masjid, Lahore

An ancient milestone lies embedded in one of Lahore's busiest thoroughfares, ignored by pedestrians but making it's point: "Delhi 311 Miles". My self-appointed guide stops the car to point this out and exclaims, "and just imagine—Amritsar is only 35 miles! We speak the same language, Punjabi. And now you have a Prime Minister who comes from Jhelum—from our side of Punjab. This is a good sign; relations will surely improve..."

The good sign perhaps is the sharing of identities. If Sardar Khushwant Singh could appropriate the Quaid-e-Azam as a former "son of India before he became the father of Pakistan", now the Pakistanis can lay claim to our Prime Minister as a son of their soil. Perhaps, the air of condescension can evaporate somewhat in this new climate, and we can build upon new futures where India forfeits its role as the big brother... But we have a long way to go before we can become once again, in vernacular English, "same to same".

The architectural ambience of Delhi and Lahore certainly evokes a remarkable correspondence—as Ajaz Anwar suggests,

'he Museum, Mall Road, Lahore

they were planned by the Mughals as twin cities, with the two Jama Masjids towering over the fort and the old city. Visiting the tombs of Jahangir and Nur Jahan on a rainy day, we cross over the village of Shahdara into open countryside. I am reminded instantly of Humayun's tomb, flushed a deep red against giant green plane trees where peacocks dance. They are repairing the tomb, and I am informed that the red sandstone has been brought here all the way from quarries in Rajasthan—as indeed, they had been brought from Agra some 360 years ago.

Even today, the buildings along the Mall are reminiscent of Delhi, and their names possess a resonance which surprises me: Dayal Singh Library, Patel Park, Macleod Road, Lawrence Road. Here is Charing Cross with its imperial facades like Connaught Place, Baba Dingha Singh building with its clock tower, Kirpa Ram Stores "who opted for Pakistan but left in the 1960s." Next to the College of Art is situated the Museum, exhibiting one of the masterpieces of world art: the fasting Buddha from Gandhara. Lakshmi Building, a celebrated centre for the distribution of films

Lakshmi Building, Lahore

is crowded with hoardings in Urdu. I learn that Indian films are banned in Pakistan—which does not of course deter the making of films with the same names like *Bandit Queen!*

Clearly, a crisis is brewing. A Film Convention is held at the Pearl Intercontinental, called by the Minister for Information and Culture. We find ourselves in the audience, five women out of perhaps sixty film makers, distributors, script-writers and technicians. In the late afternoon the question turns to the booming industry of Hindi films in video casettes. Can video parlours be banned ? An objection about these films is raised by a gentleman in a black sherwani, about "certain parts of the body" being exposed. A recommendation is moved about setting up a New Central Board of Film Censors. This reminds me of the interview with Shyam Benegal and a spicy comment by Veena Das on the "territorialization of the human body". Evidently censorship plays a similar role on both sides of the border while the real issues of violence and criminalization are largely ignored.

What of other cultural activities ? The Arts Council is housed in a magnificent new redbrick complex called Alhamra; but I learn there is no repertory theatre, no formal training for television or cinema, and few plays written for performance. Given this situation, we can only marvel at the high quality and professionalism of the television industry in Pakistan, and the initiatives taken in alternative theatre. Dance was never encouraged in the days of General Zia. Kathak dance is performed today by visiting artistes such as Naheed Siddiqui, compelled to retreat to London but now regaled in the newspapers. What will remain of the traditions of great Sufi singers like Fateh Ali Khan and Nusrat Ali?

In the old city we have a rendezvous with Iqbal Husain, who runs a restaurant with the surprising name of Cuckoo's. Iqbal is an artist whose first show was rejected in 1984; but he draws attention because he paints women from the kotha in Hiramandi—from his own community. High up on the walls are suspended large canvases of Ayesha, Lubra, Hanni, each exuding their persona. He comments: "My work is not like that of Toulouse Lautrec in Paris. I see these women not from the outside as he did, but as my own community—we speak to each other in one language, Punjabi."

Language determines the specific identity of a people. It defines their culture, their sensibility, their perception of the world. On the same evening I meet the intelligentsia at a party. Conversations are in English, occasionally branching off into Urdu but never into Punjabi. I begin to sense that great divide between high society and the rest of the world. At schools Urdu is the language medium, not Punjabi. The editor of the *Friday Times* confirms this with a devastating comment. "In the quest of that dream which is Pakistan, most of us speak to our children in Urdu—not in Punjabi, which is our mother tongue."

To my mind, this raises an interesting dilemma. Ironical as it may seem, when Pakistan was formed there were no native speakers of the Urdu language. There were peoples of five spoken languages which united into Pakistan: the Punjabis, the Sindhis, the Baluchis, the Poshtus, the Bengalis. Those who spoke Urdu were those who crossed over the border from India, mainly from Uttar Pradesh, Bihar and Madhya Pradesh. These people are described, in Lahore at least, as the Muhajirs. The term is not derogatory since it derives from "Haj", those who travel. Yet they are singled out with the implications of the traveller, the "outsider". Krishna Sobti mentions in her interview that "the Punjabis are supreme in Pakistan to this day... They see themselves as the only true Muslims."

Essays in the second section deal with the emergence of new writings, born of the soil in Pakistan and Bangladesh. Sukrita Paul refers to the debate among intellectuals in Pakistan to define Pakistani cultural identity, with reference to the roots of the Urdu language. Can the "laughing ghost" of India be exorcised? Does Intizar Husain, the gifted Urdu writer, retain a sense of alienation? Living in Lahore, he mentions in an interview that he sees himself with one foot in Ayodhya and the other in Karbala. While contributing richly to the national language, is he still searching for his identity?

The ideology of countries in our subcontinent is grounded on language. National identity is derived from language. A case is made which pleads that India is equally culpable for the same blunder. "While promoters of sanitized Hindi have the upperhand in India, Urdu, which is neglected here, has become the official language of Pakistan—although there it is a language of the minority." The confirmation of Urdu as the state language of

Election hoarding, Lahore

Pakistan, as against the plea for Bengali, is recorded in the statement made by Liaquat Ali Khan in 1951—linking the issue of language to religion. "Pakistan is a Muslim State and it must have as its lingua franca the language of the Muslim nation... It is necessary for a nation to have one language, and that language can be Urdu and no other language."

Fissures erupted like molten lava in new writings and Bengali poetry that fought against the imposition of this tyranny. Subhash Mukhopadhyay recalls that when Qazi Nazrul Islam came home from fighting in the first world war, he "assumed a new role to prove that the pen was mightier than the sword". Indeed it was: language became the pivotal point upon which the identity of the people of Bangladesh crystallised. Kabir Chowdhury's review suggests the transformation of poetry over fifty years as it became both the cause and inspiration for national liberation. The Language Movement of 1952 and Martyr's Day of 21st February acquired symbolic connotations which are relived to this day.

Recurrent images of the mother, the blood-drenched earth and the blood-red palash tree in bloom aroused the passion of a country aflamed. Language is personified as a lover in Shamsur Rahman's tender poem, "My Sad Suffering Alphabet". On the other hand, Syed Shamsul Haq says it subtly with the statement,

> My poems are my limbs.
> I grope and perceive
> time and the world with these limbs.

The overwhelming response was not in poetry alone but in a great surge of drawings and paintings which record the resistance of the country in the war of liberation. These include the spirited drawings of great masters such as Zainul Abedin and Qamrul Hasan, and the volatile paintings of a younger generation including Shahabuddin who became a freedom fighter in 1971, and whose explosive energy appears on the cover page.

Bengal's culture, according to its own historians, had always been composite, cutting across social and religious differences. You perceive this resistance to orthodoxy from earliest times in popular culture: in the early terracottas from Chandraketugarh, and much later in the songs of the Bauls who drew inspiration

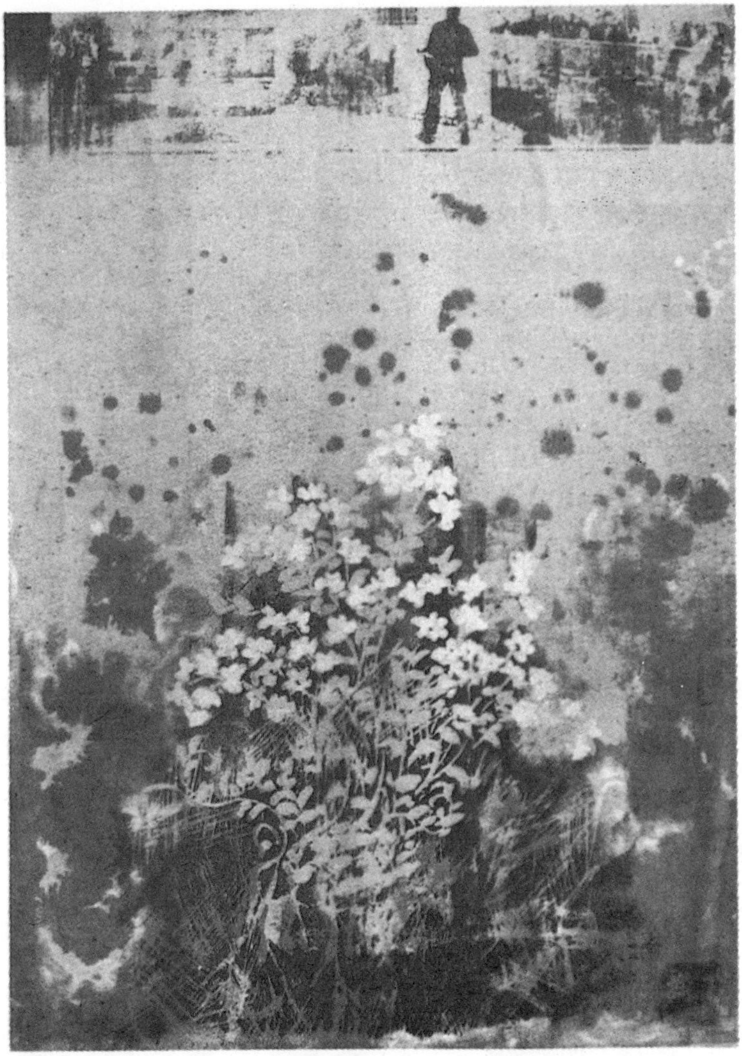

Lithograph by Abdus Sattar, Dhaka, 1971

from three different streams of religion: Sufism, Hindu Vaishnavism and the Sahaja path of Buddhism. The most recent evidence for this syncretism is seen in the novel combination of Hindu-Muslim names: Ananda Iqbal, Arani Haq, Sucheta Zaman are children of the new generation in a liberated Bangladesh.

The resistance, to absolute monotheism derives partially from Bengal's tradition. More immediate factors however, such as the draining of East Bengal's resources, feudal attitudes, and the nullifying of the democratic elections led to the events of 1971. No one can deny that the war of liberation was initiated as a grass-roots movement—as a collective voice of the people, and at their great cost and experience. Yet that Utopian dream of their "Sonar Bangla" still awaits the promise of redemption and realization.

As explored in one of our essays, the history of that war has different readings today, determined largely by the politics which followed. In 1972 the Constitution of the newly-founded Bangladesh declared secularism as one of the four fundamental principles of state policy; it also prohibited the use of religion for political purpose. In April 1977 the Constitution was amended by General Ziaur Rahman. In his seminal book *Identity, Religion and Recent History* Anisuzzaman is perhaps correct in raising the question, "Did the Bangladesh society go through a kind of change that necessitated or facilitated the move from secularism to having a state religion?" He affirms that while religious tendencies appear to have increased, there was never any clear

Freedom Fighter by Shahabuddin, Dhaka, 1996

mandate from the people but rather from the leaders, to revoke the original state policy of Bangladesh.

In one of his astute statements Gandhiji had said, "those who believe that politics has nothing to do with religion understand neither politics nor religion". Sadly, this is being proved truer by the day, and not in India alone. Ironically, religion and politics are sought to be combined to create a new identity in the entire subcontinent—this "identity" being radically different from that which given to us by language and culture.

The resistance to this new identity has come from quarters least expected—in all three countries. To resist the growing fundamentalism and state-controlled media, theatre has engaged in the wider political movement to impart alternative messages. In the absence of sites for performance, theatre took to the streets in Bangladesh "where theatre workers continue to question and challenge orthodoxy and the establishment". In Pakistan Ajoka forms part of the alternative theatre movement where the official

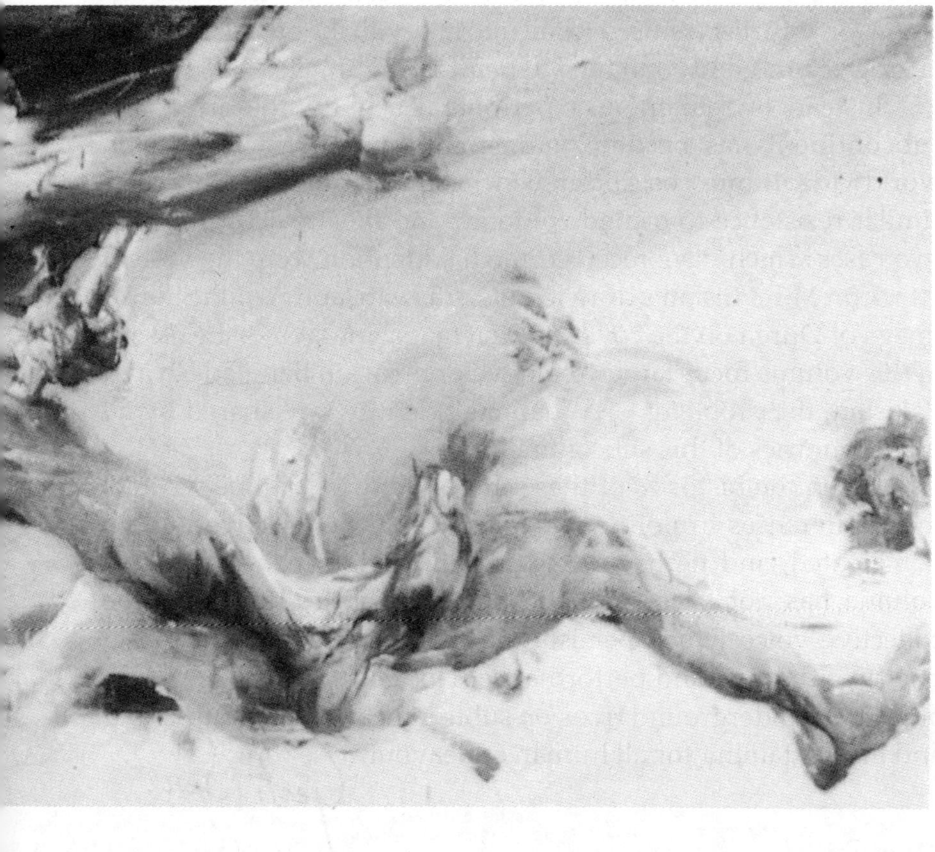

one-language policy has been resisted by introducing the dialogue in the raw local dialect of Seraiki Punjabi. If scripted plays are not available, they are devised, based on a newspaper report of a case where a wife and a buffalo were exchanged by mutual agreement by two farmers—as being of the same value ?

Essays by Meghna Guhathakurta, Madeeha Gauhar and Salima Hashmi would suggest that the voices of women, placed in the domain of the silenced, have now broken free to give powerful expression. No one can deny the controversial but substantial role played by a single woman, Taslima Nasreen in Bangladesh, in revoking the traditional attitudes towards women—by writing on topics "declared taboo by a political culture steeped in self-censorship."

Salima Hashmi comments on the paradox about "the invisibility and the visibility, and the potency of women (which) became most acute during the Zia years". Art, considered for so long as the least dangerous of occupations and relegated to women (at the Punjab University, Lahore) turned to become the most subversive. Women artists refused to fall into line with the offical art policy of Zia's regime, and continued to paint the figurative.

Instead of remaining a peripheral activity, the art of the subcontinent has become mainstream and invites attention worldwide. It must be said in conclusion that in India there is a similar resistance to orthodoxy in art and theatre activism—the two cases which have received media attention were the violent attack on M.F. Husain's drawing of Saraswati, and Arpita Singh's image of Durga on the cover of *Desh* magazine. While the essays in this volume focus largely on developments in Bangladesh and Pakistan, the problems of a "national identity" are shared by all three countries of this subcontinent.

When the histories of these three countries will be written, their differences in polity and religion and perspective will be demarcated, and perhaps exaggerated. Yet our concern in this volume has not been with the official histories, but with the collective voice which persists—in the sharing of language, in poetry and music and performance. This cultural heritage flows on, like an underground river, on subterranean levels, nourishing and life-sustaining for all human endeavour.

Geeti Sen.

Basant, *water colour by Ajaz Anwar, Lahore*

I
REMEMBRANCE OF TIME PAST

INTIZAR HUSAIN

Journey Across the Border

As I recall my journey from Meerut to Lahore fifty years back, I feel like I am travelling through history. My personal memories are fading into collective memory, handed down to us from time immemorial. I find myself travelling with some ancient caravan—forming a long row of slow moving bullock carts loaded with travellers, along with their bag and baggage bound for an unknown destination, and fearing with palpitating hearts an attack at every step. It was an unending dark night, and we, divided between hope and despondency, were passing through East Punjab. The Special carrying us was in no way different from the ancient caravans of bullock carts moving at a snail's pace. Sandwiched between travellers, sitting motionless and dumb in the pitch darkness of the compartment, I felt like I was travelling in the company of ghosts.

After long hours of moving at a snail's pace the train gained speed in a sporadic way. The mere fact of speed revived hopes in us. We could now hope to get out of this dark desolate plane, which with its hushed darkness was sending signals to us of something ominous that might happen any moment. Now we were happy and once again talking in an optimistic mood. But, lo, the train again slowed down and soon halted with a jerk. There was a sudden hush. It appeared as if we had even stopped breathing. The danger of attack lurking in our minds that had been subdued for a few moments once again loomed large. We were in a state of suspense.

With our palpitating hearts we were waiting for what seemed to us the inevitable; but what seemed to us inevitable had got stuck somewhere in the way. The moments of suspense prolonged; but the effectiveness of the moments of suspense lies in their brevity. When prolonged they begin losing their effectiveness. Something has to happen as a diversion.... And, lo, the parrot sitting so quiet in a cage by the side of a burqa-clad woman fluttered to life all of a sudden and began screaming in a shrill voice. The hushed travellers were taken aback.

"Whose parrot is this?" asked an angry voice in a subdued tone.

The burqa-clad woman tried her best to placate the bird. But the bird was in no mood to keep quiet. It went on shrieking in its shrill voice.

Saleem Ahmad, who was soon to shine in Pakistan as a poet and a critic, was sitting by me. Encouraged by the situation he began cutting jokes at the cost of the parrot. Immediately the shrieking parrot receded in the background. Angry voices were now directed against Saleem and against our whole group, who were laughing in response to the jokes.

"Young man", said an old man sitting near us, "this is not the time for cutting jokes. This is the time for asking forgiveness from God, the merciful for our sins."

"Saleem", I whispered to him "be quiet and don't try to pose as a brave man."

Just at that moment a young man sitting by the window tried to pose as a brave man in a different way. Seeing a Railway Officer passing by he asked "Guard Saab, when are we going to be attacked?"

"Don't talk rubbish and be quiet," came the angry reply from the guard.

"Yes, be quiet," chimed in the old man sitting by me "Better remember God, the merciful. Not the guard, but God, the All-Knower knows about things to come."

Thanks to the Burqa-walli's parrot, we were no more in the grip of tense moments. We were now giving vent to our anger, our suspicions and our fears in a normal way. The young man sitting by the window had a word of justification for what he had said to the guard, "I just wanted to tell him that we are not fools. We know that you are in the know of things, that you have stopped the train in the thick of the jungle with a purpose."

But at that very moment the train made a start and began moving at a slow pace. The fears and suspicions aroused by the comments of the young man were allayed by the growing speed.

Such was our journey from Meerut to Lahore. The Special moved in a normal way upto Saharanpur. After that we felt we were entering a danger zone. The rest of the journey was an unending series of tense moments, arousing in us fears and suspicions of all kinds. It was the month of October. The bloody period when the Specials moving from one country to the other were being attacked was almost over. Ours was supposed to be the first to reach its destination safe and sound.

Lahore was now a calm city. I stayed as a guest with my respected friend and distinguished critic, Mohammad Hasan Askari, who shared accomodation with his cousin, living in an allotted house in Krishn Nagar which was originally a Hindu locality. Krishn Nagar appeared to me a strange place. Most of the houses had been occupied by the immigrants, each of them accommodating more families than they had the capacity to accommodate. But strangely enough these houses humming with the noise of the families living in them paled into insignificance as compared to the houses standing empty amidst them. These vacant houses, after being deprived of the human warmth they once possessed, gave a sad look in daytime and turned into ghosts in the darkness of the night.

I still remember the three-storeyed house standing vacant on the corner of the lane where I was living. The vacant house with its windows agape still looms large in my mind. Perhaps while leaving, the residents of the house had no time to shut the windows of the upper storey. In dark windy nights as I passed by the house the violent flappings of the shutters high on my head sent a wave of fear through me.

Within a month I got a job. The famous weekly 'Nizam' of Bombay had just shifted to Lahore. I joined the weekly as its Editor. After a week or so, as I was sitting in my office on the fourth floor of Habib Bank building, a peon of the Bank peeped in my room and asked "Are you Intizar Husain?"

"Yes, what do you want?"

"Some friend of yours has come from Delhi. He failed to locate your home."

"My friend from Delhi?" I was a bit confused. "Did he give his name? Where is he?."

"No, he did not give me his name. He is standing below at the gate of the Bank."

I peeped from the window below and was wonder-struck. My friend Reoti Saran Sharma was standing below. I did not believe my eyes! Hastily I went downstairs. And now I had to believe my eyes. Reoti with a bag on his shoulder was standing before me.

I welcomed him with a volley of questions. "How did you manage to come here? Had anything unpleasant happened in the way.... And why did you not inform me? Foolish fellow, you should have waited for times to become normal!"

"How could I wait?" he replied briefly "You did not care to see me when leaving for Pakistan. I had to come to see you!"

The next moment, we were normal. I introduced him to the manager and other members of the staff, and their pleasant reaction assured me that we in Lahore were now living in normal times.

The only thing that now worried me was Reoti's vegetarian diet. I communicated my worry to Askari Sahib, who in turn communicated my worry to his mother. She promptly said, "Nothing to be worried about. Your friend's friend will be provided with a vegetarian dish, provided he has no objection to taking food cooked by a Muslim woman."

Reoti remained with me for a week or so and enjoyed his time in Lahore. He left after getting a promise from me to pay a visit to Delhi.

To get a permit for a visit to India was not an easy job in those days. After untiring efforts of more than one year, I got that permit which allowed only a week's visit, to my town Hapur and to Delhi.

I went straight to Hapur and stayed with my sister who was still living there, for two days. Then I expressed my intention to go to Delhi.

"Have you gone mad? Why are you going there?"

"To see Reoti".

"Why can't he come here? Has he got his feet plastered with the paste of *mehndi?"*

"But I want to see Sarla. If I don't go there and congratulate her on her marriage, she will mind it."

In fact, I had left India at a time when Reoti stood in need of my moral support as he was in the thick of a battle against the Brahmanism of his father. Sarla Devi, whose brother Krishan Chander we had adored as a great short story writer, belonged to a Kayasth family. Reoti however won the battle in my absence, and married her.

My sister saw no way out but to allow me to go to Delhi. At the eve of my departure she tied "Imam Zamin" round my arm and asked me to kiss the Holy Quran. In the end she gave me a piece of advice: "As you enter Delhi, recite 'Nad-ai-Ali' five times."

I readily promised her to do so. 'Nad-ai-Ali' is a kind of appeal from a devotee in trouble to Hazrat Ali to come to his rescue.

As the train entered the bridge on the Jamuna river, all the travellers in my compartment demonstrated their devotion to the river by throwing coins in it. I too did not lag behind. I took out a Pakistani coin from my pocket and threw it in the flowing water. This was a Pakistani's homage to Jamuna nadi. Immediately after that I began reciting 'Nad-ai-Ali' as advised by my sister.

Alighting from the train I went to Lodi Colony where Reoti was now living in a flat. Seeing three ladies sitting in the verandah, I went to them and sought their guidance in my search for Reoti's flat. They examined me from head to foot with suspicious eyes. I felt unnerved. And now I realised my folly. I should not have come here in my sherwani. One of the ladies reluctantly told me, "Go upstairs. On the second floor is the flat for which you are searching."

So I found the house. Reoti had not yet returned from the office; but Sarla was there to welcome me warmly in her house. But the next moment there was a knock at the door. Sarla went to the door and I heard her saying, "Don't worry, he is a friend of Reotiji and a brother to me." She paused and perhaps in reply to another query, said, "Yes, he is a Muslim, but you need not worry about it. Thank you very much." And she slammed the door.

Next day was Janamashtami. Sarla had chalked out a programme to go to Janamashtami Mela at Birla Mandir. But we, Reoti and I, got ourselves embroiled in a heated discussion on the Indo- Pakistan situation. In those disturbed times this subject was unavoidable. So much had happened and was happening around us that even friends could hardly avoid being embroiled in a bitter discussion about it. We might well be in a mood for gossip, but the subject somehow cropped up in the course of conversation. Sarla appeared very upset as if she was sensing the dangerous germs of an Indo-Pak war in our discussion. Abruptly she intruded and said, "Don't you remember we have a programme to go to Janamashtami Mela?"

"Sorry for causing delay in your programme," I apologized.

"What do you mean by 'your programme'? You have to accompany us."

"But I am a Muslim."

"Who denies your being a Muslim? But this evening, you will have to part with your dear sherwani."

She hastily went to the room and returned with a pant and a shirt. "Here is the dress for this evening. Make haste! We are already late." In those days the sherwani was my favourite dress. But Sarla was right. The occasion demanded a change of dress.

For three days I remained in Delhi and enjoyed the hospitality of Sarla. On the fourth day I hastily went back to Hapur where my sister was constantly praying to God for my safe return from Delhi. She saw me return alive and thanked God. The next day, having failed to get an extension of my permit, I left for Pakistan.

Thanks to the trials of a visa to India, it took more than thirty years to make a second visit to that house in Delhi. In the meantime, a new generation had cropped up in the house. Two sons were born, brought up and married, and were in turn fathers to children. So I was received in a house humming with new life. Only Sarla was not there to welcome me. She had migrated to the next world, for which no visa is needed.

NIRMAL SEN GUPTA

The First Days of Pakistan*

I

Sri Prakash (the first Indian High Commissioner in Pakistan) was an aristocrat from the United Provinces of those days (Uttar Pradesh today)—rich, plain-speaking and yet genial. There was therefore no dearth of friends. He was very friendly with the I.G. (Inspector General) of Police of Pakistan. ...The I.G. had a motor launch. He used to move around in his launch both on official beat and when off-duty. One day, he invited Sri Prakash for a trip on his launch to Sandspit on the sea-shore. It was quite a coincidence! I was also visiting the spot the same day. The I.G.'s launch overtook ours. Sri Prakash was sitting in it. Even from a distance of a mile, we could make him out from his spotlessly white dress and Gandhi cap.

Suddenly from the opposite side we spotted a motor launch coming in our direction. It was coming from Sandspit packed with young boys. They appeared to be students.

I waited with bated breath... I noticed that the boys were pointing out at him (Sri Prakash), and all of them were crowding on the deck to look at him. What were they planning to do? I hoped they were not up to some mischief... Those were the days when the Indian government was planning to march into Hyderabad. The Razakars there were beating their war-drums, and the Indian government was not silent either. In Kashmir, there was already a war going on between Pakistani and Indian troops.

The extremist papers of Pakistan—which were widely read—were spitting poison against India everyday. ...Besides, from the provocative talks in streets, tea-shops, drawing room

---

*Excerpted from Nirmal Sengupta's memoirs, entitled in Bengali *Prothom Diner Pakistan*, published in 1994.
Translated by Sumanta Banerjee

discussions, it was evident that the enemy was India. These boys were surely reading these papers. The discussions must be fuelling their anger (against India).

The boys' launch meanwhile had come closer to the I.G.'s launch. The I.G. was standing straight as a ramrod. It was almost like a 'war alert'; he was preparing to face any situation.

All of a sudden, the boys shouted—"Sri Prakash Zindabad!"

Zindabad? Imagine—these young boys were wishing long life to the representative of India, which was Pakistan's enemy! Many of them could be joining the army tomorrow, or aid (their government's) war plans in some way or other. Yet, here they were wishing long life to the representative of India. Could anyone in India believe this?

But it all happened before my eyes. I was not dreaming. I was fully awake, all my senses taut in apprehension of something untoward happening. Yet, there was no hypocrisy, no jeering laughter in the voices of these young boys. It was a mood of fervent amiability that inspired them.

Sri Prakash smiled and raised his hands to acknowledge their greetings. The boys shouted in happy response and went past us.

I realised that the greetings of these boys were not meant for India; but their personal welcome to this representative from India. They had come to know that ever since Sri Prakash had come to Pakistan, he had been trying to establish friendly relations with Pakistan. This had been not only through his attempt to reopen the Jodhpur railway line—the link between Karachi and Delhi—and increase trade with Pakistan, but also by his personal behaviour which demonstrated that he bore no ill-feeling (against Pakistanis). Why, only the other day, on the occasion of 'Bhai-duj' (the Hindu ceremony of marking the forehead of brothers by sisters with sandalwood paste and offering of gifts), early in the morning he went to the house of Shaista Sughra Ikramullah, the sister of (Hussain Shaheed) Suhrawardy, and presented her with a beautiful 'sari' .... Begum Ikramullah— the sister of Shaheed Suhrawardy, the architect of the 1946 Direct Action—was at first flabbergasted, and then overwhelmed; she took Sri Prakash by his hands and led him into the house.

Here is a fantastic woman! She is irrepressibly vivacious! A dyed-in-the wool Pakistani! And yet, she is equally determined to fight for her own tradition and culture. Her relations with the wife of the Prime Minister, Begum Liaquat Ali Khan are not quite warm. Begum Liaquat says that the 'sari' is a product of India and has no use in Pakistan. Pakistan women (according to her) should wear 'gharara'...

Shaista is totally opposed to this. Why should she give up the 'sari'?—she asks. She will never stop wearing it. She wants to move around proudly, to strike all with wonder, and hypnotize the onlookers with her magic power to choose 'saris' and her enchanting dexterity in wearing them. Shaista's voice, her rich vocabulary and her biting debating skills were nurtured and honed in Bengal, Calcutta. Before her therefore, Begum Liaquat could not be anything else but just a sitting duck!

Soon after the Sandspit incident, I paid a visit to Sri Prakash. There was a standing invitation from him—anyone visiting him at 4.00 p.m. in his sitting room could join him for tea and talks. When I dropped in that day, Sri Prakash in his usual affable, but loud voice, addressed me: "My dear chap! There's someone here who is importunately requesting me to send you back to India. He says that you are a Communist!" He then burst out into laughter, and said: "I told him—he may be. But then, he is an Indian Communist, not a Russian one. He hasn't done any harm to India. Why should I then send him back?"

II

From Delhi arrived Mridula Sarabhai. Among many of the tasks she chose, one was to trace, and wherever possible to restore to their families, the women who were abducted (on both sides of the border during the Partition riots)....

Mridula never lived in fear of anything. She wore—not 'saris', but 'salwar' and 'kameez' made of 'khadi', and ochre-coloured. Her hair was cut short. She used to go around fearlessly in this attire in Lahore, Rawalpindi and Peshawar. A lot of people could not make out whether she was a man or a woman. Meher Chand Khanna used to joke, and renamed her as 'Maridulla Khan'—meaning, a Pathan youth.

She came to Karachi and decided to have lunch at my place... From my office, I rang up Afzal (my cook and domestic help in Karachi—originally from Poonch in Kashmir) and told him that a lady was coming for lunch and that she was a Gujarati and a vegetarian who did not touch drinks, meat or eggs....

At around 1 p.m. I picked up Mridula-ji... and arrived home. Afzal announced that food was ready. When we reached the table, even before I could say anything, Mridula had one look at the spread and said—"Why, this is all Gujarati food for me! Where did you get a Gujarati cook?" I silently nodded at Afzal, the man from Poonch. Mridula looked at him with surprise.

There was a lot of discussion during the lunch. It was at that lunch table Mridula decided to go back and suggest to Jawaharlal to sign a 'No War Pact' with Pakistan.

Coming back home in the evening, I asked Afzal whether he had earlier worked at any Gujarati household. Afzal said—No! But then, how could he have produced an authentic Gujarati meal? He told me that soon after receiving my telephone call, he had gone to one of his old acquaintances—a Bohra Muslim butler (Bohras being a Muslim community inhabiting the western part of the sub-continent, and the butler therefore being familiar with Gujarat food habits). He taught him the intricacies of Gujarati cooking—within just one hour!

III

War was continuing in Kashmir. But it was not an officially declared war. Diplomatic ties between India and Pakistan therefore were not severed.

(Indian) films continued to be shown in the cinema halls of Karachi. One day I saw an advertisement announcing the exhibition of Uday Shankar's film 'Kalpana' in one of the halls. I immediately bought a ticket. By the time I arrived, the hall was jam- packed.

The film began. There were lots of dance sequences. One of them showed a Sikh 'chimta' dance.

The Sikhs were the most hated people among the Muslim refugees who had arrived from India in Pakistan. ....There were a lot of Muslims from Punjab among the audience in the hall that day. The moment the 'chimta' dance scene began—with the rows of lungi-clad young men dancing with handkerchiefs— the Punjabi viewers broke into wild jubilation. They had not watched the Sikh dance for a long time. I wondered—where did their bitter anti-Sikh sentiments disappear ?

IV

Many years ago I saw a picture in a war museum in London. It was entitled 'The Enemy'. A battlefield. Everything is hazy, indistinct. There are only smoke and dust. Through that some people are coming forward. Who are they? Enemies? Their faces cannot be made out. Everything is obscure and shadowy. That they are also human beings like us, and have their mothers, fathers, friends, relatives, that they also have love and affection—all that has been overcast by the dust storm of the gunpowder explosion. They are just enemies. In their eyes also, we are their enemies—nothing but enemies!

I always remembered this whenever I heard outpourings of hatred against Pakistan—as if the whole of Pakistan is filled with our enemies, as if there is an impervious solid wall between 'them' and 'us' .... But, who made them enemies? Wars? Who manufactured the wars?

Shahnama *(detail) by Mohammed Imran Qureshi*

ZOHRA SEGAL

Theatre and Activism in the 1940s*

Since the early 1940s Bombay had a nucleus of talented writers who formed themselves into the Progressive Writers' Association. Its glittering stars were Khwaja Ahmed Abbas, Mulk Raj Anand, Sardar Jaffrey and Rajinder Singh Bedi. Among this group was a young journalist from Bangalore, Miss Anil de Silva, who had the brainwave of starting a people's theatre movement. The idea caught on like wildfire, and the Indian People's Theatre Association (IPTA) was born.

IPTA was a non-profit voluntary organisation whose aims were to raise artistes' voices against the injustices of the country's present rulers. Songs, poems, ballets and plays were all directed towards this goal and every artist of any significance became part of IPTA. The association drew talent like honey does bees and every branch of art was represented by the most honoured in the land.

Among the stage actors and actresses were Prithviraj Kapoor (twice nominated IPTA's president), Balraj and Damayanti Sahni, Chetan and Uma Anand, Uzra and Hamid Butt, Dina Gandhi, Habib Tanvir, Krishan Dhavan, Safdar Mir, Hima Kesarkodi, Romesh Thapar, Sarju Pandeyu, and Shaukat Kaifi. Apart from the writers mentioned earlier, IPTA's membership boasted of Krishan Chander, Ismat Chughtai, Kartar Singh Duggal, Vishvamitter Adil, Balwant Gargi and many more. Amongst the dancers were Shanti and Gul Bardhan, Narendra Sharma, Shanta Gandhi, Debendra Shankar, Sachin Shankar, Prabhat Ganguly, and the musicians included Ravi Shankar, Salil Chowdhry, Sachin Dev Burman, Sisir Sovan, Nagen Dey, Jatindranath Goloi, Abani Das Gupta and a host of others. The film world was represented by such celebrities as David, Mubarak, Shahid Lateef, Shyam,

*Excerpted from *Stages: The Art and Adventures of Zohra Segal* by Joan L. Erdman with Zohra Segal, Kali for Women, New Delhi, 1997.

Agha, Sajjan, and Khan. Poets dedicated their work to this cause, and included Harindranath Chattopadhyaya, Faiz Ahmad Faiz, Niaz Haidar, Akhtarul Iman, Miraji and Prem Dhavan. Folk singers like Binoy Roy and his sister, as well as Amar Sheikh held mass audiences spellbound with their powerful voices. In short, every artist who lived in Bombay between 1940 and 1950 was connected with IPTA in one capacity or another.

The organisation was left-oriented and, as was fashionable in those days, many members were Communists, but only the Cultural Squad was supported by the Communist Party. A central committee planned the day to day affairs of the association and nominated a president and vice president who were changed every two or three years. We all met in the evenings after our regular professional activities. Such was the zeal of IPTA's members that no one begrudged the extra hours devoted to this task. Sometimes, if we were lucky, we performed in a regular theatre but most of the time the performances took place in halls, since they were cheaper to hire. A great number of shows were held anywhere in the street or neighbourhood where an audience could be assembled. The novel idea of a theatre of this kind soon mushroomed in all the main towns of India. Calcutta's IPTA became one of the foremost—Utpal Dutt, Shambu Mitra and Tripti Mitra were outstanding examples of its acting and directing talent. Just as IPTA in Bombay had used the folklore of Marathi theatre, taking tamasha and pawada as forms of expression, so the Bengali artists employed jatra, their provincial folk theatre, as their medium.

Zohra as "the Foreign Woman" in the Prithvi Theatres' production, Deewar, *1946 (photo by Raj Kapoor)*

With India in the last stages of the freedom struggle, song and play themes were radical and left-oriented, inspiring and uniting us to action. Having joined IPTA almost as soon as I arrived in Bombay in 1945, I took an active part in these plays. In 1947, during the Interim Government when Jawaharlal Nehru was appointed vice president, some IPTA branches were harassed by government bans which censored certain plays and called for the arrest of their performers. I had recently been nominated vice president of IPTA and wrote a most foolishly presumptuous letter to Pandit Nehru, "I am writing to you as one vice president to another..." describing the harassment and requesting his mediation. Just imagine the cheek! He wrote back in a most considerate manner, saying he was not aware of the harassment and would see what could be done about it. And sure enough, the aggravation stopped after some time.

Gradually the impact of IPTA declined, perhaps because a number of its artists became popular in Indian films and were no longer inclined to slave away without monetary compensation. Or maybe quite a few of them felt the organization was influenced by the Communist Party of India and because they had different political convictions, decided to leave IPTA. Or possibly, because the country had gained freedom and the imperialists been expelled, there was no longer a rallying cause!

To my mind, the two outstanding achievements of the Indian People's Theatre Association of that period were the Cultural Squad and a film, *Dharti ke Lal* (Children of the Earth). It dealt with the Bengal Famine, and was written and directed by K.A. Abbas with a stupendous cast and technicians composed entirely of IPTA members. The Cultural Squad was a troupe of dancers and musicians, housed in very reduced circumstances in suburban Andheri, who toured all over India with a marvellous ballet called *Discovery of India*, based on Jawaharlal Nehru's book of the same name. In 1946 P.C. Joshi, secretary of the Communist Party, had asked me to take charge of this troupe but I had to refuse, as I could not simultaneously continue working with the Prithvi Theatres, my primary commitment.

From my family's point of view, what would perhaps have been ideal was for me to stay home and look after husband and children. Since we had ayahs and servants I could manage the household fairly well when I was in town, but the family was definitely disrupted when our tours began, and Kameshwar was not at all happy about it. As a result there was constant tension in the house. Considering that my career came before anything else, I gave as much as I could to the children, looked after them and had them with me wherever I could—but I did go on those tours, except when I was expecting my second child, or if I had to act or direct a dance in a film. Of course there was the other side of it: absence makes the heart grow fonder! Whenever I came back our reunions were wonderful.

For the next fourteen years, my life was in acting. I was like a sculptor taking a rough sort of clay and moulding it into a certain shape. A lot of snobbish nonsense fell off me during this period because of Prithviraj. Rather than teach anybody he related anecdotes and stories, and by his sheer presence and example one learned a way of living. With Uday Shankar I had been treated as a star, always travelling first class in India, staying in the best hotels. All this ended when I joined Prithvi Theatres. Prithviraj travelled with his company in the third class compartments engaged for the troupe. In spite of the fact that he had a first class pass as a Member of Parliament, he still travelled with us. All our food was cooked together and he ate exactly what we did. We all slept in dormitories on the floor when we were touring, either in rented accommodation just above the theatre, or a rented house. I started to appreciate these things and thought, wonderful, this is the true way of living.

Other adjustments also had to be made. I thought I had my own views about theatre and drama, though I was quite naive. From whatever concepts or theories I'd developed, I disagreed with the length of the plays, thinking some too long. Up to a point improvisation is all right, and our improvised dialogue was incorporated in the text of the play, but sometimes I felt Prithviraj himself would go on for hours and hours, so that the play stretched from two and a half to four hours! My acquired concern for punctuality did become an example for the company, though some remained immune to it.

A whole book could be written on Prithviji and his extraordinary effort in keeping his theatre alive, almost single-handed, for sixteen years. His work inspired me to write magazine articles on this period of my life and this great character who taught us not only the art of acting but a way of life. No man is perfect—if he were then he would be God—but I have yet to come across a single person with so many godly attributes, while at the same time being so human, lovable, humble, sincere and solid as a rock, physically and morally.

The seed of Prithviraj Kapoor's career was planted in a little village estate called Samundri, in the Lyallpur district of the Punjab. Young Prithvi Nath, grandson of a Hindu Pathan zamindar, enacted anecdotes from the epics Ramayana and Mahabharata inside the buffalo shed. Most of us have put up such curtains in our childhood, performing for relatives and friends, but how many have become a *Natya Ratna* (Jewel of Dramatic Arts) and received the highest title and award for an artist in India, the Padma Bhushan? The grand old Diwan Saheb was a strict disciplinarian, instilling democratic values in his kith and kin as well as in his large retinue. Each evening, little 'Prithvi' was made to polish and light the innumerable kerosene lamps of the entire estate. He would rub shoulders with the sweeper's son while playing *kabbadi* in the fields. This was the foundation of his love for the outdoors and sports, and it inculcated in the young man the belief that all men are equal in the sight of God. Later he went to college in Peshawar and Lahore, where he was always the first to thrash out any communal ill-will. His great love was the theatre and he set himself the task of learning passage after passage of Urdu and Hindi poetry in order to strengthen his memory and perfect his diction. Being slim and extremely good looking, he was usually cast in female roles, something one could never imagine, seeing him in later years when he had developed his physical powers to the utmost.

Contact with personalities such as Mrs. Nora Richards, wife of his school principal, nourished dreams of having a theatre of his own. She initiated him into the world of the great western plays, always encouraging him in his acting. This great old lady later became a recluse living entire on her own in the Kangra Valley, but she took an avid interest in all Prithviraj did and, indeed, all that transpired in the theatre in India and the world. The other person who provided timely guidance to Prithviji was his old teacher, Professor Jai Dayal of Edwards College, Peshawar, who developed him into a versatile actor, polishing the many facets of his talent and helping him choose his career. Naturally Jai Dayal was the happiest of men when Prithvi Theatres was launched and his favourite pupil received national recognition. In his book, *I go South with Prithvi Theatres*, Jai Dayal wrote, "I had hoped that an actor-manager would appear who would bring about a revolution in the minds of men by his plays and his acting, who would hold the stage to the people as a mirror in which to behold themselves, one who would have the courage to say to the people 'This is YOU!' This man was my dream. It has found fulfillment in Prithvi."

After graduating from Lahore, Prithviraj joined the films taking his young wife, Rama, with him to Calcutta. Though his acting ability was never questioned, it was an uphill struggle. Films were made in double versions, in Bengali for Bengal and in Hindi for all-India distribution. Invariably a Bengali actor replaced Prithviji for the regional version. Perhaps he was too outspoken for directors in Bengal, expressing his own ideas about the art of acting; so after making some memorable films he left Calcutta to fill an opening in the company of Grant Anderson, an English director-manager who toured with a small group of Indian actors performing the plays of Shakespeare and Shaw. This experience gave Prithviji a taste of the touring life, though many days he went without sufficient food because box office returns were low.

Having toured in several towns Grant Anderson finally disbanded the enterprise in Hyderabad, and Prithviji went to Bombay to try his luck there, starting again from scratch. He joined films as an extra and was spotted immediately for his personality by Ermeline, reigning beauty of Ranjit Talkies. She asked the owner-producer, Seth Ardeshar, to let this handsome young man play opposite her. From that moment his name caught on and he starred in one success after another, reaching the height of his popularity in *Sikander* (Alexander the Great). Although he had always loved the stage and dreamed of having a theatre of his own, he never actually planned one, being a believer in fate and saying, "Nature determines the right moment for everything." Eventually he was almost pushed into it when a writer friend came to him one day in distress. He had written a play, *Shakuntala,* in Hindustani, but the director who had commissioned it had rejected the script. Prithviji said he would produce the play himself and paid Betabji, the playwright, a thousand rupees as an advance.

So it happened that without any previous preparation Prithvi Theatres came into existence on January 15, 1944. Actors, dancers, actresses, musicians, singers, make-up men, tailors and carpenters attached themselves to this venture. Because Prithviji could never say no to anybody they were all welcomed, until he had a collection of about sixty people! Rehearsals for the play began, conducted by an assistant director since Prithviji was busy honouring his film commitments. Six months later when Uzra Mumtaz was discovered playing Zubeida in Ahmad Abbas' play of that name for the Indian People's Theatre Association, a heroine was finally cast.

The first performances of *Shakuntala* on March 9, 1945 resulted in a financial loss of nearly a lakh of rupees, but to celebrate this first show Prithviji paid a bonus of two months' salary to the entire cast and management from his own resources. All his earnings from film contracts were put into the theatre. "What next?" was the question. The existing Sanskrit plays he found too long and impractical for stage production, despite the beauty of their language and minute detailing of character. The more modern plays of Agha Hashar were mostly adaptations of western classics and had outlived their importance for contemporary theatre-goers in India. So he decided to have new plays written for his theatre.

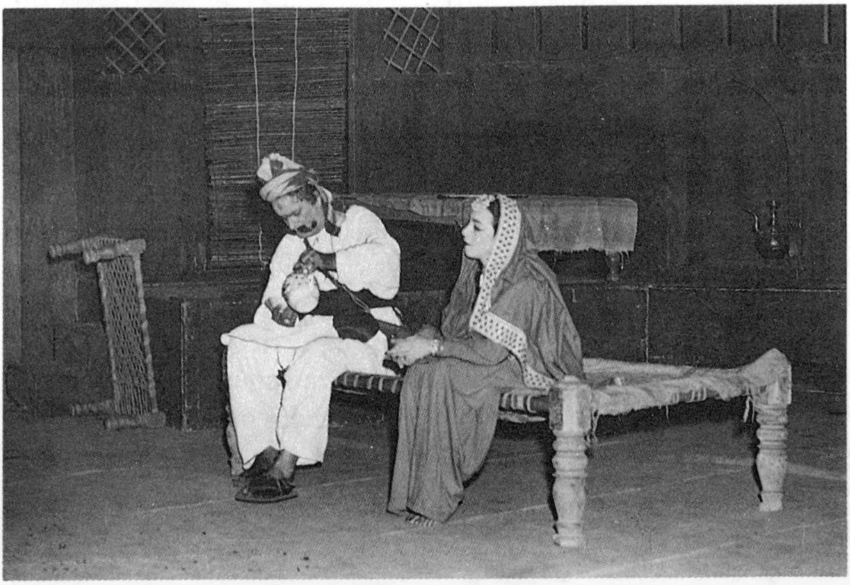

Prithviraj Kapoor and Zohra in Pathan, *as 'Sher Khan' and 'Khairunissa', Prithvi Theatres production, 1947*

Sitting with writers Prithviraj disgorged his ideas, his plots, his experiences. The plays were to be understood all over India and have essentially Indian themes. His nationalism yielded a play in the form of a warning. *Deewar* opened on August 9, 1945, and pointed to the impending partition of India. The play's allegorical theme portrayed a wall of enmity created by a foreign vamp between two brothers, who had until then lived in complete harmony and trust. She plays the emotions of one brother against the other until they can no longer bear to live in the same house. Their daily bickering reaches its culmination in the partitioning of the joint property by a wall. In the final act a united revolt of peasants and women of the country pull down the hated wall, while the two brothers realize their mistake and are happily reconciled, allowing the foreigner to stay in the capacity of friend rather than enemy. Alas, such an ending was not to be, and the wall has become a permanent fixture. The dialogue of the brothers and the vamp consisted, in part, of exact translations of the speeches of T.B. Macaulay, Gandhiji and Mohammed Ali Jinnah.

When I first saw the play, a young and talented actress, Damayanti Sahni, was playing the foreign vamp, but this attractive girl was soon snatched up by films. I was already installed as the theatre's dance director and offered myself for the part, which I played till the very end of my employment with the theatre.

Eventually the company was installed at the Royal Opera House, a cinema with a large stage. But our performances could only be given in the daytime and then too, just on holidays and weekends since the cinema was used for film shows every afternoon and evening. Gradually a work schedule evolved from our daily morning meetings, beginning at ten with an hour of singing and voice production, an hour of dance practice and an hour of classes in Hindi and Urdu. We all called Prithviji 'Papaji', which means elder brother, and when he was not filming he would take the voice production class himself. Otherwise Ram Gangoli, the music director, rehearsed songs from the various plays with the entire cast. The dance class was taken by me: half an hour each of limbering up and dance composition, either connected with the forthcoming play or simply to ensure correct deportment on stage for the cast. After this preliminary work we had actual play rehearsals for about two hours.

Before starting rehearsals each play was read to the entire cast and company technicians, inviting suggestions and criticism.

Except for *Shakuntala* all the plays were inspired by Prithviraj, partly dictated, sometimes written and mostly added to in the form of extempore dialogue by Prithviji. They were truly his creations, a product of his imagination, voicing his lament for injustice and the ills of his motherland, and showing ways of rising above it all to a glorious future. The themes of the plays were uncomplicated, the language predominantly Hindustani, a simplified combination of Hindi and Urdu understood all over north India, and their style was naturalistic, with melodrama overtaking some of the climaxes.

After an extremely successful run of *Deewar* in Bombay, we took this play and *Shakuntala* on a tour of some neighbouring towns, creating an unprecedented sensation wherever we went. Carrying along our own cooks and utensils, we stayed in rented houses, younger children and their ayahs travelling with mothers. During the holidays even school kids joined the cavalcade, so my daughter Kiran took part in almost all the plays when on tour with me. One tour followed another and as the years progressed, we collected humanity to this nucleus like a massive avalanche... poets, writers, convicts or mere observers, all were welcome. Prithviji was never able to deny anyone anything.

What I tried to bring to the troupe was the professionalism I had learned with Uday Shankar. His punctuality, the seriousness of applying our make-up, and exercising before the performance. For a theatre troup we naturally didn't have any dance or physical limbering up before the show, but Prithviraj incorporated regular dance classes in the routine so that whenever we went to a new town, we all assembled at a certain time in the morning after our baths and breakfast, and began with my dance class. Classes in Hindi and Urdu followed—an excellent addition because we had to have perfect diction and pronunciation for the Hindi—and sometimes Sanskrit (at which I was terrible). Even my Urdu was pretty bad in those days, but eventually all these things were corrected. Our language class was taught by an excellent scholar called Manik Kapoor who knew both Hindi and Urdu, as well as English. His written record of each performance as it went on gave us an account of all the plays, their chief actors and understudies, where each was performed, the number of performances and how many towns we visited in which year. This record was made into a chronology by one of the actors, Sajjan, as a gift to Prithviraj for his 60th birthday, which is how I have a copy.

PRAKASH TANDON

*The Jajmani System**

Khatris and Aroras were the two props of our Hindu society, and around them was built the structure of the service castes, both Hindu and Muslim. All the service castes were hereditary. Some of them worked on the jajmani system whereby each family was hereditarily attached to a group of jajmans—families to whom they ministered. We had a family barber, whose father before him had been our family barber, and so the barber's family and ours were indissolubly bound. Good or bad we could not get rid of him, nor could he refuse to serve us, unless we went to live in another place and adopted a local barber family. But whenever we returned to our home town the old barber was there, and there was no changing him.

The first and most important in the jajmani system were the Brahmins. That they could be the leaders of society, in a position of privilege, I only discovered when I went to live outside the Punjab. With us the Brahmins were an unprivileged class and exercised little or no influence on the community. Perhaps the Muslims had so discouraged temples and external worship that the Brahmins had no place left from where to exercise their authority. In towns like Gujarat, and more so as you went further west of the Jhelum river, there were very few temples of any size. Only in Lahore, and that too in the deep heart of the city in Hindu mohallas, did one come across any big temples; mostly our temples were holes in the walls or little shrines under pipal or banyan trees, easily demolished and just as quickly set up again. The importance of the Brahmins was therefore limited.

Our Brahmins did not as a rule even have the role of teachers, because until the British opened regular schools, teaching was done by Muslim mohallas in the mosques or by Sikh granthis, scripture readers, in the gurdwaras. Our Brahmins were rarely

*Excerpted from *The Punjabi Saga* by Prakash Tandon, Viking, Delhi, 1988.

erudite; in fact many of them were barely literate, possessing only a perfunctory knowledge of ritual and knowing just the necessary mantras by heart. As the occasions requiring their aid and knowledge were few, to earn their living they had developed a system of charity. Every morning members of a Brahmin family would visit the homes of their jajmans to collect cooked food— a chappati, some cooked vegetable or lentils, and buttermilk. The food would last the Brahmin family for both meals of the day; sometimes there were chappatis left over which they would dry and eat later soaked in hot milk. *Handa*, as such gift of food was called, was always cooked food. It could never be claimed in its equivalent of raw food, for that our women would have considered an imposition. While mother could always manage the handa out of whatever was cooked for the family, to give it raw would have meant dipping into her stores. While the handa took care of the family food, gifts in money and clothes on ceremonial occasions helped the Brahmins to eke out a thin living. It was a frugal life, and there were rarely any affluent Brahmins.

Without erudition and because of their daily dependence on the other castes, there was a touch of mild derision towards the Brahmins. The very address 'oh Pandita' or 'oh Brahmina' had gentle sarcasm about it. They were never elders of the community, nor was their advice sought on mundane matters. On the other hand some respect was shown to the astrologer pandits, who were the elite of our Brahmins, or the learned pandits who gave religious discourses, but astrologers and learned pandits were few. To the astrologers we went for establishing auspicious moments for betrothal, marriage, a business venture or a journey. They interpreted the almanacs, called jantris, and advised on the influence of the heavenly bodies upon individuals. These jantris, produced by the great pandits of Banaras and Hardwar, were essential for Hindu homes, sometimes the only book a family might possess. They were calendars with information about stars, planets, moon and the sun, whose interpretation was the specialised task of astrology. The basis of each individual's life, as it was governed and influenced by the heavens, was his horoscope which the astrologer cast at birth and consulted before all important moves and occasions in life. Astrology was the preserve of Brahmins.

The other Hindu services castes were the artisan castes of Sonars, the goldsmiths; Tarkhans, the woodworkers; Jhewars or Mehras the cooks, chars and water carriers; and Kalals, who sold liquor and were on the fringe of the social scale. Of these only the Jhewars were included in the jajmani system, and were in daily contact with us. A woman or girl from a Jhewar family would come every morning to clean and wash the utensils, while a man would bring water from the nearest well, and later from the hand pump on the ground floor. At weddings, or when we had a lot of guests, their men came to do the cooking.

The goldsmiths and carpenters were independent and dealt with whoever needed their services. The Kalals, before the British introduced liquor, sold opium, hemp and other narcotics. Liquor among us was practically unknown and addiction was mainly to eating opium, although even that was an uncommon habit.

There were no Hindu untouchables in the West Punjab, and such work as that of sweepers , skin-flayers and leather workers was done by Muslims. They were presumably untouchable Hindus who had at one time become Muslims to escape their lot, which they apparently did not manage to do even though they acquired some kind of theoretical equality with their Muslim brethren. They had the right to worship in mosques and to mix at an uneasy distance with poor Muslims, but they were compelled to retain their unwelcome professions.

As a boy I would feel quite ashamed when my mother, asking for a glass of water at some Muslim house, would be told with ingratiating courtesy that both the glass and the water had come from a neighbouring Hindu family. But slowly I saw the change come in. Our father made no bones about eating with Muslims and bringing them home. Interestingly, this problem was solved in our home, as in many other homes where a similar change was at work, by the introduction of chinaware. Our women, who objected to Muslims eating off our metal utensils, willingly shared china plates, cups and saucers. These were somehow considered uncontaminable. Their gleaming white, smooth surface, from which grease slipped off so easily, somehow immunised them from contamination. My mother would not at first use the chinaware herself and reserved it for the menfolk and for Muslim, Christian and English guests, but she soon began to weaken. This led to the next stage, that of accepting unpeeled fruit in non-Hindu homes.

Then followed the acceptance of tea and manufactured biscuits and the English bottled lime cordial, but mother never reached the stage of eating cooked food with Muslims or even with my father's English colleagues. This also used to puzzle me, because I could understand the traditional taboo on Muslim food, but how did this taboo attach itself to the English? I think it came from the discovery that like Muslims they ate beef, and that only Muslim cooks would serve them. As a child I could never understand how the Muslims and the English swallowed such insults from us and did not retaliate. It took the ideal of Pakistan and a separate Muslim nation in the 1940's to create an occasional feeling in Punjabi Muslim minds that they should also not accept food or water from the Hindus. The English, I suppose, just left it as one of our idiosyncrasies and bothered no more about it.

There were a number of other Muslim service castes who plied hereditary professions. Two of them were in the jajmani system. I have already mentioned the barbers. In addition to his professional chores of haircutting, shaving and some surgery, the barber enjoyed the important function of go-between for arranging betrothals. At the weddings the barber, Raja, as he was always courteously called, had a place of honour second only to the Brahmin. As a barber we children of course never took to him because he always knew better than we how our hair should be cut. Just at that time the English style of hair-cut, known to us as the 'Bengali fashion', was becoming popular, but our Raja insisted on giving us a close crop. To add insult to injury, he said it was good for us because it did away with the need for dressing the hair and thus losing valuable time every morning which might otherwise be spent on studies. We despised him, but dared not say so, and in any case his argument about work appealed to our father. But whatever his skill as a barber, the Raja enjoyed much prestige among his jajmans for arranging betrothals, when he literally held the honour of a family in his hand.

Another Muslim caste in the jajmani system was that of Mirasis. The Mirasis beat drums and played the shehnai, a flute with a trumpet end, at weddings and other auspicious occasions, but their speciality was wit and repartee which they could exercise with traditional immunity on the highest and the lowest in the society. The victim could not take umbrage at the Mirasis' wit. They would come to weddings and other gatherings, invited or uninvited, and begin to poke fun at guests and hosts alike. Their wit was inherited down the generations and practised from childhood; it was sharp and very quick, and at times brilliant. Woe betide a man who tried to retaliate and get the better of them, for they could reduce him to rags before a company. A problem with the Mirasis was how to send them away satisfied; anything short of that would lead to a special session against the poor host; and it was the respected custom to let the Mirasai say whatever he liked without showing anger and rancour. In any case, retaliation could only lead to an admission of lack of humour; the Mirasi had nothing to lose. The Mirasi women also worked, playing small drums and singing, but they never excelled in wit, only in vulgarity. Men and women sang praises of the family and recited its genealogy at weddings. They were also the vehicle of old ballads and songs. The word Mirasi in the Punjabi language has come to mean witty and funny in an overdone, vulgar manner. They lived as a close community in their own mohallas. Although Muslims, other Muslims never intermarried with them. Their women were slim and attractive in a brazen way, and of easy virtue.

The Mirasis moved with the times and took to brass bands, an influence from the army, which gradually replaced the shehnai and the drum at weddings. Dressed in the quaintest uniforms which were a mixture of those of the regimental bands and of the court dress of the King Emperor as shown in pictures, the Mirasis led the wedding processions and gave their customers the maximum value out of their new instruments, drowning the din of the party and even challenging the fireworks.

Not far removed from the Mirasis were the Kanjars, the community that bred prostitutes, singing girls and nautch girls. They were of course not in the jajmani system. Their men lived like drones, condemned to this because illegitimate birth of such low origin prevented them from going into any occupation. They were also Muslim, although the ranks of prostitutes drew castaways and fallen women from all communities. As with the Mirasis there was no inter-marriage between them and other Muslims. The professions of singing, nautch and plain prostitution were graded in that order in their community, on account of the requisite skill and talent required. It took only good looks to make a prostitute, while dancing, despite the low level to which it had dropped, still required some years' training and a lithe figure; but singing needed both talent and intensive training of many years. The singing girls were the elite of their community. They were no common prostitutes, and gave their favours only when they wished. The Mirasis provided them with musical accompaniment.

Other professional castes of interest were the Bhands, Bazigars, Saperas, Madaris and Behroopis. Bhands and Rasdharis were a community of clowns and jokers whose specialities were farce and impersonation. At weddings and parties they gave traditional performances or improvised skits on the company present. They were ingenious in both humour and farce, and never performed anything serious or classical. The word Bhand in Punjabi is synonymous with clown.

Bazigars (acrobats) and Madaris (jugglers) were also hereditary professions. They moved from place to place, the Bazigars as a troupe but the Madaris always single. Sapera, the snake charmer, must also have formed his own caste, but somehow one never knew where he came from.

A Behroopia's speciality was to disguise himself and act a role in such a realistic manner that people did not suspect it to be play-acting. He might arrive at a party as an old toothless hag, and no one would know until the end, when he suddenly threw away his garb and declared that he was a Behroopi. People used to be so taken in that they would gasp with wonder and reward him suitably. They were consummate artistes. The word Behroopi in Punjabi has come to mean someone with a deceptive appearance. Rasdharis on the other hand went about in groups and put up plays and dramas. Dressed in colourful costumes they would arrive in a town and give short performances of old legends, stories or plays at street corners and at weddings.

The trades of weavers, tailors, washermen, blacksmiths, potters, oil pressers and vegetable growers were also practised only by Muslims. In some cases there was probably no question of caste involved, for when the British brought Hindu regimental tailors and barbers, some Punjabi Hindus also took to this work. To some trades like blacksmiths and weavers, resistance was broken by the arrival of machines; but to others like oil pressing, pottery and vegetable growing the Hindus never took. Even the agricultural

Hindus never practised market gardening. For this there was a special Muslim caste of Arains who only grew vegetables. An ordinary farmer might grow some vegetables for himself but never a surplus for sale.

All these castes did not make ours a multi-layered society; it would be more apt to describe it as a multi-unit society, in which each caste had its functional place without oppression by a high caste. The different castes were united into biradaris, literally meaning brotherhoods. There was an overall Hindu biradari; there was a Khatri biradari, an Arora biradari, and biradaris of sub-castes and of each service caste, Hindu or Muslim. These biradaries were loose and undefined, but in time of need they formed themselves into close-knit groups. They gave you certain rights and expected some duties. They were led by elders of the group, not formally elected but just the senior and most respected men. Your rights were your duties. At weddings and funerals everybody helped the family ungrudgingly. At a daughter's wedding the biradari members served the guests and helped with many chores; at death, when the immediate members of the family were too stunned to be of much use, the whole biradari was a source of strength.

N.N. VOHRA

91, Garden Town

My father and his four elder brothers had built houses on adjoining plots in Lahore city in an area which had acquired the rather unusual name of 'Paisa Akhbar'. It was close to Anarkali Bazaar and virtually adjoining the rear boundary wall of Government College, one of the leading educational institutions in the country whose high academic standards had been established by Cambridge dons. A science graduate from this college, Father was also the best athlete of Punjab University in his time, with the rare distinction of being the best short distance runner as well as the record holder in the marathon race. He had supported his own education from school onwards, having run away from his home village Vaniaki (in the Amritsar district of undivided Punjab) when he found that his elder brothers were not interested in educating him. My four elder brothers are also distinguished alumni of this once eminent seat of learning.

Father was highly allergic to dust and smoke and hated congestion of any kind. As an officer of the Survey of India Department, he had spent all his service life in remote areas, amidst nature. When my mother's first cousin, Sukhdev (member of the revolutionary group which included Bhagat Singh and Rajguru) was arrested and subsequently hanged to death with his compatriots in the Lahore Jail after a rigged up trial, the British had summarily discharged Father from government service because of his family links with a terrorist! Thereafter he had been virtually confined to Lahore.

With the passage of time the Paisa Akhbar area had become very congested. Not being able to bear the rapidly deteriorating environment, Father decided to shift well away from the city. So, just before the commencement of World War II, we found a new home. It was a spacious house in a still to develop colony called Garden Town. It had about five houses in an area of about 500

Paisa Akhbar Street, *Lahore, Water colour by Ajaz Anwar*

acres, the largest being one owned by Raja Narendra Nath who also owned one of the best mango *bir* (orchard) some miles further away from our colony. Our new address was 91 Garden Town, Post Office Model Town (a large and quickly developing colony about 3-4 miles beyond Garden Town), Lahore. In those days the southern limit of urban Lahore was well short of the Canal, on the highway leading from Lahore to Ferozepore. This highway, the Grand Trunk Road, was better known as the Ferozepore Road.

Between Garden and Model Towns was a considerable tract of *kalar* (land eroded with the surfacing of sub-soil salts) with just one large and lonely bungalow owned by Sir Chottu Ram, a notable leader of undivided Punjab. When we shifted to Garden Town, work had just commenced for the construction of the new campus of the Foreman Christian College (better known as the FCC) along the southern, Ferozepore side, of the Canal. The site was partially under an old forest. A detachment of the city police was almost permanently deployed near the Canal bridge, on the Ferozepore Road, to eliminate a tiger (one of the several whose habitat had been disturbed by the FCC project) which was on the prowl in this area. Beyond the bridge, towards the city, there were two prominent agglomerations, Ichra and Muzzang, almost entirely inhabited by Muslims.

Between Garden Town and the Canal there were some cultivated areas and a sizeable grove of *ber* trees but no habitation. On the western flank was a small Muslim village, Jiunhana (which the locals pronounced as Jeewanhana) comprising about 30 households of tenants and day wagers, and a beautiful mosque.

Our family spent over eight years in Garden Town, till the Partition came and we were compelled to flee. For me, personally, this was an idyllic period even though I had to get up very early every morning to walk to the Ferozepore Road (about a kilometre from our house) and be in time to catch the special bus (of the Model Town Bus Service) which took school children from Model Town to various schools in Lahore. With several stops on the way, the journey took well over an hour. I studied in the St. Anthony's European School which used to have separate sections for English and Indian students. However, by the time I joined this school—where all my brothers had studied and also successively taught for brief spells and Father, after his sudden retrenchment, had taught for several years—the separatist policy seemed to have been circumstantially dissipated.

This appeared to have happened because almost all the younger Reverend Brothers, enlisted to fight the War, had been killed or seriously wounded. Consequently, the vacancies had been filled by the best available Indian Christian and non Christian teachers. Also, the attention of those who were expected to enforce the segregation policy was diverted to more pressing concerns generated by the War. The section to which I was admitted had no English boy—our class comprised Hindu, Sikh, Muslim, Anglo-Indian and a lone Parsi. Barring those who instructed us in Urdu and Drawing all our teachers were Indian Christians and one Reverend Brother, straight from Ireland—from where he had brought a fresh stock of canes to discipline us.

Father remained quite ill, refused to receive proper medical treatment, and died at home in early winter 1946, leaving the large family ship rudderless. The refusal of the Muslim League to agree with the Congress and agitate a collective approach to gain freedom from the alien yoke had engendered growing suspicions and hatred among the communities. This had led to large scale communal violence, arson and killings in Bengal, the North West Frontier Province (NWFP) and Sindh. As stories of these killings spread and those who had managed to escape started arriving in Punjab, to seek refuge with their relations, the Province virtually went up in flames. The traditional good health and vigour of the Punjabi was transformed into tireless enthusiasm and ingenuity to kill those who had been his long term associates, neighbours and trusted friends. The alibi of the killers—not that one was needed in the prevailing environment—was that with so many of their relations lost at the hands of the Hindus in other Provinces they were compelled to level the score!

Violence in Punjab, which began on this rather simple arithmetical basis, assumed a frightening scale and gruesome modalities. Dusk to dawn curfew imposed by the district authorities was extended for days at a stretch in many parts of Lahore. This, however, did not deter those overtaken by the communal frenzy. Tear-gas, lathi charge and police firing became routine phenomenon. Thousands were being killed every day and lakhs of Hindus, including government employees at all levels of functioning, were seeking the shortest route to safer areas.

Mountbatten's meticulous planning to relieve himself of his task by a pre-determined date had not reckoned a situation in which organised communal violence would need to be controlled by police forces comprising one of the warring communities.

By around April-May most of the government offices in Lahore, specially police stations, were manned largely by Muslims. The Hindus who had not been killed or wounded had fled or were cooped up in their community majority localities.

Father had a profound conviction that regular and large intake of cow's milk contributed to good health and cerebral development! Irrespective of his bank balance he invariably succeeded in buying the best pedigree cows so that his many sons and daughters could drink unadulterated milk, consume home made butter and curd and drink *lassi* around the year! Thus, we always had 4-5 cows of which at least two would yield immeasurable quantities of milk.

Life had become terribly insecure even before Father died. Though killings had not yet commenced on an organised scale, as happened from early 1947 onwards, cases of theft and looting had been on the increase. Prudence would have counselled that the cattle were disposed of—each cow would have sold at anything between Rs.900-1000, a phenomenal price in those days. However, our family believed that the worst would soon be over and nothing should be done in a hurry! Around early June an unknown person visited the house and offered Rs.40 for our best cow, a prize winning animal which Father had bought in the Punjab Cattle Fair in 1941. Mother felt insulted and asked this man to go away. That night both our milk yielding cows were stolen and two days later the remaining stock. With human beings being killed by the thousand there was no question of the Police registering a case regarding the theft of cattle!

The situation deteriorated with every passing day. Serving government employees were asked to indicate the areas they would wish to serve—those likely to comprise India or Pakistan. My eldest brother, serving the North West Frontièr Railway in Karachi, was shifted to Ferozepore. As a senior officer he was entitled to several wagons in which we could have moved all our household baggage, including our prized cows, from Lahore to Ferozepore. Failing to persuade Mother to leave Lahore he took away our sisters with him. As subsequent events showed, all of us may have been killed if the girls had not been shifted from Lahore when they were. My second eldest brother, then serving as a Civilian Gazetted Officer in the Army Base Depot at Avadi, got himself posted to Lahore. My other two brothers were already in Lahore, one serving in the Military Accounts Department in Lahore Cantonment and the other in the local Radio Station. All of them believed that normalcy would be restored and we would never have to leave Lahore.

Having lived in Lahore for many years, all our friendships and connections were with Muslim families. All our domestic staff was Muslim, from the next door village. The thought of emigrating could not even be entertained. Sher Mohammed, who looked after the cows, and Chagan Bibi, who washed clothes, repeatedly warned Mother to at least temporarily shift to a safer place in the city. This was not to happen till 14 August when the next door house was looted and burnt, and Sher Mohammed sent us a message to leave immediately, as we were next on the list. One of Father's nephews, a journalist, seriously risked his life in driving alone from the city to Garden Town to take all of us to our uncle's house in the heart of the city, a Hindu majority area. In the evening the sky was aglow on all sides—Lahore was burning.

That midnight we heard Nehru's "tryst with destiny" speech. It was not till several weeks later that we could get to Ferozepore by road, leaving Lahore and all we had behind. The only clothes we had were those which we were wearing. Mother was carrying some little jewellery and cash tied in a silk handkerchief. The car in which we were travelling was stopped at Kasur, not far from the Indian border. The vehicle and all of us were subjected to a thorough search and Mother was relieved of whatever she was carrying. We crossed the Indo-Pak border checkpost at Hussaini Wallah late in the afternoon and were at my brother's house in the Railway Colony in Ferozepore Cantonment by early evening. The family was now "32 carat" refugee, bereft of all it ever had. However, thanks to the Lord, we were all alive!

In the subsequent years our family faced numerous trials and tribulations. With sustained effort, all of us "resettled" ourselves, in the course of time. However, we have no "family home". All of us are scattered in various parts of India and some abroad, propelled by individual destinies.

I joined the Civil Service in 1959. In 1987, when I was serving the Defence Ministry, I had the opportunity of going on an official visit to Pakistan. Our talks were in Islamabad. Our delegation made the customary call on General Zia, the Pakistani President. On knowing that I hailed from Lahore, he graciously asked the Punjab Governor to make arrangements for me to visit my old school and our house in Garden Town. This was exactly forty years after we had left Lahore. The staff car driver was very happy to take me wherever I wished to go. However, after crossing the Canal, I could not identify any of the landmarks of four decades ago. I found that the entire area beyond the Canal had since been fully built up and, as in India, without any planning whatever. There was wall to wall construction in Garden Town which was beautiful countryside four decades earlier. The house numbering also did not help. I succeded in identifying No.91 but it was not our house.

We went round and round the colony but I could not find any structure even remotely resembling our old home. As our delegation was to catch an early evening flight to Delhi I gave up the effort and asked the chauffeur to return to the Governor's House. As he reversed the car, I chanced to sight a pillar in an adjoining house. Stopping the car I hurriedly got out and entered the premises. The very extensive front lawn of our house had been divided in half by a barrack type building, behind which our house stood in all its grandeur, just as it was forty years ago. It now housed a government middle school. The semi-circular front verandah had three supporting columns, two of which were now hidden by the new construction. It was my chance sighting of the third pillar which had led to my discovering the house associated with all the memories of my early youth. The teacher in charge of the school, on learning of my connection with the building, very kindly showed me around. He also explained that as an evacuee property the premises did not carry the original house number which, apparently, had been assumed by an adjoining plot owner!

The visit to the house where our family had lived till Freedom compelled us to leave our hearth and home brought a rush of memories of all that had happened before and after 15 August 1947. While it would be naive to expect that erstwhile refugees, Hindus and Muslims—such of them as still remain—will have the opportunity of returning to wherever they had once belonged,

I hope that one day, not far from now, displaced families on both sides of the fence will at least be able to freely cross the borders and show their grandchildren where their grand parents had once lived and belonged. The day such a change comes about, I shall be the first to cross the Wagah or Hussainiwallah border posts to take my grand-daughter to Lahore, and show her the home of my youthful dreams—**91, Garden Town.**

Memory and History

KRISHNA SOBTI
In conversation with Alok Bhalla*

Alok Bhalla: *Most novels about the partition are autobiographical, drawing upon personal memories. This raises a few interesting questions. What kind of language and tone does one use so that what is written is not merely a record of horror but an attempt to understand something of ourselves? Most novels about the partition were written much after 1947—for example, Bhisham Sahni's* TAMAS *was written about 25 years later. How are memories recast imaginatively in a fictional text? And most importantly, why do you think that the partition occurred?*

Krishna Sobti: The partition of India is three generations old. For my generation of writers, it was not so much a happening or historical event as living history, easily the most massive experience of a kind that became an encounter between man and reality, a collision between a political agenda and a long tradition of pluralism. Writers on both sides soon realized that after so much of hatred, violence and killings, human values had got to be affirmed and restored.

After the great divide much has been written about the difference and distance between the Hindu and the Muslim culture but any of us can vouchsafe that in spite of political undercurrents and religious overtones, the two communities had lived for centuries in a workable harmony almost like cousins.

Fiction writers of the post-partition period have testified to this truth in novels such as *Jhoota Sach, Tamas, Aag ki Darya, Kale Kos,* and *Udas Naslein.*

We are quite familiar with the coercive jargon of social scientists. Politicians also spin out reality as

*Excerpted from a longer interview with Krishna Sobti.

fiction. Memory of those times could always be falsified, distorted with an ideological bias. That is why writers wrote their major novels only after they were rid of their mental and physical clogging and could see the partition with clear sight.

A creative writer has to transform experience into something that is history from below. When politics, religion and humanism are transmitted in literature, human faith is transformed. Alok, I do feel in my inner recesses a certain richness that is part of our common heritage. Nanak, Baba Farid, Amir Khusro, Jayasi, Bulleh Shah, Waris Shah, Shah Latif—can we divide this whole lot of poets between yours and ours? No doubt we divided the territory—but tradition, music, art, literature are not like geographical areas: they continue to remain undivided, indivisible.

A novelist makes use of his or her experiences many years after the event. I am surprised that till recently I had not paid much attention to this fact. I had not realized it even when I reread my story *Sikka Badal Gaya* recently. I am not sure if I still understand the creative process. Maybe, earlier, I was much too close to the events. I was a part of them and didn't have the skills to deal with them. I did, however, sense even then that it was necessary to look beyond the immediate horror—that it was necessary to salvage something that remained untouched by violence.

The fiction written about the partition in India and Pakistan has made an attempt, despite the enormity of the horror it describes, to preserve essential human values. This attempt is remarkable. Because there certainly existed hatred between the communities. It led to the destruction of property, migration of populations and a lot of killings. Yet the writers were convinced that it was essential to preserve a sense of humanity, to affirm human values.

AB: *How do you now interpret the character of Shahni in* Sikka Badal Gaya *in the light of what you have just said, about preserving value systems?*

KS: The story is autobiographical and was written in 1948—immediately after the partition. It is about my Naani who, for more than two months after the partition, had refused to leave her home, in spite of news of killings of Hindus and Sikhs in neighbouring villages. One afternoon she got a message that Shahji's friend, one Cheema Sahib, a Superintendent of Police from Jullundhar, had come to see her. She hurriedly asked her maid to light the tandoor and cook for him things he liked. However, there was no time for cooking and Cheema Sahib came up and asked her to collect whatever valuables she could and go with him to the camp.

When she came out of the haveli to sit in the Police Superintendent's jeep, all the Hindus and Sikhs of the village who had stayed on with her, left their homes on foot, to go to the camp.

The story appears to have assumed a cold profile, an uncanny neutrality perhaps born out of the enormity of pain. Human emotions seem to have been drained out. The finality of the great historical divide was aptly summed up by the Muslim village elders in two short sentences: "Shahni, we could not protect you. *Raj palat gaya, sikka badal gaya.*"

In contrast to this story, I wrote *Zindaginama* thirty years after the partition, even though I had made the first draft in 1952. This time it was like memories recollected in tranquillity. Time is a strange chemistry. First we wanted to forget and then we wanted to relive the life that was!

AB: *Two things strike me about the story. The first thing is that the police inspector who decides to rescue her is a Muslim. The second, that despite the violence, the first thing that occurs to Shahni is not that he is a Muslim, but that he must be hungry. There is still a deep sense of humanity left in both of them.*

KS: Yes. He took Shahni to a refugee camp near Gujarat. Once in a refugee camp, things happened to people the same way, with no exception. It was not a personal tragedy and one did not need any sympathy, however terrifying or agonizing one's experience might have been. Shahni's own working hands had looted her home along with other Muslims but they had also reached her ration, clothes, blankets and other necessities in the camp. When my Naani's *kafila* reached Amritsar and from there she was brought to Delhi, whatever was uppermost in her mind she poured in a letter to her 'home-hands', giving instructions to the boys. The last sentence ran like this: "Dear *puttar* Mohammad-Din, when things settle down and it is calm on both sides, I shall return and join you. After all that is my home and the home of Shahji's fore-fathers. I should like to die there only."

AB: Sikka Badal Gaya *is slightly different from the account you have just given. In the story you don't describe what happened to Shahni after she had left the village and found herself in a refugee camp. Nor do you talk about the police inspector. What you describe instead is that the people whom she had trusted and regarded as her own were the ones who had looted her house.*

KS: Yes. They were deeply concerned about the woman who had been the mistress of the haveli and the owner of the village lands. Now, when I look back and think about the experience, it seems to me that there wasn't anything personal about what happened in those days or what people did to each other. The historical events were so overwhelming that small personal tragedies were insignificant.

When one of my aunts arrived in Delhi after a difficult train journey, she had lost her son and was in a state of shock. She sat in silence all day. My mother offered her tea and food and tried to do what she could do to comfort her, but she gave no response. Finally, my mother dragged her to the bathroom, and opened the shower, and said to her sternly, "Look here, forget all that has happened. Everyone has suffered. Now change. Drink your tea and eat something." My aunt cried like hell. She had not shed any tears before.

Alok, have you read Balwant Singh's novel *Kaale Kos?* How closely he visualized and depicted the drama of partition! He shows amazing insights and sense of history.

A convoy of trucks covered with tarpaulin is carrying Hindu refugees from Pakistan to the border. At one place, the driver gets down from the truck and walks down to a group of people standing on the road. When he returns after talking to them, the refugees want to know who they were. He remains silent. They insist, "Tell us whom you were talking to." He replies, "Strange! Can't I talk to my Muslim brothers?" The people in the truck are terrified. The truck stops once again. The refugees wonder if the people on the road are going to slaughter them. When the driver returns, they ask him once again, "Are those people policemen or soldiers?" The driver gives them an evasive reply. However, when the truck stops for the third time, the driver tells the refugees, "Why are you afraid? They are only scoundrels in hired police uniforms. Yaar, it doesn't matter if they also make a little money on the side, does it?"

Each refugee had paid three or four thousand rupees to the driver. Those people on the road got their share of the money to allow the refugees to pass through safely. It was likely that the regular police would not have let them through. Those people actually helped the refugees across the border ... So you see, a sort of parallel economy existed even in those days ... Anyway, when the trucks approach Lahore, the refugees plead with the driver, "Don't go into the city. There will be Muslim crowds and we'll be killed." The driver refuses to oblige and drives the truck into the city. Suddenly, they see a huge crowd before them. Someone says, "There is a crowd. We'll be killed. Why did you drive into the city?"

The driver says, "Don't worry. They are not Pakistanis. They are Hindustanis."

"They are Muslims!"

"Yes, but not Punjabi Muslims, they are Hindustani Muslims."

"Why do you say so? Muslims are Muslims anywhere."

"Not so, brother. A Punjabi Musalman alone is *asl* Musalman."

Balwant Singh was looking beyond immediate time and events. He was aware of religious and political complexities generated by religion but he was aware of racial tensions also.

AB: *That people defined themselves as Punjabis, Muslims, and Hindustanis?*

KS: Yes, the Punjabis are supreme in Pakistan and they are arrogant. They have military clout. They have still not conceded the status of equality to non-Punjabis and the migrants from India.

AB: *There is one thing that I still don't understand—an explanation that some historians still offer is that the Pakistan movement was primarily instigated by the zamindars or by the educated people who were aspiring for jobs in the bureaucracy, etc. The zamindars wanted to hold on to their lands and were afraid that if the Congress came to power, it would snatch them away. It was, therefore, a movement of the rich and educated. The ordinary man and woman really didn't play a major role in it.*

For instance, when I read Rahi Masoom Raza's Adha Gaon, *I got the sense that the Pakistan movement was launched by those educated at Aligarh—by people who spoke Urdu. The language spoken in Ghazipur was different and was common to both Hindus and Muslims. Thus, in the novel, when students from Aligarh come to propagate the idea of Pakistan, the people in the village tell them to go away. They are not interested in leaving the place where they were born and grew up. Still, it seems that the demand for Pakistan was in the air—that the winds of change had touched ordinary people before 1946–47.*

KS: Yes, indeed, Aligarh became a formidable centre for the propagation of the idea of Pakistan, and the Muslim masses were influenced by the cry of a separate homeland for Muslims. It is true, of course, that the majority—minority question and the demand for a separate nation for Muslims turned very important. Still, I feel, it was around the more important, larger economic issue that these crystallized. Let me tell you that there was a time when people—Hindus and Muslims alike—used to buy goods from any shop in the market. But from 1944–45 onwards that was no longer the case. Hindus were asked to buy only from Hindu shops and Muslims were urged to buy from Muslim shops—earlier they would buy from Hindu shops, too. After 1944–45 there was a great change in their collective psyche—and it turned anti-Hindu.

Hindus had begun to feel apprehensive about the disturbances. Yet they were not sure if Pakistan would actually come into being. Hindus, as in the past, still had money. They were also intelligent and educated.

Do you know about Todar Mal who was from Punjab?

He advised Hindus, "If you want to prosper, learn Persian, learn Arabic." Hindus learnt both. They were sure they could tackle any situation. But what happened in the 1940s was so vastly different and cataclysmic that it was beyond their political vision and intellectual abilities. The debates over land reforms, for instance, had far-reaching, profound effects. Hindus had money and land; they owned the newspapers. Barring a few who were very big landlords, Muslims were primarily poor labourers and peasants; they earned just four annas a day. They did all the work, and yet were always in heavy debt. As reported by one of the Lawrence brothers who was given charge of the revenue in Punjab, Muslim peasants were so deep in debt that even if they worked for fifty years, the debt they owed the moneylenders would not be repaid.

AB: *You spent your childhood in Gujarat. Did your family own land there? Who tilled it—Muslims or Hindus?*

KS: Yes, we had lands. Muslim labourers and peasants worked on them. In those days the custom in the village was that peasants did everything with the help of the landlord or Shahji, who had money and means. They borrowed from him. If they didn't have the money to pay the revenue officer, Shahji paid it for them. He also helped them meet expenses during ceremonies like marriage. In reality, the peasants were slaves of sorts, although they were called *muzarei* and *Kammis*.

AB: *Didn't the Unionist Party in Punjab come into power as a result of the support of peasants? In those days there was no real support for the Pakistan movement. Hindus, Sikhs and Muslims had jointly supported the Unionist Party. Is it possible that the Unionist Party was the party of zamindars, but the pretence was that it was a party of peasants?*

KS: Yes, you are right. But an additional factor which helped to sharpen tensions was the religious revivalist movements—which first started in Bengal. The Punjabi Hindus responded to them favourably. One such revivalist attempt, which Hindus adopted as their own, was the Arya Samaj movement. There was a time when there was a deep suspicion between the Arya Samaj and Muslims. The entire regional press, including the *Zamindar* and *Paisa Akhbar*, was full of stories which helped to sharpen the identities of Hindus and Muslims—to ensure that the differences between them were absolutely clear. Slowly, they even began to write about how different the two were in their nature and character. This was true both of the Arya Samaj press and the Muslim controlled press.

AB: *Did Iqbal support the Pakistan movement?*

KS: Yes. Absolutely. It was his vision to a large extent. He consolidated Muslim thought.

It is an irony of history that the same poet who gave us an evocative vision of Hamara Hindustan also visualized Pakistan. For singing and reciting these beautiful lines of his—

Sare jahan se achha
Hindostan hamara
Hum bulbulein hain uski
Voh gulistan hamara

we had to forgo the territory which now is known as Pakistan.

AB: *The first riot in Punjab was, perhaps, in Rawalpindi in 1926—at least that's what Bhisham Sahni told me. You were born and grew up in Punjab. Did you ever feel that the antagonism between Hindus and Muslims there was so great that they could never live with each other?*

KS: No, not really. People didn't think like that in those days. In *Zindaginama,* I wanted to examine why the partition happened and why it had to happen, although the novel itself ends a little before the partition.

In the novel there is a villager who watches both the communities and wonders, "I don't understand one thing. God distributed the sun and the air equally. How is it that He couldn't distribute wealth the same way? Why should there be such an unequal distribution of wealth?" The man is completely illiterate. He is bitter. What Shahji says in reply to his question is typically Hindu. He says it is the Law of the Almighty that he who works with mind and intelligence is paid better than one who works with hand. Those who hear Shahji feel that he is right. However, the peasant is questioning the basis of class differences. He has become conscious of the fact that in spite of doing all the labour, he is poor ...

Once the crop had been gathered, there would be a feast. The landowners would spread out durries and khes in their courtyards and serve the labourers the best basmati rice, sugar and ghee. The feast was worth watching. The members of the landlord's family served the labourers. Food was served generously. But even during the feast the relation between the landlord and the labourer was clearly defined. Slowly, however, this entire way of living was derailed—it jumped off the tracks.

The differences between Hindus and Muslims didn't emerge very strongly during British rule. As long as the British were in power. Hindus knew that there would be no change in their status. Once the Pakistan movement started, Hindus felt that since they had lived through Mughal rule they could also adjust to Muslim rule. They were, in fact, sure that they would not be thrown out of their homes.

AB: *You are right in saying that in Punjab the conflict was between the peasant and the zamindar. This conflict was not confined to Punjab. It was an economic conflict. But did it ever seem to you that an economic conflict would turn into a religious one?*

KS: Yes, that was the greatest danger in the past—it still is. Remember that if a poor Muslim student wanted to get a seat in a medical college, he could not. That was also true of engineering colleges. Indeed, only the children of the Muslim aristocracy could get education. The children of the poor could never go to school.

AB: *Wasn't that also true of Hindus? Surely, the children of poor Hindus rarely got a chance to go to school!*

KS: No, not in the same way. The children of poor Hindus could go to school. There was a reason for it. An average Hindu's priority is to educate his children. He is hardworking (*laughs*) and doesn't unnecessarily waste money. He never says to himself, let me fulfill all my desires at once—today. He tries to save what he can. An ordinary Hindu designs his life carefully and intelligently.

AB: *Were you as a child told by your parents, "Don't play with that girl because she is a Muslim? Don't go to her house or eat food with her."?*

KS: No, I was never forbidden to do so. In our houses at Delhi and Shimla there was no discrimination. Nor was there any discrimination in Gujarat. We addressed the Muslims who worked in our house as 'mamus'. In villages they never entered the kitchen in Hindu households. No one minded this till the politics started playing it up as an example of Hindu arrogance. Whenever we went to the houses of our Muslim friends, we had no hesitation in eating food with them.

AB: *There was, however, talk about "Hindu Paani" and "Muslim paani."*

KS: Oh, yes! Although separate plates and glasses were kept for Hindus and Muslims, the same dhaba could serve eats to both the communities. No one stopped us from going to Muslim areas, only we were not allowed to wear frocks and skirts. I suspect social tensions increased once Punjab came under the influence of the Arya Samaj.

AB: *I would like to know a little more about why you think the emergence of Pakistan was inevitable, Historians like I.H. Qureshi in Pakistan have maintained a similar position. They claim that historically Muslims were always distinct and separate from the Hindu community. Therefore, after independence, the formation of Pakistan was a foregone conclusion. Is that assertion true? Is there sufficient historical evidence to suggest that the Muslims of India always saw themselves as distinct enough to form a separate nation state of their own? Weren't a majority of the Muslims here converts? Further, do we have authentic communal records of communal riots before the 1880s? There were, of course, incidents of violence between the two communities. There were, however, social mechanisms also available for contain-*

ing the tension. Indeed, it is also arguable that till about the 1890s there was a viable composite culture in India.

KS: I think that when a historian decides to take sides, he can justify anything (*laughs*). Memories of those times can always be falsified. In the histories of the partition, culture is one word that has been abused constantly and mercilessly. 'Secular' is not the expression I would like to use for the way of life that existed before the partition. The weave of that common culture was so strong and dense that it still lingers in us not as a memory but as source of inner strength.

In spite of political overtones people lived in harmony. Each respected the other's otherness. Both were wholly self-assured about the threads that held them together, threads like a common language, dialects and a way of life, none of which bore any reference to religious identity.

The relations between the communities were complex. It is on record that Jinnah was never in favour of partition of Punjab and Bengal. He said that he couldn't imagine these areas being divided. Our people ignored that statement. Even the Viceroy was surprised by it.

AB: *When I interviewed Intizar Husain a few years ago, he said two important things in this context. First, that he saw himself as a person who still had one foot in Ayodhya, one in Karbala. Second, that he always felt that there was a Hindu sitting inside him. I feel that it is because of this kinship between Hindu traditions that when he thinks about questions of tradition and history, he insists that both Hindus and Muslims talk about Meera Bai and Kabir, Amir Khusro and Tulsi Das as a part of the same heritage. He is sure that we can still learn from the Hindu and the Muslim traditions of the Indian subcontinent.*

If he is right in asserting that there was so much give and take between Hindus and Muslims throughout our history, that they could exchange ideas at the profoundest philosophical levels, then it is difficult to talk about the emergence of Pakistan as inevitable. There seems to be a contradiction between Intizar Husain's version of India's composite culture, and Qureshi's history of Muslim separation.

KS: Alok, I am thankful to Intizar Husain Sahib for spelling out our cultural complexity in such a beautiful way. He is right when he invokes Kabir and Tulsi Das, Meera Bai and Bulleh Shah and Baba Farid to talk about our heritage. Sakhi Sarvar's shrine was regarded as a holy place both by Hindus and Muslims. But they didn't make concessions to each other even as they lived with each other.

You must, however, remember that once people become conscious of their separate identities, their modes of living and their expectations also change. If we go back in time, we find the National Congress and the Muslim League moving in contrary directions. The Muslim League was working for a separate state for Muslims, and Hindus in the Congress with their defensive psyche were protecting some of their cherished ideals. Whatever their political strategies, their symbols too, were very different indeed.

The relations between Muslims and Hindus underwent a sea-change with the rise of political awareness. Once upon a time there was an accepted and traditional way of defining these relations. Now political awareness brought with it new expectations and new challenges—it also raised new questions about our inherited assumptions.

AB: *What was the reaction in your home when it was announced that India was going to be partitioned? You told me that your parents wanted to live in Pakistan. Why?*

KS: I was in Delhi in March 1947. All government servants had been asked to fill up a form stating in which country they would prefer to live and work. My father opted for Pakistan. There were two reasons for that. My family owned lands and properties there. An old haveli and other properties also needed looking after. The other reason was that my family members thought there would be better opportunities in Pakistan. There were, of course, lots of Muslims, too, who opted to stay on in India—particularly those who had property or small landholdings here. I think everyone was under the impression that since they had lived together, they could continue to do so.

Anyway, my father was persuaded to change his mind by a friend of his who was a Muslim and was holding an important seat in the Home Ministry. He thought my father was being naive. Unfortunately, it soon became clear that it was no longer possible to continue existing as in the past. Many Muslims who had opted to live here also decided to migrate to Pakistan after some time.

AB: *Did people feel that the demarcation of new boundaries and the emergence of new nations did not call for the exchange of populations?*

KS: Perhaps yes. But I am not sure if everyone felt that way. The Punjabi Hindus certainly did. They had witnessed many changes of power. They remembered the times when invaders slaughtered one village, burnt down another, and converted the third—to demonstrate their power. In those days, Muslims were an imperial power and Hindus were their subjects. It was only after 1857 that Muslims lost control over the nation. The British squashed them. They no longer felt that they had a "mother nation." We had; we could assert that we belonged to this land. Muslims too had political aspirations, but they knew that they could never regain their old power.

AB: *Was this sense that India was not their land true of all the Muslims? Surely, there were many nationalist Muslims for whom India was home? Consider Dr. Ansari, Maulana Azad, etc.*

KS: Yes. That was also true of the Khilafat supporters. The Khilafat movement certainly cemented the bonds between Hindus and Muslims, though only for the time being. Many Muslims did say to themselves, "If Hindus can support our cause, we can also live with them, be with them."

But I do feel the relations between the two communities had started worsening after the repeal of the partition of Bengal. It made Muslims feel that the nationalism of the majority community was Hindu nationalism. This made them take the next step, which was to demand the partition of the country.

AB: *Do you really believe that the national movement was an expression of Hindu nationalism?*

KS: Yes, to a great extent, it was Hindu nationalism. Consider works like *Anandamath* or songs like *Bande Mataram*. Hindus were upset by the reorganization of Bengal; but the reorganization of states was not a new thing. The North West Frontier Province had been carved out of Punjab by the British. Surely, there was nothing wrong with the division of Bengal. It would have come to be accepted, had there not followed such a fierce, almost hysteric opposition to it from so many parties. That certainly upset Muslims. They felt that Hindus were likely to oppose any move that favoured them. It is likely that if the partition of Bengal had not been repealed, Muslims would not have demanded Pakistan later on.

AB: *You must surely have known many Muslims who felt that this was their land as much as it was the land of Hindus.*

KS: Yes. There were many Muslims who felt the same way as Hindus. However, once we began to play the politics of separate electorates, etc., the British seized the chance to increase the rift between the communities.

At the social and cultural level, the two communities were quite close to each other. I would like to repeat that in spite of the political noise, both Hindus and Muslims continued to show reverence for saints like Khwaja Khizar, Baba Farid and others. Khwaja Khizar was considered to be the pir of life. It was said that his eternal boat, though invisible, always floated on the rivers and helped people to cross. Our family had great faith in Baba Farid and nothing was done without invoking his blessings.

AB: *Recently, I met Sant Singh Sikhon, who told me something startling. He said that in rural Punjab no Muslim was allowed to read the 'azan' publicly. Was that true?*

KS: Certainly not. My novel *Zindaginama* opens with the *azan*. It was an important part of village life. There was no hostility towards the practice. We respected it. Absolutely. Remember that Hindus always went to the holy places of Muslims to receive blessings. Pregnant women visited the *mazars* of the pirs, etc.

AB: *Did Muslims visit the holy places of Hindus?*

KS: Yes, I have seen Muslims in city and village Gurdwaras—in red Turkish caps—sitting along with others. This was not an unusual sight but this created curiosity and interest among us children. It was their otherness which fascinated me.

AB: *Where were you in August 1947?*

KS: On August 15th, 1947, we insisted on going to the Red Fort. When we reached Daryaganj, we saw a sea of humanity all around us. That day the Jama Masjid seemed a bit forlorn. There were a few lights on the minarets, but it wasn't as well-lit as the Red Fort or the Gurudwara Shish Ganj. As we stood near the tram tracks, we noticed a Sikh boy who had lost his right arm. He was in his early teens, or maybe even younger. He was singing a song to a group of refugees standing around him. I still remember that song:

Jai, jai Jawaharlal
Tu ne kar diya kamaal
Desh phaad ke de diya
Hamey yeh rumal ...
Ke jao ankhen ponchh lo!

When people heard that song, tears sprang to their eyes. Even we cried. It was obvious that the boy had composed this ditty himself. Everyone gave him coins.

The tensions on both sides of the border in the aftermath of the partition had been unbearable. We had left everything behind, had lost everything. In addition, our Muslim friends in India, friends we were so fond of, were leaving for Pakistan. Yet, one could not discuss the situation with anyone. The events of those days had a terrible effect on all of us.

When the killings started in Delhi, we were very worried about the families of Muslim friends living in Delhi and New Delhi. When we heard from someone that the family of a well-known Muslim doctor had been killed in Karol Bagh by rioters, we became really anxious about our friends. Our house was in one of the lanes near Barakhamba Road and I decided to visit our friends.

When I reached their house, I was shocked to see a lock on the door. Locked doors always produce strange emotions, but in those days the sight of a locked door was an ominous sign. I was weeping as I walked back home. Later that evening we received a brief letter from Haider Sahib saying that they had reached Purana Quila and were safe. He wanted us to send his family some food and clothes. There was a discussion in our family as to who would visit them in the refugee camp. The situation even in New Delhi was very bad, so bad that even the India Gate area was not considered safe. People were afraid to go out in the evenings. Anyway, we packed some food and clothes for them and managed to send them across. The conditions in the camp were very bad.

They were awful times. Each community was very frightened. People did not have the courage either to speak up or do anything. Bitterness lingered for a long time on both sides, especially with those who had been politically uninvolved and yet had been caught up in the conflict.

AB: *Did you ever see Gandhiji?*

KS: Yes, twice. The first time I saw him here, in Shimla. I saw him again at the Birla House in Delhi.

When he came to Shimla, I was a child. Like every child, I had seen photographs of him and was familiar with his face. My father was working in the Shimla Secretariat in those days. When the news came that Gandhiji was to visit Shimla, all those who worked in the Secretariat decided to attend his prayer meeting. The British government did not want that any of the staff should attend it. An order disallowing their participation was issued. However, someone saw to it that it was not circulated till 5 p.m.! Thus no one 'saw' it before the office closed! The staff also resolved to tell the British that they had all gone to a prayer meeting and not to see Gandhiji.

Gandhiji was staying in the house of Mohanlal Sood who was a lawyer and lived on the way to Chota Shimla. I went with my father to the prayer meeting at Sood Sahib's house and saw Gandhiji.

Alok, perhaps you are unaware that after Gandhiji was assassinated, it was first rumoured that he had been shot by a refugee. Later, it was whispered that he had been killed by a Muslim. It was many hours after his death that the name of the assassin was announced. It is a sign of our common tradition to pay homage to the departed. The programme broadcast by Radio Pakistan on Gandhiji's assassination brought comfort to people, and washed away the bitterness for the time being. One could clearly hear the announcers sobbing. You see, Pakistan was also shocked. Its citizens also regarded Gandhi as someone of their own. The announcers' voices on Radio Pakistan were full of anguish, and one could hear between words a stifled cry. I think this was one happening during those times when a divided people were brought very close to each other. The tragedy had made them one. I wonder why the tapes of those announcements have not been made available in India.

AB: *You mean, those in Pakistan also saw him as a Mahatma?*

KS: As a great human being! I remember another small incident. When our neighbours were leaving for Pakistan, we went to see them off. The grandmother cried and said, "We spun the charkha and wore khadi because Gandhi asked us to. Who could have imagined that we'd have to leave our home someday." Unfortunately, they left. Many did. We were concerned for the safety of our friends. We were worried lest their train should be attacked by violent hordes.

AB: *After the partition, there were many Hindus who stayed back in Pakistan. In order to survive, they converted to Islam. Muslims in India didn't, however, have to convert to Hinduism. Do you know people whose relatives stayed back in Pakistan. Did they ever meet each other again? What were their feelings when they did?*

KS: Yes, I knew many people whose relatives had stayed back in Pakistan. There was a woman whose family used to live in Dera Ghazi Khan. Her parents and brothers had got left behind. Many years later, when she learnt from people who travelled to Pakistan that her mother was still alive, she contacted her and went to visit her. Her mother had changed her name and was called, if I am not mistaken, Fatima. Anyway, Fatima's neighbours welcomed her as a daughter. They gave her gifts of clothes and money. She stayed at her mother's place for a while. When it was time for her to return to India, her mother asked her to visit her father's grave. He too had become a Muslim. She refused to do so. She told her mother that as far as she was concerned, her father had been killed in the riots. She couldn't bring herself to go to his grave and pay homage. When I asked her about it, all she said was that she simply couldn't accept the fact that he had been buried according to Muslim rites. "I have tried to find the reason for it, I have scratched my soul to discover if there was a hidden cause. All I can say is that I simply couldn't..."

AB: *I have a difficult and painful question to ask. Did you know or talk to women who were victims of the partition? How did they deal with their trauma? As a novelist, have you been able to find the language to talk about the experiences of women as victims?*

KS: Well, normally, I wouldn't talk about them. It is difficult to do so. When families of migrants meet, they don't talk about the partition because it is a painful subject. It troubles everyone, especially the women. Most families have let time help them forget the past, forget even the names of the women who were killed or left behind. I have never heard anyone mentioning the girls who either killed themselves or were abducted. It is a forbidden subject. In our family there were two girls who got left behind. We don't know what happened to them. We like to believe that they are dead. The fate of women during the partition was a great burden on the Hindu mind. Well, not just on the Hindu mind, but on the minds of all those who migrated.

AB: *I am sure Muslims are equally troubled.*

KS: Yes, sure enough. It is terrible to think about the entire subject. Women on both sides had to pay very heavily. They were the victims of mob violence.

Muslim women rescued from India and sent across were accepted in Pakistan more easily. They were somehow rehabilitated in society. Hindus, as a whole, did not accept their women back. There were some families which surrounded such women with deep silences.

It seems to me that those people who tried to defend their women—Sikhs especially had a sense of masculine pride in doing so—were able to deal with the women who had suffered, better than the others. They showed a greater sensitivity to the fact that these unfortunate women were a part of their families, that they were their wives, sisters, daughters...

AB: *How did we deal with the entire issue socially?*

KS: Those were abnormal times and abnormal situations: people faced them in their own way. The Governments of India and Pakistan had agreed to the repatriation of women left behind but we don't know how the cases of children were handled.

Let me tell you the story of a man called Buta Singh. It is a true story. One day there were riots in the small town where he lived. A young Muslim girl trying to escape from a mob that was chasing her came running into his house and hid herself under a large heap of straw in the courtyard. Later that evening when Buta Singh returned home, he sensed that there was someone hiding under the straw heap. He saw the corner of a chunni sticking out. He persuaded the girl to come out of hiding. He assured her, "Don't be afraid, nothing will happen to you. You are safe here. Stay indoors till the riots are over."

The girl stayed in his house for many days. During the entire period, they didn't talk to each other. Buta Singh, who was old but a bachelor, cooked food for her.

A few days later, a young boy playing on the roof of a neighbour's house saw the girl in Buta Singh's house. He told his parents about her. Soon the entire neighbourhood knew that Buta Singh had given shelter to a Muslim girl. When Buta Singh came back home, his neighbours asked him about her. He defended her with great courage and warned his neighbours not to harm her. The girl was touched by his honesty and courage. She continued to stay with him. Soon they fell in love with each other. In any case, her situation was desperate and she didn't have many choices.

One of the neighbours said to Buta Singh, "Now that the girl is living in your house, why don't you marry her?"

Buta Singh said, "I have no objection, but you should ask the girl too."

The girl thought that Buta Singh was a decent human being. She agreed to marry him. The marriage was performed in a Gurdwara. In due course, a daughter was born to them, and the family was complete.

After some time, her brothers came to the town with military escort, looking for her. When they found her, they insisted she return with them to Pakistan. According to the agreement between Pakistan and India, she had to go with them. Buta Singh pleaded with the authorities to allow her to stay with him. He told them she was his legally wedded wife and that she had married him of her own free will. She was, however, forced to leave with her brothers.

After some time, Buta Singh went to Pakistan in the hope of bringing her back. He showed the girl's brothers the proof of his marriage to her. The girl also declared that she had married him because she had fallen in love with him. The brothers didn't agree to let her go. The matter went to court. The girl appeared in court, but refused to utter a word. Buta Singh pleaded with her. He told her she was his wife and that he would die without her. He was in a terrible shape. The girl, however, didn't say a word. She had obviously been threatened by her brothers. It was not difficult to imagine her psychological condition. Buta Singh was shattered and committed suicide.

There were many such incidents in those days.

AB: *The one text I know where the fate of women during the partition has been dealt with in great detail is Bhisham*

Sahni's Tamas. *I am thinking in particular of the scene where women throw themselves into a well. The incident is based on a historically authentic event.*

KS: Bhishamji's novel is remarkable. It helped people to look at the partition with some clarity. For instance, it made them realize that those who had suffered and migrated were ordinary people, and had their roots in the soil.

Tamas had another quality. For example, the scene in which the women jump into the well was written with such restraint that it was not sensational. It made one cry, but it didn't arouse any desire for revenge. A less mature novelist could have faltered here.

The partition is now in the past and it should be possible for writers of the new generation—on both sides—to write about it with some clarity, especially since the fog of emotions has lifted.

One day someone came to see me. His language was so chaste—certainly so much more chaste than mine—that I was sure he was from Lucknow or Allahabad. Anyway, he was a second generation migrant from Pakistan. He wanted to talk to me because I had written about the Gakkhars in *Zindaginama*. His ancestors, he claimed, were from Pakistan; he wanted to know more about them because he felt a sense of kinship with them. The point I am trying to make is that for him the partition was already history, something he could talk about unemotionally.

AB: *Was the main emphasis in many of the fictional accounts written about the partition on violence?*

KS: Yes, it was. Yet most of them never forgot to emphasize the basic humanity of people. They also spelled out in detail the fact that the partition was a political decision.

AB: *Is it the function of the novelist to give solace to people?*

KS: No, but it is, perhaps, important for the novelist to show that people had not lost sight of what was right.

AB: *Manto didn't do that. His work about the partition is full of rage.*

KS: True, but only a major writer is capable of expressing that kind of rage. Manto knew that when people are expelled from their homes and forced to live in camps, they have no capacity or inner resources for rational thought left. All they can do is recall their homes, their lands... After some time, however, it does become possible to think about the past in more complex ways...

Perhaps, the most significant and profound comment on the relationship of the two communities is that Rahi Masoom Reza wrote the script of *The Mahabharata* for television. That, I think, should be seen as a great event. It has wiped out all differences. It is worth noticing how profoundly he has absorbed our culture and how profoundly he has been absorbed by it.

AB: *When I was in Pakistan a few years ago, I didn't feel that I was in a strange foreign country. Everything around me seemed familiar. Indeed, when I asked Intizar Sahib whether I could send him anything from India which wasn't available in Pakistan, he only asked for some Hindi books.*

KS: It is so very exciting to know that Intizar Sahib has asked you for Hindi books from India. I would love to send him copies of *Zindaginama* and *Dilo Daanish*. Do bring some Urdu books from Lahore when you go there next. Give my salaams to Lahore and Intizar. When I think of Lahore, I go back to the days of my youth just before the partition. Life then was so romantic, slow, deep and beautiful. Really, they were good times, they were great times.

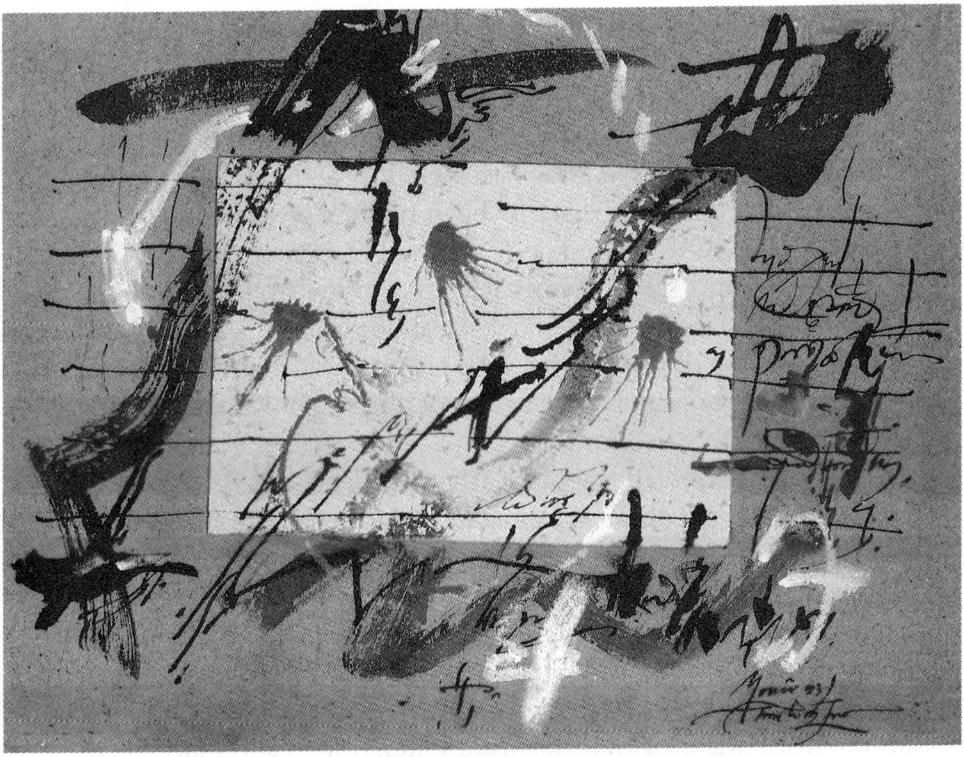

Blood-drenched, *watercolour by Monirul Islam, Dhaka*

II
NEW AND OLD WRITINGS

SUKRITA PAUL KUMAR

Cementing the Fissure: Urdu Literature from Across the Border

The political declaration of the birth of a separate geographical domain cannot create a separate cultural identity overnight. For a culture to acquire its own identifiable shape and colour, it has to remain in the womb of history over a period, when it is protected, fed and cherished. While the political dividing line after partition had to be functionally realized, many aspects of the cultural baggage could not but remain undivided.

The Partition was traumatic: for those displaced and the generations that followed. Hysterical communal violence and mass migration of people created a psychological imbalance and the uprooted could not come to accept the idea of Pakistan. In the introduction to a volume of Urdu short stories Kamleshwar writes with the sensitivity of an artist when he says: "I'd take the risk and say that though Pakistan may be the name of some country, but for us writers, meaningless hatred, fear and suspicion, directionless 'ahumanity' are only the other names for political manipulation."[1] According to him, Manto issued a 'Fatwa' on this very truth by writing the story *Toba Tek Singh.* Manto in fact draws a historical question mark on the thinking and political ideas of Nehru, Sardar Patel, Jinnah and Liaquat Ali Khan. Toba Tek Singh is a character from the lunatic asylum; ironically, what emerges through his madness is a very sane rejection of the insanity of political decisions. He dies on no-man's land rather than crossing the border. And Deewane Maulvi Sahib of *Khwabro*, a novellete by Joginder Paul, actually crosses the border, carrying his Lucknow in his mind; while he settles in Karachi, he thinks he is in Lucknow and does not recognize it as 'Pakistan'.[2] With a deep-seated desire for the continuation of life in his own homeland, Deewane Maulvi Sahib escapes into insanity.

For a long time the reality of Pakistan remained with the people of the subcontinent as a metaphor more than a specific land or culture. The metaphor got defined through the way in which a person experienced 'Pakistan'. In Kamleshwar's story *Kitne Pakistan*? (How many Pakistans?), Pakistan becomes a gruesome metaphor for violence, vengeance and anger.[3] It is a curse thrown at a person. The same Pakistan evolves as solace and home for Mirasin of Joginder Paul's short story *Panahgah*.[4] Mirasin has been gang-raped and later when taken to a hospital, the compassion and love of the young doctor arouses a gush of maternal passion in her. She perceives him as her "Phattu". She was told that all Muslims had been packed to Pakistan along with her dear ones. For her, Pakistan was home then; and indeed, wherever there be solace, there'd be home, her Pakistan.

Wazir Agha, an eminent critic and poet of Pakistan, published an article on *25 Years of Urdu Literature in Pakistan* in a literary journal called *Auraq*, with a focus on post-Partition writings.[5] Feeling quite lost and homeless for sometime after the Partition, the Pakistani writer woke up later to the concrete reality of the land of Pakistan with all its natural and urban environs. This consciousness of their surroundings projects itself in the Urdu ghazal written by such poets as Majeed Ahmed, Shehnaz Ahmed, Muneer Niyazi, Parveen Shakir and others.

Leaving Persian and related imagery behind, the new Urdu ghazal was vitalized by the freshness of new local images and symbols. The social and natural specificity of Pakistan was thus brought within the ambit of direct human experience through poetry.

> The yellow bird darted out of the bush,
> paused on a trembling branch for a second,
> flew off into the sky, then came back to earth.
>
> The branch of the henna bush bowed.
> A faint and sweet fragrance spread.
> Your hands, knitting a shawl, stopped.
>
> (Wazir Agha)[6]

Wazir Agha's poem *Apprehension* grows from a direct relationship with the local "yellow bird" and the "branch of the henna bush." The poem lifts itself to a philosophical apprehension about the stability of the earth itself, yielding a quick glimpse of the dark and silent void beyond. What brought about a fundamental change in the artist's perception was a psychological proximity to one's new land. A feel for that land developed into what some commentators misconceived as "the Cult of Earth worship". Wazir Agha had really felt the need to highlight the importance of the geo-social roots of a culture. This was known as the Sargodha school of thought.

Agha traces the origin and development of Pakistani culture by going to the roots of the culture of Mohen-jo-daro, perhaps to silence the rather aggressive noise produced by the religio-political leaders in the country. He hinted at the possibility of a link with Iraq and other semitic cultures if lower layers of Mohen-jo-daro were to be further excavated. The constant recurrence of the ghost of India evidenced in music, painting, literature and in the very ethos of their people unnerved those from the "establishment." To quote Fahmida Riaz on this:

> Pakistan was a fait accompli, for whose creation further slogan mongering and breast beating was hardly called for. Yet the bureaucracy persisted in its quest to 'justify' the creation of Pakistan. Debate on Pakistani culture was supposedly the last mantra to exorcise the laughing ghost of India. It did not work."[7]

To go back to Wazir Agha, the essence of his school of thought in fact pointed towards the common and shared roots of the sub-continent to be located in the ancient civilization of Mohen-jo-daro.

Where can one discern the beginnings of Pakistani culture: in the arrival of the Muslims in the sub-continent? Or then, do the roots spread in the distant past, in the ancient Indian civilization? For the intellectuals of Pakistan, this becomes an ongoing debate. Waheed Quaraishi, Jameel Jalibi, Ajmal and others joined the discussion in their attempt to define Pakistani cultural identity. Though Maulana Iqbal's concept of "Khudi" never became a popular reference point, self-identity and national identity have been a matter of major concern in both Indian and Pakistani Urdu literature.

> Aali apne des ki likhe aur todi kehlayen
> Surma log bidesi paise khaye aur itrayen[8]

Jameeluddin Aali, a Pakistani poet, exploring the folk lyricism of *doha*, used a form of poetry reminiscent of the medieval times of the subcontinent. By adapting *doha* as the form of his poetic expression not only did he revitalize a traditional cultural practice, but he also revealed a latent dimension of his own consciousness: the input of a generic North Indian cultural form into the evolving of his own cultural reality as much as the consciousness of an entire people. The discerning of this lineage effectively bridges time-gaps and indicates a deeper continuity of shared concerns, irrespective of disruptive political happenings. Aali's collection *Pakistan Katha* sings the story of Pakistan emerging out of a collective cultural consciousness and moving creatively towards a future that could work out the contours of the specific Pakistani culture eventually.

Memory and myth play a definite role in understanding contemporary life as an extension of the past. Qurratulain Hyder's novel *Aag ki Dariya* places the cognition of living characters of today against the backdrop of ancient history. So does Abdullah Husain's novel *Udas Naslein*. The invocation of the rich resource of cultural memories can indeed arouse a nostalgia for the past. But then, that also, is a real enough psychic context to confront rather than pretend that one is free of it.

After all, when a writer like Intizar Husain migrated to Pakistan, a storehouse of memory went along with him to the new land. In his fiction he goes beyond the memory of a few individuals and digs into the vastness of racial memory; as Wazir Agha puts it, he sees today's atmosphere and characters walking about in the mirror of old mythical tales.[9] In form and content, some of Intizar Husain's stories are the cultural legacy of medieval times. Both in the telling of the tale and the tale itself, the writer creates the present through the formidable shadow of the past, wherever he can. That certain human concerns and predicaments remain the same despite the difference of space and gaps in time becomes a poignant realization in such stories as *Kashti* (The Boat)[10]. Problems of human and animal survival amidst the Great Floods in mythical history are as impending as the problems of the human predicament today. Technology and scientific progress have in no way reduced the struggle for existence.

It is the inverse of the above experience that one derives from a poem such as *Shakkerpariyon ki Pahari* by Muneer Niyazi. From a very concrete geographical and local reference, the poem yields the experience of a rather abstract painting of blue dreams and winds captured in pathways. It is *Shakkerpariyon ki Pahari,* the title of the poem, which makes the setting real and the atmosphere of the poem convincing. From the purely imaginary Persian locales, the Pakistani poet's mind began to relate to the land of Pakistan. The emotional involvement in this land and the creative rendering of it, is what in a way announces the arrival of a specific Pakistani Urdu poetry.

Mohammad Hasan identifies three points of axes around which the literature of Pakistan revolves: (a) Islami (b) local, native culture (c) historical.[11] The basis of the Partition of the subcontinent was religion, even though with secular ideas; soon after the birth of Pakistan, Urdu was made out to be the language of the Muslims. The language of the people became merely the language for Islam. Unnatural boundaries were drawn around the vibrant, live language, caging it within religio-political bars. In Pakistan, Urdu took firm roots as the national language and Sindhi, Baluchi, Punjabi, Siraki became secondary; and in India even though Urdu was later accepted as one of the state languages, its linkage with Islam hampered its free growth. The tendency to restrict the language with religion has done more harm than good to Urdu, whether in India or Pakistan. Pakistan is not one cultural and linguistic entity. The misconception that it is so, grows out of an indifference to the diversity of local cultural entities.

The year 1947 brought an influx of migrants into Sindh, Punjab and other states of what became Pakistan. These migrants called themselves *mohajirs*—a word derived from 'hijrat' meaning the holy Prophet's migration from Mecca to Medina. Sindhis preferred to call them *panah-geer* meaning 'refugee'. While Urdu used by Sindhi, Baluchi or Punjabi writers gained by acquiring the hues of various local languages, as Fahmida Riaz points out, Punjabi was relegated to the position of a 'folk language', a language of the masses. In the Punjab, Urdu was used by the intelligentsia. Iqbal, Manto, Faiz Ahmed Faiz, Ahmed

Nazim Qasmi, Balwant Singh of *Jagga* fame and others lent the Punjabi idiom to their Urdu. A strong sense of bilingualism reflects itself in their use of Urdu. Punjabi writers in Urdu churned out massive literature on the Partition depicting communal carnage, atrocities and salvaging humanity by portraying moments of compassion amidst the deluge of violence. Ahmed Nadeem Qasmi's story *Permisher Singh*, for instance, unfurls love realized through intense suffering. Urdu language and literature sensitively synthesized with Punjabi culture and language and accommodated within its folds more and newer layers of meaning and experience.

Unfortunately, in the wake of meaningless and gruesome political happenings, an atmosphere of suspicion and fear takes over and sometimes what is churned out instantly as literature is generally a representation of alarmist sensitivities. The Indo-Pak war of 1965 fanned animosities and hatred. Even such fine writers like Ahmed Nadeem Qasmi of *Permisher Singh* or Ashfaq Ahmed, the writer of *Gadariya*, and Mumtaz Mufti, climbed onto the bandwagon of war propagandists breeding mistrust for the "Other". The "Other" for Pakistan was India and all that was on the other side of the border was to be despised.

The connection of Urdu with 'Islamiat' and 'Islamiat' with 'Pakistaniat' was strengthened by Mohammad Hasan Askari who perceived the foundation of Pakistani culture in 'Islamiat'. On the other hand, the new generation of progressive writers in the post-Partition era remained indifferent to religion and aligned themselves with the material conditions of the subcontinent. To quote Mohammad Ali Siddiqui from a discussion on *Modernism in Urdu Fiction*: "Some of the writers were modern and progressive and on the other hand some of them were modern and retrogressive."[12]

What distinguishes Pakistani modernism from the Indian is the fact that while in Pakistan the progressives could also be modern, in India the progressives and the moderns confronted each other. But in both, to be modern indicated that the creative writer began to strip life-experiences of the half-truths built by old beliefs. The dynamism of the new experiences could be realized only through a direct confrontation with the starkness of reality. Nikka of Enver Sajjad's story *Gaae* (The Cow) resents the harsh truth that his people are callous and mercenary and that they would sell the cow to the slaughter-house rather than spend money on her treatment. "At last one day, they huddled together and decided it was time to write off the cow—a case fit for the slaughter-house."[13] The story begins with such a tough and matter-of-fact decision by the 'herd' of elders; only Nikka, the child who is emotionally attached with the 'mother' cow, questions the decision of the 'wise' old men. When as a strategy to get the cow on the truck, her maternal pull for the calf is cleverly exploited by them, Nikka revolts in a frenzy, runs inside and gets Baba's double-barrel gun.

> I don't know what happened next. At whom did Nikka aim his gun? At the cow, the calf, or at the driver? Or was it at Baba or at himself? Or is he still standing there with his gun aimed at the target?
>
> Would someone care to go there and and come back to tell me what had happened next? All that I know is that one day they had put their heads together and had decided that....[14]

The answer to the questions raised at the end of the story is really not relevant. What is pertinently brought home is the total absence of compassion and the completely mercenary approach of the "wise elders." By implication one would conclude then, that domestic, social and political decisions too are taken precisely in the same fashion; innocence, sensitivity and relationships are slaughtered and sacrificed on the altar of petty selfish gains in the name of maturity and wisdom. Enver Sajjad's story works as much at a symbolic and suggestive level as the realistic.One is led into wondering: what does the anguish of the cow represent?

Mansha Yad, another Pakistani writer, projects a similar vision of relatedness involving a child and an animal and contrasts it with the seasoned and tough indifference of the elders. In his story *Dangar Boli* (Language of Animals), the child understands the language of the lamb to be sacrificed. They seem to live in their own isolated world, understanding each other's language because it is the language of love.

Earlier, the progressive Urdu writers of the forties and fifties were creating a literature of commitment with an increasingly radical outlook. The style became realistic and the content very material. In that the human personality became real, flesh and blood, but it soon began to "lose its shadow"![15] For a character to acquire a convincing fullness of being it has to coexist with his shadow. The modern writer awakened to the existential subjectivity of the character and took journeys into a person's inner reality. The shadow became visible and Urdu fiction abounded in symbolic, psychological and modernistic tales of human existence. Rasheed Amjad, Mirza Hamid Beg, Ahmed Daud, amongst others, told such tales with a lot of creative fervour to come to terms with the complexity of human life in modern times.

Both in India and Pakistan, the modernist stance in Urdu literature evolves from some common sources of creative tension—the problems of survival and poverty in the subcontinent, the struggle for expression of the marginalized, the exploited and the deprived, the stresses of modern life and the question of the rehabilitation of a whole generation of Partition refugees. Indeed, in Pakistan due to the non-democratic political atmosphere, modes of resistance and pursuit of freedom sought to find guised expression through symbolism and abstraction.

Khalida Asghar's story *Saathi* written in the first-person singular in the voice of the performer-animal catches the delicate moment of transference of consciousness: the performer becomes the involved spectator. Such a feat of psychology could be convincingly presented only by a writer with a modern sensitivity evolved from a literary ethos that could accommodate and explore such an unseen and unexplained dimension of human consciousness.

The woman writer in Pakistan saw the possibilities of defining her own identity with the newly acquired awareness of the dignity of her own female individuality:

> My mind talks to me, and I know, that is the court of loneliness...I see the pain of solitude on the face of God... I do not seek the king of the world. I am merely a girl with eyes that are waiting and I wait for the ocean, but it does not come up to me...when my feet do not move, I remember that my lower body is made up of dust and breeze... how shall I come out of the circle of my existence, my eyes are looking at me.[16]

Dipping into the depth of her female self, Zahida Hina, in her story *Meri Aankhein* (My Eyes), unmasks that aspect of a woman's life which is traditionally expressed only in a private diary. Hina shows some courage in offering her own female perceptions in fiction meant for public consumption. Ismat Chughtai and Qurratulain Hyder had paved the way for a woman to become the central concern of the writer. The absent and the mute had to be made visible and articulate. What Ruksana Ahmad says about women poets is true of women fiction writers too:

> ...the literary establishment always implies that women poets are a special case : they achieve publication and, sometimes, celebrity because they are women rather than because they are poets... They are easily marginalized by the implication that the interest in the work derives from its rarity rather than from intrinsic qualities the work may possess.[17]

The human spirit demands a natural flow of expression for an authentic realization of its predicament and experience. The process of socialization may constrain and confine the spirit for a while; but brave departures in the form of protest soon begin to burst the masks imposed by conditioning. Feminism too is first an awareness of the disadvantages and constraints faced by women and second, it is a recognition of their need and desire for freedom and change. In *We Sinful Women*, Rukhsana Ahmad puts together some of the more significant poetic voices of the recent past resisting the onslaught of patriarchy in a traditional and politically non-democratic society:

> It is we sinful women
> who came out raising the banner of truth
> up against barricades of lies on the highways
> who find stories of persecution piled on each threshold
> who find tongues that could speak have been severed.
>
> Kishwar Naheed[18]

As an editor of *Maah-i-Nau*, a prestigious monthly, Kishwar Naheed ceaselessly asserted the voice of the woman against the stranglehold of the oppressive social and aesthetic values of a male dominated society. Fahmida Riaz, the editor of *Awaaz*, wrote *The Body Lacerated*, a book which is a vigorous exploration of female sexuality. Defying the notion of 'ideal woman' perpetuated in a romantic, ornamental style in traditional Urdu poetry, fresh and live images of women emerged through a wave of self-aware and highly politicized women poets. They knew what they were up against.

In the name of religion and Islamisation, a nationwide campaign called 'Chadur aur Chardiwari' was carried out in General Zia's time to assure the exclusion of women in public affairs and keep them confined to their homes. Women became the subject of a major revival of oppressive laws. The retrogressive changes provoked the feminists into action. The Women's Action Forum launched itself in Karachi, Lahore, Islamabad, Rawalpindi and Peshawar. More and more women became conscious of the need to resist attempts of further oppression.

In Sara Shagufta's poetry, the gush of poetic energy combines with outbursts of woman's experience, violating all conventions of form and content. An evidence of how she gave creative vent to her feminist anguish and anger lies in the biographical letter she published along with her only collection of poems, *Eyes*:

> I had a temperature of 105 degrees. I got on to the bus and went home. My breasts were overflowing. I filled a glass with milk and kept it on the table. The poet and the other scribes returned. I said to the poet, 'I gave birth to a boy but he has died.'
> He heard it casually and mentioned it to his critics.
> There was silence in the room for two minutes.
> What do you think of Freud?
> What does Rimbaud say?
> What has Saadi said?
> Warris Shah was the greatest.
> I used to hear these things everyday but the words sounded clearer today.
> As if all these great people had stopped in my blood for a little while. And as if Rimbaud and Freud were snatching my baby from my womb. That day knowledge entered my home for the first time and was screaming with laughter in my blood. Look at the birth of my child.[19]

No wonder Sara Shagufta committed suicide. Although in numbers there may not have been many women poets and writers, qualitatively the small minority of these poets have substantially contributed towards the questioning of the existing female role models. The silent and the invisible were brought under the focus of their vital spotlight, seeking not just to redefine their contours but also actually 'see' them and their deprivation.

Poets like Zehra Nigah, Ishrat Aafreen, Saada Gazdar joined others already mentioned above, to sustain and support each other and create a register of resistance through poetic sensitization. If left resting on the edifice of exploitation and inequality, society would slip into a world of perversion or a gruesome psychological underworld.

Faiz Ahmed Faiz had appealed to serious writers in Pakistan to speak truthfully without fear and exercise their right to express themselves. The writer, he said, cannot compromise and is not an opportunist. He should not betray his own experience and its specific cognition.[20] Literature then becomes a very useful reservoir of authentic human experience salvaging humanity from offensive and inhuman practices perpetuated in the name of religion, politics etc.

For an effective dissemination of Urdu literature in Pakistan, journals have consistently and formidably built a creative and critical consciousness among general readers. The sustained efforts of such journals as Ahmed Nadeem Qasmi's *Funoon*, Wazir Agha's *Auraq*, *Naqoosh*, *Sareer*, *Afkar*, *Maah-i-Nau* have gone a long way in according a vital space for Urdu literature in Pakistani society. There are avid readers of these journals in India as well. They are keenly sought after and their non-availability is actually resented. Well brought out, they are substantial in both their creative as well as critical output.

Bahav, a recent novel from Pakistan, covers a whole range of emotional geography when the author Tarad excavates distant civilizations of ancient history to uncover our shared past. Writers and readers reach out to each other across the borders, imbibing each other's experiences and creative ventures and building strong cultural bridges. Irrespective of political hostilities between the two countries, the rapport between the two peoples is strong and can remain so. One of the ways to assure this is to keep Urdu alive and make Urdu literature from across the borders available. Urdu literature from the two countries helps build channels of communication. The shared sentiment connects the subcontinent once again as a unit containing diverse local realities with a common heritage and a common set of contemporary problems. It is simply a question of prioritizing such an understanding over political complications contrived through hostility imposed externally or fanned by narrow communalism. The fire and the passion have to be conserved as energy for progress rather than hatred.

Notes

1. Kamleshwar, ed., *Bhartiya Shikhar Katha Kosh: Urdu Kahaniyan* 2, New Delhi: Pustakayan, 1992.
2. Joginder Paul, *Khwabro*, Delhi: Rajkamal Publications, 1990.
3. Kamleshwar, "Kitne Pakistan", *Bharat Vibhajan: Hindi Ki Shreshtha Kahaniyan*, ed. Narendra Mohan, New Delhi: Satsahitya Prakashan, 1984.
4. Joginder Paul, "Panahgah", *Kahan*, New Delhi: Kitabghar, 1995. p.195-208.
5. Wazir Agha, "25 Years of Urdu Literature in Pakistan", trans. Sheesh Khan, *Pahal: Pakistan Mein Urdu Qalam*, 17-18, ed. Gyanranjan, p.22-23.
6. Wazir Agha, "Apprehension", trans. C.M. Nain, *Urdu Canada, ed. W.A. Shaheen*, vol.1, no.3, Ottawa: Urdu Canada Publications, 1987, p.84.
7. Fahmida Riaz, *Pakistan Literature and Society*, New Delhi: Patriot Publishers, 1986, p.87.
8. Ibid., Jameeluddin Ali, "Pakistan Katha", *Pahal*, 17-18, p.78.
9. Ibid., Wazir Agha, *Pahal*, 17-18.
10. Intizar Husain, "Kashti", trans. Avtar Singh Judge, *Breakthrough*, ed. Sukrita Paul Kumar, Shimla: IIAS, 1993.
11. Ibid., Mohd. Hasan, "Tahzibi Shinakht ka Masla", *Pahal*, 17- 18, p.13-16.
12. Sukrita Paul Kumar, *Conversations on Modernism*, Shimla: IIAS, 1990, p.119-129.
13. Enver Sajjad, "The Cow", *Contemporary Urdu Short Stories*, trans. Jai Ratan, Delhi: Sterling Publishers, 1991.
14. Ibid., p.141.
15. Ibid., Wazir Agha, *Pahal*, 17-18.
16. Zahida Hina, "Meri Ankhein", *Pakistani Urdu Kahaniyan*, ed. Aziz Indori & Ajay Didan, New Delhi: Seemant Prakashan, 1987, p.118.
17. Rukhsana Ahmed, trans. & ed., *We Sinful Women*, Introduction, New Delhi: Rupa & Co., 1984.
18. Ibid., Kishwar Naheed.
19. Ibid., Sara Shagufta.
20. Ibid., Faiz Ahmed Faiz, *Pahal*, 17-18.

Portrait of Nazrul, pen and ink by Qamrul Hasan

SUBHAS MUKHOPADHYAY

Open Sesame

In today's India, the fetish over language does disservice to our national integration. How language changes hands with the change of time and place can be illustrated with the lives of two literary giants of Eastern India: Jyotiprasad Agarwal and Kazi Nazrul Islam. The Agarwal family settled in Assam and, in course of time, Jyotiprasad became one of the makers of modern Assamese literature. In a similar way, the ancestors of Kazi Nazrul Islam emigrated from Patna in Bihar during the reign of the last Mughal emperor, to settle down in Churulia village in Burdwan. Who could dream in those days that one of their progenies would be in future the stormy petrel of Bengal, presaging Indian independence!

When I first stepped into Calcutta in the early thirties, the city was in turmoil. Close upon the non-cooperation movement, self-immolation of revolutionary heroes was almost a daily affair. On one of those days, as a child, I attended a Tagore lecture in the Senate Hall on prosody, without understanding a word. Another time, I accompanied our landlord to visit his imprisoned brother at Alipore Central Jail. As a bonus I had direct access to a vivacious Subhas Chandra Bose greeting a fresh batch of young volunteers in person.

As a newcomer to the city, I thanked my stars when my father directed my attention towards a car and said with excitement, 'Look! It is Nazrul..." Agape, I had only a glimpse of the glowing face of the long-haired man. I cursed my luck as the car approached the same place which we had left only a few minutes ago. It was the residence of Sabitriprasanna Chattopadhyay, the well-known editor of *Upasana,* and author of several books of poems. We hailed from the same village.

I have cherished that fleeting vision of Nazrul throughout my life. In our early days, Tagore was revered by all. But close to our hearts was Nazrul. At a time when Tagore overawed and overshadowed everybody, to make a mark in Bengal was not easy. Nazrul found his way through the vicissitudes of life as being one with his people. He contended against the dark forces both within and without. For the most part self-educated, his command over folklore, mythology, scripture and history helped him to gain access to the hearts and minds of his audience with ease. His mode of language and rhythm always agreed with his content. Nazrul engendered in the Bengali language a vigour and firmness which was badly needed at the time.

Throughout his life Nazrul had to sail against the wind. His academic life was discontinued due to adversity; but he never failed to educate himself. Learning the languages of Urdu, Persian and Sanskrit, he became conversant with the ethos of our people. When still a boy, he wrote songs for *Leto,* a local form of folk drama. During the First World War, he joined the Bengal Battalion as a havildar. Away from home, he got a larger view of life with multiple languages and different cultures. Later, he put to use this knowledge to augment his power of innovation. As a combatant, he came face to face with all shades of tyranny, bigotry, disparity and hypocrisy. When he came home, Nazrul assumed a new role to prove that the pen was mightier than the sword. In his case, indeed it was.

Nazrul brought out a bi-weekly, *Dhumketu,* the Comet—calling to mind his own abrupt comet-like appearance in the firmament of Bengali literature. Tagore sent a blessing for this paper in verse, hoping that it would build a fiery flyover across the enclosing darkness and, that after storming the stronghold of misery and despondency, that it would some day come out in flying colours.

Soon Nazrul was behind bars for a year, having written a seditious poem. During the trial he pointed out that, "A poet gives voice to the truth, which no power on earth can throttle. The tyrants can take away his flute, not his music, for it is in his soul, not in the flute."

Born into an orthodox Muslim family, he married Pramila Sengupta, a Hindu woman he loved. He believed in universal brotherhood and in the reconciliation of all religions. He fought bigotry and apostasy in every field. Nazrul's answer to the 'divide-and-rule' policy of the British was 'unite-and-fight'. It was his 'open sesame' strategy to unlock the doors of freedom. He honoured his words by living up to every word that he uttered.

Nazrul's career as a poet was short-lived. He took to writing songs which won him fresh laurels. As a composer he proved his uniqueness, as he could seamlessly shift from poetry to music. Just when the public at that time began to make a fetish of this image of him as a rebel poet, Nazrul chose instead to set free his fine sensibilities in the field of music. As a result, Bengal's world of music cashed in—with the loss to Bengal's poetry.

When his cherished independence came a few years later and knocked on his door, there was no response! In a cruel twist of fate, he had lost his voice and memory. Breathing his last in Dhaka, Nazrul bequeathed to the people of India and Bangladesh the need to stand together.

Nazrul was spared the agony of partition. But his contemporary and counterpart in Urdu, Josh Malihabadi, a poet of the revolution and a relentless fighter for social justice and human dignity, found himself on the horns of a dilemma. For almost a decade, he shuttled between India and Pakistan without being able to decide to which country he should belong. For it involved separation not only from his near and dear ones but also from a vast audience fond of his poetry.

Those in power in Pakistan cajoled him to cross over. They wanted to profit from his popular appeal. Josh was smitten by all kinds of doubts and misgivings, as he fretted and fumed over the fate of Urdu in India. Recounting his cogitations of those days, Josh wrote in his autobiography:

> ...I then comforted myself with the hope that mutual hatred and prejudices would be overcome. A Socialist government would be formed, one that would put an end to divisive forces. That is when religious fraternity will be replaced with universal brotherhood.

He hummed:

> This is the agony of the night, let the dawn come
> Paradise will descend on earth
> Desires spread wing over heart's domain, for the dust to rise
> A chevalier will surely pass by.

But Josh could not hold out for long. The great poet died in Pakistan totally crushed and crestfallen.

Joining the Progressive Writers Movement, I earned a lifelong friendship with the Hindi writer Amrit Rai, without knowing at the time that he was the son of Munshi Premchand. I feel that Amrit could not do justice to his great promise as a *littérateur* because his father's fame overshadowed him.

Sajjad Zaheer will be remembered in posterity as the father of the Progressive Writers' Movement in India. He laid the basis of a platform where writers of different Indian languages could meet and fight for a common cause. After independence this movement was further enlarged and brought within its scope writers from all Asia and Africa. During the Alma Ata Conference of Afro-Asian writers Sajjad Zahen was happy to find that delegates from India, Pakistan and Bangladesh were united as one.

Independence, the partition and growing globalism have affected our languages in diverse ways. While promoters of sanitized Hindi have the upperhand in India, Urdu, which is neglected here, has become the official language of Pakistan—although there it is a language of the minority. The most adversely affected language is Sindhi. Under the impact of devious conditions, its development has followed different courses.

For national integration in multilingual India, we also must necessarily come out of our shell. The friendship between writers also helps their respective readers to broaden their vision and open their minds.

A unique situation occurred in East Bengal, when young people gave their lives for the sake of their mother-tongue. From the letters received in those days, I could imagine how deeply this stirred people's minds. Even in remote villages posters were pasted on roadside trees with inspiring lines quoted from Bengali. Poems set to tune were sung in market-places. Because of the dearth of books, handwritten copies were circulated among the readers.

The movement acted as a great spur to the creativity of Bengali writers. In an ode to the Bengali language, Ashraff Siddique wrote:

> A bud, that is hope, blossoms sharply in this language.
> The river Padma runs along
> Swinging in the melodies of this language.
> We are born into it and shall close our eyes for good

The birds of the forest sing, calling it sweet.
In the endearing words of this language
My mother cries out and laughs.
It is my speech and yours and our mother's too,
It is Bengali.

(tr. Animeshkanti Pal)

Begum Sufia Kamal did not fail to remember the martyrs:

The tears of night on this blood-smeared track
can never wipe out
the red streak of blood
which burns again
on this day of falgun
when flowers blossom in many forests.
When a mother waits with anguish
for her prodigal son to return,
unknown fears gather in her breast.
The young bride lights a lamp and waits
anxiously, with longing eyes.
But they shall not return. ....

(tr. Pritish Nandy)

During the Bangladesh war, an impossible reign of terror was unleashed on such a massive scale. Many writers had to stay in exile. Prominent intellectuals were liquidated in a most gruesome way. How did the stay-at-home writers feel in those furious days? One can find their anguish expressed in some lines by Shamsur Rahman:

Of course, a street dog, he is.
... Wagging his tail oft and on
Rolling on the dust, when gay.
At times he ornates the Still by his bark.

I am locked-up in my room.
... Soldiers are moving all over the city
Firing at random, cannonading and
  driving tanks everywhere.
People are dying on streets and lanes
like bleeding plagued rats.

We are a few
Waiting—perhaps from eternity.
And all on a sudden falls
the sharp bark on our ears,—slowly I move to the window
—half dark.
That very street dog, I see,
rushing towards the olive-green jeep, armed with soldiers.
Oh! If only I could be a pariah dog! I fancied.

(tr. S.K. Mitra)

From 1958 I met Faiz Ahmed Faiz countless times, in the course of our work in the Afro-Asian Writers' Association. I came quite close to him in later years. Born in Sialkot, in the Punjab, he loved Pakistan. But at the same time, he regarded India as his own. Faiz was soft-spoken and a very lovable person. His incarceration and suffering at the hands of the rulers could not take away the elegance of his lyrics.

But I must own that for an understanding of his life and work, I had to depend much on what I heard from his interpreters who had a very good rapport with him. I know from my long experience, how an interpreter can build a bridge between writers who write in different languages.

In Jalalabad, in Afghanistan, I found him to be nostalgic after seeing the portrait of his father in the local royal museum. He also remembered his father's friend, Sheikh Abdullah, who acted as his godfather in his childhood. His varied career as college teacher, army officer, journalist, political leader, trade unionist and broadcaster could not hold back his devotion to poetry. Being a humanist to the core, he could give full play to his personal feelings and social commitment with equal ease. Sometimes he would fuse the two by impregnating new meaning to time-honoured images.

Besides being a world famous poet, his ghazals are immensely popular both in India and Pakistan. In Calcutta I found one singing girl regale her listeners with ghazals of Faiz. I was told by one of his Moscow interpreters that a renowned *baiji,* a great admirer of Faiz, used to regularly visit him in jail and bring food specially cooked by herself.

When for years together he was out of home and moving from place to place, I met him a number of times. In the days of the invasion of Lebanon, Faiz was editing *Lotus*, heedless to repeated bombardment and gunshots. After his return to Pakistan, I met him last in Moscow. We were invited to an Indian home. I sat next to Faiz, noticing that he was neither smoking nor drinking, because of his heart condition. I also decided to be restrained. The next moment someone pushed a glass into my hand. I looked up and it was Faiz. Then he lighted a cigarette for me with a beaming face. That evening Faiz recited a poem which still rings in my ear:

> The road of memory you have walked so long
> will end a few steps further on
> where it turns on the way to oblivion.
> Neither you nor I exist there
> My eyes can't bear it:
> They don't know if you might return,
> step into thin air and disappear,
> or look back over your shoulder.
> ... there is no turning, nothing
> to hide you from me.
>
> So let the same road
> go on as it does, with you on it,
> and if you never look back
> it doesn't matter.

Shahabuddin, oil on canvas, Dhaka

KABIR CHOWDHURY

Of History, Nationalism and Poetry

The 1930s signalled a turning point in the evolution of Bengali poetry. Buddhadeva Bose, Jibanananda Das, Bishnu Dey, Sudhindranath Datta and Amiya Chakravarty are generally recognised as the pioneers who brought a new flavour and set a new trend in Bengali poetry. They freed it from the overwhelming influence of Rabindranath Tagore—although it must be acknowledged that towards the end of his amazingly fertile literary career, Tagore himself had experimented with certain techniques of modern poetry.

Modern Bengali poets of the thirties abandoned the path of platonic romantic love, the adoration of serene nature and the lure of mysticism. The second world war, the devastating famine of 1942 and the social, economic and political unrest of the period made their inevitable impact on poetry. In addition to the five stalwarts of modern Bengali poetry named above, poets like Samar Sen, Subhas Mukhopadhyay and Sukanta Bhattacharya brought new elements into it. Buddhadeva Bose once characterised this modern poetry as the poetry of "rebellion, protest, hesitation, boredom, quest, while expressing at the same time the awakening of a sense of wonder, the joy of life...." Perhaps one could say the same thing about contemporary poetry in Bangladesh.

After the partition of the subcontinent in 1947, public leaders, politicians, poets and intellectuals and the common people of Pakistan thought that the ordinary people of Pakistan would now be considerably better off, both economically and socially. They fondly believed that the motive force for this new transformation would be provided by Islam. The poets of the then East Pakistan, which emerged in late 1971 as the sovereign and independent state of Bangladesh, had inherited a rich cultural heritage. Theirs was a composite Bengali culture that cut across religious or social differences between the two major communities, the Muslims and the Hindus. But, after the emergence of Pakistan, deliberate efforts had been made to bring about a change in this field. Some poets of East Pakistan felt that now that the country was divided, that since West Bengal was a part of Hindu India and East Bengal of Muslim Pakistan, their culture too was divided. They felt that they should try to give their poetry a new shape and content. Not all, but some.

Instead of the secular Bengali tradition, these poets made the Muslim tradition their major concern. Keenly aware of the religious and cultural heritage of the Muslims, the issue of religion was indissolubly mixed in their psyche with a newly awakened nationalistic urge. In the use of imagery, symbol and myth, as well as in the liberal use of words of Arabic and Persian origin in their writings, they pursued a course of sterile revivalism, erroneously thinking that it was the course of a healthy renaissance. Gholam Mostafa, Farrukh Ahmed, Talim Hossain, Mofakkharul Islam and Roushan Izdani belonged to this group. For convenience's sake they are often labelled as Islamic Traditionalists.

Among them Farrukh Ahmed (1918-1974) was the most talented. He had a fine poetic sensibility and a highly evocative style. He sought the sources of tradition in two directions: in Islam through its prophets and saints, and in the myths and romances which had a Muslim setting. In his use of words of Arabic and Persian origin and in his choice of similes, symbols and images, he revealed his commitment to Muslim reawakening. Farrukh was a powerful poet; but preoccupation with the past and an excessive concern with an idealised religious sensibility led to the neglect of many other important regional realities. His efforts to create symbols and myths from materials that had no roots in the soil often led to mere rhetoric, where the generality of emotion blurred the total picture.

There were, however, others who were not inclined to overemphasize the Islamic tradition. They did not want to talk much of the past that took one back to Hera and Hejaz. Instead they concentrated on the contemporary world and the land in which they lived. Such dissimilar poets as Abul Hussain, Ahsan Habib, Syed Ali Ahsan, Sikander Abu Jafar, Sanaul Huq, Shamsur Rahman, Abdul Ghani Hazari, Hasan Hafizur Rahman, Al Mahmud, Syed Shamsul Haq, Mohammad Maniruzzaman, Zia Haider and Abdul Mannan Syed belong to this category. The above list is not exhaustive. All these poets were conscious of the importance of form, and a number of them were influenced, either directly or indirectly, like the modern Bengali poets of the 1930s, by the literature of the west—notably by the works of T.S. Eliot, Baudelaire and Rimbaud.

Abul Hussain, (born in 1922) is not a prolific writer; but his poetry is distinctive in many ways. He is clearly an urban poet. He makes effective use of understatement, controlled satire and sophisticated irony. His language is terse and free from the familiar trappings of maudlin sentimentalism. Abul Hussain is a socially conscious poet, keenly aware of the economic, social and political problems of the middle class in today's disturbed world. To a certain extent so is Ahsan Habib (1917-1986), although it is the lyrical grace and quiet tone of his poetry and his projection of the heartache of the lonely individual that appeal to most readers.

The Bengali Language Movement of 1952 brought a significant change in the literature of this region, especially in the field of poetry. The movement, however, was already there in embryonic form as early as 1948, that is less than a year after Pakistan was born. One simply has to recall the historic words of Dr. Muhammad Shahidullah (1855-1969), a great scholar of Bengali language and literature and a widely revered Muslim. In one of his Presidential addresses delivered at a literary conference held in Dhaka in 1948, he said that we were more Bengalis than Hindus or Muslims. He said that Nature had seen to it.

This identity of ours as Bengalis was threatened when the Pakistani rulers tried to impose Urdu as the only state language of the country. The people of East Pakistan rose in revolt demanding the recognition of Bengali as one of the two State Languages, Urdu being the other. It was a most reasonable demand; but the voice of reason was not heeded. On 21 February 1952, bullets were fired on a procession of unarmed and peaceful protesters. The martyrs of the Language Movement became national heroes. The history of the 1952 Language Movement is too well known to be recounted here in detail. It inspired our writers to create a significant body of writings, where not only the issue of Bengali language and literature but of Bengali nationalism in a wider context occupies a central position.

The Language Movement of 1952 was the first major movement in Pakistan that was completely secular in character. It highlighted the link between cultural rights and emancipation from autocratic political bondage. It inevitably led to the struggle for autonomy and, in course of time, to the mass non-cooperation movements of 1969 and 1970 led by Bangabandhu Sheikh Mujibur Rahman. Finally it led to our Liberation War of 1971.

The '50s and the '60s constituted a period of unrest. Our poets responded to it by declaring with passion their love for Bengali language and culture. They did so in a way where the note of protest and rebellion was explicit against all forms of authoritarianism and tyranny. This poetry was nationalistic in a new way. Firmly rooted in the soil, it spoke against communalism and autocracy in no uncertain fashion. It also strove to achieve a certain level of technical excellence, notwithstanding its rich emotional content.

The impact of the language movement on the poets of Bangladesh was all-pervasive. Though there were some common elements in the poems inspired by it, there was diversity. Among the poems dealing with 21st February 1952 that immediately come to my mind are:

> Jasimuddin's *Song of the Twentyfirst;* Sufia Kamal's *Such a Wonderful Day;* Alauddin Al Azad's *The Monument;* Hasan Hafizur Rahman's *The Immortal 21st;* Abu Zafar Obaidullah's *To a Certain Mother;* Shamsur Rahman's *Mother* and *Alphabet, My Sad Suffering Alphabet;* Shaheed Qadri's *Confession on the 21st;* Fazal Shahabuddin's *Bengali Language, O Mother Mine,* and of course, Abdul Ghaffar Chowdhury's beautiful song *Can I ever Forget 21st February Incarnadined by My Brothers' Blood,* immortalised by the haunting tune provided by singer and composer Altaf Mahmood, who was cruelly tortured and killed in occupied Dhaka during Bangladesh's bloody nine-month long liberation war.

New poems, too, are being written to celebrate 21st February which has now acquired mythic proportions. The Language Movement of 1952 and the Martyrs Day of 21st February have transcended their association with Bengali language, to become a powerful source of inspiration for our people to fight against injustice of all kinds. Some of the poems inspired by the Language Movement specifically mention the names of the martyrs, as in

Hasan Hafizur Rahman's *The Immortal 21st*, a long elegiac poem that brings together the emotions of grief, hope and determination. In many poems the mother image recurs again and again, becoming an archetypal figure as in Shamsur Rahman's *Mother*. Recurrent images with symbolic overtones, such as spring, fire, flaming krishnachura, palash and blood, are constantly mentioned in these poems.

From 1948 to 1971 political and cultural movements in our region went hand in hand, drawing sustenance from and mutually reinforcing each other. The same trend continued after 1971. From 1972 onwards these two movements in Bangladesh merged with each other to become integrated. The horizon of the post-liberation poets was, of course, wider. Naturally the poets of newly-liberated Bangladesh dealt with the theme of war—as the poets of the pre-liberation subjugated Bangladesh concentrated on the theme of Bengali language. Before I speak more about the characteristic features of our poetry from 1971 to date, let me go back a little and say something more about our poets of the '50s, and the '60s.

By the end of the '50s, Shamsur Rahman, Al Mahmud and Shaheed Qadri had established themselves in the vanguard of Bangladesh poetry. Rahman and Qadri were particularly inspired by modern Western poetry. They brought into their poetry various experiences of the alienated urban man, as well as certain literary techniques and associations used by some modern poets of the West. Al Mahmud, however, was more drawn to pastoral romanticism, succumbing at a later period to the lure of Islamic mysticism.

In the early poetry of Shamsur Rahman one clearly detects the influence of Jibananda Das and Bishnu Dey, particularly of Jibanananda Das. Soon he outgrew their influence and showed his individuality, both with regard to theme and technique. Shamsur Rahman still writes about his childhood memories, nature, love and universal humanism; but he has moved more and more into the fold of public events. Consider, for example, his poems entitled *The Shirt of Asad*, *To get You, O Liberty*, *A Certain Pride*, and *My Native Land is Riding on the Back of a Strange Camel*. It is Shamsur Rahman more than any other poet who has put Bangladesh at the heart of our poetry. As years roll by he grows in stature, as much by the thematic content of his poetry as by its artistic quality. He has by now established himself as the doyen of Bangladesh poetry and the most adored chronicler of our times. One of our poet-critics and reputed academics said, perhaps too eulogistically: "He (Rahman) discovered and developed a new idiom and a new cadence for poetry and in the process purified the dialect of the tribe."

Poetry in the '60s showed a rich harvest and new sophistication. It was amazingly varied and defied any simple categorisation. In 1963, four poetry volumes by four poets, namely, Shamsur Rahman, Al Mahmud, Hasan Hafizur Rahman and Zia Haider, were published. In some of these poems the theme of loneliness, the painful contradictions of urban life and a note of bitterness and frustration are easily detected. In others one notices a yearning for the attainment of an unrealized dream. In still others one sees a desire to explore the technical possibilities of the language, to experiment with words and to exploit the surrealistic. Rafiq Azad, Mohammad Rafiq, Nirmalendu Goon, Mahadeva Saha, Khaleda Edib Chowdhury, Asad Chowdhury, Abul Hasan, Muhammad Nurul Huda, Shikdar Aminul Haq, Sanaul Huq Khan, Abdul Mannan Syed, Syed Shamsul Haq, Habibullah Shirajee and many others endowed the poetry of this period with technical and thematic richness.

Inevitably, a substantial segment of the poetry of the '60s was protest-oriented. The early sixties saw a dictatorial military regime bent on crushing the economic, political and cultural aspirations of the people of Bangladesh. We see quite a few 'angry poems' by Shamsur Rahman, Abdul Ghani Nazari, Sanaul Huq, Nirmalendu Goon and Mahadeva Saha. Satire predominates in some of these poems, as in Hazar's *The Wives of a few Bureaucrats.* A tone of serenity prevails in some, as in Shamsur Rahman's *For a Poem.* Shamsur Rahman wrote poems titled *Liberty, You are, Samson*, and *I Curse Them.*

Some said that the Bangladesh poetry of the '70s had drifted into decadence and frustration. I would not say so. Rudra Mohammad Shahidullah, Mohon Raihan, Helal Hafiz, Abid Azad, Ruby Rahman and Shihab Sarker, among others, wrote some fine poems during this period. During the early years of independence, a note of joy and hope predominated; but later, as the keenly awaited fruits of independence seemed to recede further and further, it was replaced by one of disillusionment, satire and criticism.

The liberation war of Bangladesh was waged with certain principles and ideals in mind. Bengali nationalism was one of them. The other three major ideals were democracy, secularism and socialism. The concept of civil society was indissolubly linked with these ideals. It was quite natural that the poets of independent Bangladesh should write with feeling against fundamentalism, communalism, autocracy, economic exploitation, denigration of women and other forms of violation of human rights. It was also natural that independence would bring in a breath of fresh air from the wide world beyond the national frontiers. As a result of these circumstances, poetry became multifaceted and multidimensional in new ways.

Several of our poets, and at least one verse-playwright, made creative use of the myths and legends of both Muslims and Hindus of the subcontinent, as well as those of the ancient Greeks. Shamsur Rahman exploited the myths of Daedalus, Icarus and Aphrodite and made effective use of Telemachus, Agamemnon and Electra in his poems. He related them effectively to our own situations and broadened the appeal of his poetry. Poet-playwright Syed Shamsul Haq in his verse-play *Their Footsteps can be Heard* and Abu Zafar Obaidullah in his long poem *I am Speaking of Legends* used mythical associations in a refreshing way. Some of our poets referred to Hiroshima and Nagasaki, Nelson Mandela, Lenin, Vietnam and Kampuchea while writing on themes of world peace and anti-imperialism. The widening of the thematic horizon linked Bangladeshi poetry with world poetry and gave our writings a certain universal appeal.

Let me now draw the attention of my readers to another matter which made a deep impact on our poets. In August 1975 the newly independent nation of Bangladesh was overwhelmed by a disastrous event. Bangabandhu Sheikh Mujibur Rahman, the President of the country and the Father of the Nation, was killed in a coup led by a small band of army officers and a coterie of conspirators who did not believe in the principles and values of the liberation war of Bangladesh. Sheikh Mujib's death sent shockwaves throughout the nation.

The promise of Bangladesh developing into a secular democratic country strengthened by the spirit of Bengali nationalism was rudely thwarted by the events of August 1975. The successive governments that ruled Bangladesh from mid-1975 to mid-1996 used the religion of Islam for blatant political purposes. It preached the strange doctrine of Bangladeshi nationalism as opposed to Bengali nationalism. Their activities encouraged the growth of religious fanaticism. The rulers of the day de-emphasized the concept of secularism. In fact, the principle of secularism was dropped from the constitution of Bangladesh, and Islam was proclaimed its state religion.

The leaders of the coup failed to assume power; but for the next twenty-one years the reins of the government passed into the hands of those who did not believe in secularism, Bengali nationalism and socialism. They paid lip service to democracy but their conduct was autocratic and dictatorial. In course of time the people grew restive. Popular discontent mounted, and finally in June 1996 the party that had led the country to freedom in 1971 reassumed power after winning a decisive victory in Bangladesh's fairest-ever general election. These events could not but affect our poets. Hundreds of poems were written on Sheikh Mujib. They were mostly elegiac, but quite a few incorporated in them other moods. As in the case of the Bengali language movement of 1952, the killing of Bangabandhu in August 1975 also led to a large and varied crop of poetry.

Some of the images and symbols created by the poets are as wide in their philosophic implications as they are deep in their emotional appeal. Shamsur Rahman in his poem *The Song of Electra,* in reality mourned the death of Sheikh Mujib. Assuming Electra's role he said that as long as she saw every morning the play of sunlight and shadow, felt the kiss of the wind on her cheeks, and watched a frolicking young deer, she would not cease to grieve for her slain father Agamemnon who now lay in his grave. Nirmalendu Goon's poem *How the Word Independence became Our Own* and *Mujib means Emancipation,* Mahadeva Saha's *That Poem has not yet been Written* and *Was I able to write that Poem?* evoke the image of Mujib. Many other poems written by senior poets like Sufia Kamal, Sanaul Huq and Zillur Rahman Siddiqui as well as by younger poets like Shihab Sarker, Muhammad Nurul Huda, Zahidul Huq and others make up a special corpus of our contemporary poetry. In many of these poems Mujib's image is evoked both by open association and suggestive references to 'Jesus', 'Shepherd King', 'father', 'poet', the 'red lotus', 'the rose' and 'the river'.

After the independence of Bangladesh, her women had begun to play an increasingly active role in the social, cultural and economic life of the country. But after mid-1975 Muslim religious fanatics rose up against that trend and perpetrated many acts of injustice against the womenfolk, particularly in the rural areas, through fatwas and other reprehensible means. Shamsur Rahman, Nirmalendu Goon, Mohammad Rafiq, Asad Chowdhury, Mahadeva Saha and many others spoke out against the activities of the fundamentalists in their poems. They also wrote against the economic exploitation of the poor and the under-privileged. If one looks at the titles in some of Nirmalendu Goon's books, such as *Before That, We want Socialism; The Verse for the Peasants and Their Kind*, the poet is concerned with certain basic issues brought to the forefront.

Antifundamentalism and the liberation of women two important themes of contemporary Bangladesh poetry, are brought to the fore by Taslima Nasreen. In poem after poem she attacks, society, the state and religion and the male—declaring that all discriminate against women. In her poem entitled *The Female* she points out that the male considers the death of a woman as good riddance of a nuisance. Voicing the need for women to be bold and free herself of all restrictive inhibitions created by a male-dominated society, Nasreen writes in her poem *I Shall go a Long Way*:

> I shall walk on and take that route.
> My father said,
> turn back if you are my daughter.
> I said, if I have to
> turn back because I am your daughter,
> then I am no daughter of yours.

In *Noorjehan* Nasreen pours out her anger, hatred and bitterness against the fatwa-giving mullahs who watch the scene of a poor girl being stoned to death on trumped-up charges of adultery, who watch the scene with great satisfaction and laugh noisily, stroking their beards and swinging their canes.

Muhammad Nurul Huda's poetry is steeped in the past history of the Bengalees, not the history of events but the history of the flowering of the national identity of a people. Consider, for example, his poems *We are a Coppery Race* or *The Story of Mr. Tree.* Asad Chowdhury, too, sings the hymn of the soil, often using folk elements in innovative ways. The concern of the poets with themes as Bengali nationalism, women's liberation and secularism does not mean that they neglect the eternal themes of love, nature, beauty, life and death.

Which way is Bangladesh poetry moving? What paths will it take now? It seems to me that without neglecting the universal themes of poetry mentioned a little while ago, it will continue to be largely socio-politically oriented. It may also reveal a greater awareness by our poets of the importance of form, structure and words. Some of our younger poets have already started consciously to eschew sloppy sentimentalism, loud propagandist tone and slogan-like utterances. They are more introspective and inward-looking; they try to fuse intellect and emotion in their works, accommodate 'wit' in their writings, and endow their poems with a certain post-modernist flavour.

The poetry of Bangladesh and India's West Bengal are, and will continue to be, similar in many ways. After all, the language with its roots and sources of inspiration are the same, and no political division can negate or undo them. Having said this let me add that in certain ways they will be different, too. Not only because of the differences in landscape and some aspects of the life-style of the peoples of the two regions, but for other more important reasons.

The Bengali language movement of 1952 and the Bangladesh liberation war of 1971 at once lacerated and invigorated the psyche of our poets. The poets of West Bengal experienced nothing of this kind. Maybe vicariously they did, but not directly. Besides, Bangladesh is a sovereign independent country with Bengali as its one and only national and state language, while

West Bengal is one of the many states of India on which impinge the Hindi language and various aspects of Indian culture. These naturally will have an impact on West Bengal's literature, including its poetry. Nonetheless, I am confident that in the coming years the poetry of Bangladesh and that of West Bengal will flow as two close neighbouring streams, often mingling with each other to produce a rich body of composite Bengali Poetry.

Valiant Freedom Fighters, *water colour by Zainul Abedin*

SHAMSUR RAHMAN

Mother and other Poems

Mother

She lived in her quiet remote village
engrossed in a thousand and one
domestic chores.
She hardly noticed the sun throbbing in the sky
or rafts of clouds sailing by.
Time flew without her ever noticing it.
The whole scene was intensely familiar:
the pot of rice boiling on the oven,
and a fish or two and some spinach
ready for the modest schoolteacher husband.
Now and then she glanced up and laid her eyes
on the gourd-creepers climbing over the fence,
and there sitting on a branch of the jack-fruit tree
a yellow bird wagged its tail ceaselessly.
Hours rolled by.

After her bath with the water drawn from the well
she combed her hair, liberally streaked with grey,
and thought of her small son in the local school,
learning by rote his multiplication table.

And then she packed in a jar home-made country-cakes
shaped in ornamental designs,
and she thought of her eldest son,
the one with ever-shining bright eyes,
studying in the remote city-school.

She hardly ventured outside the bounds of her small home
Her life was simple, serene, self-effacing.
Only the recollections of her long dead parents
sometimes brought an ache to her heart.

And then the entire country reared its head
like a wrathful god.
News came pouring in from all corners.
Many sacrifices crimsoned the native soil.
The blood-spattered clothes of the son
gripped the village mother inexorably.
The green gourds, the river and the meadow, the *kalai* field
and her old familiar pond were left far behind.

Today one finds her footprints on the wide city roads
and on the narrow side streets,
on all highways and alleys.
Losing her son, the mother has now mingled the bright
tears of her stricken heart
with resonant slogans.

Translated by Kabir Chowdhury

My Sad Suffering Alphabet

In my very being you live
fluttering your flag like a cluster
    of shining stars.
A soothing tenderness always holds you
    in a loving embrace.

From my very childhood
you and I have lived inseparably,
wrapped in each other's love.
You have been my companion
since my birth.
Every moment you have helped build
    the bridge of my dreams,
    and that is why the whole universe,
    turning into a ship, anchors today at
        my port.

You visit me even in the bower
    of my sleep.
From the little hollow of a huge big tree
you come down jumping
    in the shape of a squirrel,
and, dressed as an elephant, you descend
from a bouquet of clouds.

You are always there.
I feel your presence in the very depth
    of my heart,
an eternal green spot of bliss,
    the rhythmic fifty-one letters
of my remote school days
    of early childhood
or, some times turning into a beautiful
parrot with a scarlet beak,
you suddenly come and softly touch
the rim of my dream-laden consciousness.

You are the precious pupils
at the center of my eyes.
    In the raging fire of wars,
    in the holocaust of epidemics,
    in deluge or drought,
    in the ringing steps
        of a dancing girl,
    in the tender embrace of a loving daughter
    in anger and hatred,
    in the hullabaloo of anarchy,
    in the profusion of creativity,

O the pupils of my eyes,
you are always open and awake,
every moment of my life.

If you are plucked out, tell me,
what of me remains?
Nursing at your breast
the floral offerings of a few martyred youths
you live in eternal glory.
Today I shall allow no one
to pluck a single petal of those flowers.
But at present they are playing with you
    a dirty game,
they are engaged in a low, lascivious prank,
the bastards are having the time
        of their life,
and I cannot bear to look at your face,
O my sad, suffering alphabet.

Abridged and translated by Kabir Chowdhury

Invitation to a Reading and Other Poems

Invitation to a Reading

To read a poem in translation is to kiss
a girl in a photograph.
It has no life, it's not dead either.
At best it's an echo. At best
a memory. But echo minus the original sound, memory
never lived at the source.

My poems are my limbs.

I grope and perceive
time and the world with these limbs.
I have to grow them
constantly.
They die after each use, each
experience.
Poems come to me in summer months
when Bangladesh burns
under a fierce sun. In bad times
I clutch onto them to survive.
In monsoon time, in cyclone time, in mad
tidal-bore time

I chant them.

All hopes leave me
in winter time. In winter I believe
they will not come again.
Yet they come, they come
in summer time
they come again.

Black ink on paper by Qamrul Hasan

Our greatest endeavour through time
has been to reach out, to break through.
In creating these echoes and memories of my poems
I reach out towards, lightly
I touch you.
I redeem my birth.

Translated by Jeni Couzyn

I Die

I have buried all the dead but me.
My moon face brother at six years old
Fell between his truckle bed and the wall
And choked.

 Outside in the yard in the
Summer heat I sweated over lines like
"Then Rama went to the forest" to improve
My Bengali script.

 Dry wind turning to a
Mother's sob of grief.

 In the orchard green mangoes
Held their hypnotic scent and looked like
Tear drops.

 Like a sun behind cloud my
Father sat quietly and recited a few
Verses from the Book.

 Words like shot birds.
I saw them spiralling down to a wasted
Death.

 We carried him in a small barefoot
Procession through bamboo groves, under

The laughing tree of Nagakeshara to a
Cemetery on the right of the village-inn
And we buried him just as the sun was
going down.
That
summer I buried part of me.

Then at
9.13 in the morning it was my father.
He clutched at my icy hand and in a hoarse
Whisper croaked. I'm going son I'm going.
That was New year's day and men were dancing
In the square.

My father's leg had been
Bad with gangrene.

In winter we used to sit
On the sun drenched yard and listen to
Tales of when he was young.
Hills of Assam.

He on a fog shrouded virgin peak
Seeing
The village below through a break in
The mist and then gone again.
By the olive
Grove and the Mount of Sinai and the
Peaceful Town, so the sun touches the
Highest peak.

We buried him as if we
Were hiding a treasure chest of gold.
Now I am here standing with my head
Bent, powdered with the dying sun's pink.
I have lost my own treasure map my
Own gold dream coins.

Once again I have
Buried part of myself.

And then her
Who was to be the mother of my child.
She who was the bridge, the sputnik
in space that lurched in orbit and was
burned to cosmic ash.

I left her beside
Those who had gone before and scratched
Her name on the blackened wax from
Candles watching over the long dead.

Wrote an elegy but my editor cabled
Me to send something better.
Writing I
Realised is part of the living.
That day I
Buried only what was part of me.
And only
Yesterday I saw stars falling on my
City in revolt. Or, are they pieces of
Sculpture carved on stone of passion
By translucent hammers and drills

By a sculptor whose name is Hope?
I asked them in whose likeness they'd
Been made.
They answered, you and you
And you.
I asked their names and they
Replied, I.
Where do you live?
In everyman.
Address?
In tales and ballads sung
in days to come.
Height?
Freedom tall.
Colour?

Same as the great river's silt.
Distinguishing marks, if any?
The 3rd
Eye on your forehead.
Where shall you go now?
They replied,
To your soul.
I buried them
There and I buried them there.

Day after day and month after millennium
I have watched
Myself
Dying in particles
And parts
And have returned to the elements.
Every time.
And every time you die
I die and at my death
You too
Will die a little.
All save death is measurable.
Let us take one birth
And hold death in
Our hand like a child in fear
And pleasure holds his GOLDENRAIN
Flowers
And suns
spewing
laughing flowers

Of fire
Sugar white
dancingdancingdancing.

Translated by the Author

KISHWAR NAHEED

The Grass is Like Me and other Poems

The Grass is Like Me

The grass is like me.
It learns to love life
Only after feet have crushed it.
By becoming wet
Does it mean to show
Modesty's warmth, or
Passion's heat?

The grass is like me.
As it lifts its head
The mower
Promising to turn it to velvet
Levels its lifting top.

You really labour
To put women down,
But the desire to grow
Dies neither in the earth
Nor in the woman.
Hear me.
The old idea to make a track was good.
Those who shy from the heat of courage
Will still be trampled
To make tracks for authority.
But they are straw,
Not grass.
The grass is like me.

Translated by Baidar Bakht and Derek M. Cohen

A Thought Before Going to Bed

Do not leave me like the November sunshine;
Basking in it you are drenched in warmth,
Away from it the cold crawls in every joint.
Do not love me like the rainy season cloud;
Its shade soothes and quenches every thirst,
But it is wind, one moment,
And water, the next.
Do not love me like the evening twilight;
My cheeks are now crimson like the sky
But shortly after the union,
They will become pale like the night.
Do not love me like the wind
Whose stagnation is suffocating
And whose fast gait dislodges firm feet.
Do not love me like the still water
Because I cannot live like a lotus in it.
Just love me enough
To awaken the desire of love in me.

In Memory of My Birth Place

In Memory of My Birth Place

There was a cry from the moon,
And the eyes of the wind shed tears,
The grave was built in the river,
On the pitcher made of raw clay.

When the age forgot its journey,
The cuckoo called from the mango tree,
The branch of the neem tree gifted a tooth brush.

Whiter than the sun in the shade,
A shining form in scanty head cover,
The trembling form,
And the banyan tree,
The ghost saw me from a distance
He smiled,
I had come after a long time.

The earth could not control itself,
All patience was lost,
My mother put the mascara in my eyes.

Translated by Nuzhat Naqvi

Amir Khusrau Dehlvi, Calligraphic drawing by Ameena Ahmad Ahuja

III
STREAMS IN MUSIC

RAKSHAT PURI

Bulleh Shah in Punjabi Poetic Tradition

This essay proposes to discuss in a brief and necessarily general way the place of the Punjabi mystic poet, Bulleh Shah, in Punjabi poetic tradition and his verse in relation to the Punjabi language. Bulleh Shah lived from approximately 1680 to 1758. His verse is so deeply embedded in Punjabi thought and language that half a century of separate and almost exclusive literary progress on the Indian and Pakistani sides of Punjab has not been able to remove his accent and idiomatic inflection in Indo-Pak Punjabi expression. No thanks for this are due to the authorities on the two sides. Their building up of a wall between linguo-cultural developments on the Indian and Pakistan parts has resulted in the odd situation of Punjabi writers being able to get together in a free and natural way only in Britain or wherever else Indo-Pak Punjabi communities reside outside the sub-continent.

On the Indian side the authorities built a separating wall by officially decreeing that Punjabi would be written and taught in only the Gurmukhi script. They excluded the Persian alphabet in which Punjabi had been written traditionally, since at least the time of Sheikh Farid-ud-Din Masud (or Baba Farid) in the twelfth and thirteenth centuries: his poems are the earliest known literary work in Punjabi. Gurmukhi is said to have come into use only in the time of the Sikh Gurus. In addition, the authorities in Delhi and eastern Punjab seem at various levels to have given quiet and implicit encouragement to writers and others to introduce Hindi words into Punjabi, even when Punjabi equivalents are available. Some Punjabi poets and writers appear to have been only too willing to do this—in the expectation of awards and status.

On the Pakistani side after 1947 there was, to begin with, obvious officially encouraged emphasis on some kind of over-all "Arabization" which affected Punjabi among other languages. It led to the use also of outlandish and utterly un-Punjabi Persian words. The reasons were a new enthusiasm about "the Islamic religion", and a tendency to be different at any cost from "Bharati" Punjab. In fact, a number of Pakistani Punjabis— inspired by curious official attitudes in Pakistan—even began to describe themselves, somewhat ludicrously, as belonging integrally to "Arab" or "Iranian" or "Turkistani" culture. But history, geography and cultural tradition cannot be altered or evaded on order. Fortunately, the more sensible elements in Pakistan realised the absurdity of it and the phase did not last too long. Bulleh Shah, Waris Shah (whose version of *Heer* and *Raanjha* is veritably part of the Punjabi psyche, like the poetry of Bulleh Shah who was his contemporary), and the other Punjabi mystic poets triumphed, as it were—as they did on the Indian side of Punjab too. This was not surprising. Since the Punjabi language and idiom are the warp and woof on the loom of Punjabi attitudes and temperament, Punjabi accent and articulation have remained essentially unchanged despite contrary efforts and politically-directed pressures by authority on both sides. So Bulleh Shah continues to live in the idiom of eastern as well as western Punjab.

In the general and space-restricted discussion here, it will be difficult to touch on the work of the three most important earlier poets who helped create the Punjabi poetic tradition which Bulleh Shah furthered: Baba Farid, who lived approximately from 1173 to 1266 and whose Punjabi poems are included in the Sikh Granth Sahib; Shah Hussain who lived approximately from 1539 to 1593; and Sultan Bahu, who lived approximately from 1630 to 1691. However, while it is difficult to detail here the work of the three earlier poets, it would be necessary to dwell as specifically as possible, even though very briefly, on some aspects of the Punjabi language out of which their poetry grew.

Bullah was the pet name in childhood of Abdullah Shah. But the name stuck as he grew up and he continued to be known as Bulleh Shah. In his poems he uses it as his *takhalus* or *nom de plume.* Subsequently, he was described reverently as Saayi'n or Baba Bulleh Shah. Son of a spiritually inclined scholar, Shah Mohammed Dervish, he was born in Uch Gilaniya'n near Bahawalpur in south-western Punjab. The Bahawalpur State gazetteer lists Uch as "an ancient city once situated on the banks of the Indus in Bahawalpur State, identified by historians as the Alexandria established by Alexander the Great. ... (Uch) is three cities in one: Uch Gilaniya'n, the quarter settled by the Qadiri saints: Uch Bukhariya'n, settled by the Suhrawardis; and Uch Mughla'n settled by the descendants of the Moghul administrators of the region".[1]

Bulleh Shah was still a child when his father moved from Uch Gilaniya'n to, first, Malakwal near Multan, and then Pandoke Bhatia'n near Kasur, just across today's India-Pakistan border at Ferozpur. Here, primarily because he came from a family of pious Syeds, he received "a strictly orthodox religious training".[2] His teacher was Khwaja Ghulam Murtaza, who "trained two rebellious personalities; the other was Waris Shah, author of Punjab's greatest romance in verse, *Heer*".[3] (*Heer* is pronounced like 'deed' not like 'deer'.)

But Bulleh Shah's spiritual preceptor, his Guru or Murshid or Master, was Inayat Shah Qadiri, an Araai'n[4] who earned his living as a gardener but who was also a scholar and author of a number of books on mysticism, including *Dastur-ul-Amal* and *Islah-ul-Amal.* In *Dastur-ul-Amal* he has mentioned "seven spiritual stages: the ancient Hindu rishis considered passing through these stages as necessary for God-realisation".[5] Shah Inayat is said to have passed away in 1728.

Many tales are told, apocryphal and other, of how Bulleh Shah—who it is said did some spiritual practice and had attained a degree of supernatural power even before he met Shah Inayat—became Shah Inayat's disciple, or shishya or murid. One of these tales, in the *Baang-e-Auliya-e-Hind*[6], says, for instance:

> In the city of Kasur Patthana it happened to a man of God, ... that he achieved greatness from Hazrat Shah Inayat whose tomb lies in Lahore, south of the city. Bulleh Shah said to himself, 'I must get my Master after testing him. I must fully satisfy myself, I must drink water after straining it.'
>
> In his intense search for his Master, he first looked towards Lahore, then he came there and took his residence where the garden of Shah Inayat was situated. There he saw a mango on a tree at that time; he looked at it, invoked the name of God, and the mango fell on the ground. Shah Inayat called to him and said, 'Listen, you wayfarer, you have stolen my mango. Give it back to me!'

Bulleh Shah replied, 'I did not climb up the tree; your mangoes are far from my reach. It is with the wind that the mango broke from the branch and came into my lap!'

'No. Invoking the name of God, you got the mango. You have committed theft!'

Bulleh Shah realised the spiritual power and knowledge of Inayat Shah. He fell at his feet, was graced by initiation from the Master and attained the secret knowledge.

Concern in this essay is primarily with the poetry of Bulleh Shah, and not with his mysticism—even though, in relation to mystics and mysticism, it is said the song may not easily be separated from the singer. Because of this, and its probable relevance in interpreting the work of Bulleh Shah, it may not be out of place to indicate very briefly the meaning of mysticism preferred here. For this, I should like to rest on a quotation from the late Prof. J.R. Puri, who headed the Department of Philosophy at Punjabi University in Patiala from 1969 to 1976.

In a work on the mystic teachings of Guru Nanak[7], he says *inter alia* that the focal point which lies at the centre of mystic teaching is

> personal *experience* of the Divine (emphasis supplied). It is this experience that leads to the consummation of all desired ends. It takes one beyond the realm of time and space and all its attendant evils. Negatively, it gives one release from sorrow and suffering, release from the cycle of birth and death. Positively, it produces bliss, beatitude and eternal peace. Since it is a state of timelessness, it is a state that has no beginning, no end, no growth, no decay. And since this consciousness transcends time, of necessity it rises also above the level of cause and effect, for these terms signify nothing but events that occur earlier and later in time.

Since reality, or truth, *experienced* mystically is to be presumed as being indivisible, the nature of mysticism and mystical *experience* might be considered everywhere to be identical. The poems of Bulleh Shah, and of other Punjabi mystic poets, have been read and understood by the author of this essay in the context of such an interpretation of mysticism.

Bulleh Shah's poems employ the Punjabi language in a way that is remarkably contemporary. His poetry came when the language had moved a good way towards its present-day character, driven forward in the works of Baba Farid, Shah Hussain and Sultan Bahu. In fact, Punjabi literary expression is considered to have come into its own with Waris Shah's version of the tale of *Heer:* Waris Shah, as already noted, was a contemporary of Bulleh Shah.

Punjabi is usually divided into six main dialects, which of course have their minor variations and admixtures. There is, first, the Doabi dialect, spoken mainly in and around Jullundur, in the area generally between the Beas and the Sutlej rivers. Secondly, there is Malwai. This is spoken in Ludhiana and its environs. Thirdly, there is the Majhi dialect, spoken in central Punjab, in the Amritsar-Lahore-Faisalabad (formerly Lyallpur) area generally. Fourthly, Saraiki, centred on Multan and spoken with secondary modifications in the quadrilaterial formed by Jhang, Mianwali, Bahawalpur and Mithankot. Fifthly, Potthohari, centred on Rawalpindi and spoken generally in the area including Jehlum, Attok, the Hazara district in NWFP, and the Mirpur and Muzaffarabad districts in Jammu and Kashmir. The sixth dialect is a form of Dogri, spoken in the area past Sialkot and neighbouring on Jammu and western Himachal Pradesh.

Mystic poets in the Punjab have employed words and expressions freely from all the dialects, to serve the purposes of precise communication in poetry and discourse. From the time of Bulleh Shah and Waris Shah a distinct literary Punjabi diction, in essence "of the soil", seems to have evolved which today is described as Maanjhi, that is, 'central' or 'standard' Punjabi.

Though essentially of the soil, taking its cue from home-bred gesture and idiom, Punjabi has of course borrowed from its eastern and western neighbourhood. It has taken mostly from Persian in the west and from Braj in the east. The borrowing from Braj seems to have come about mostly in the time of the Sikh Gurus, whose hymns tend to be an admixture of Punjabi and Braj. Possibly, Braj was then a kind of 'link language' in the sub-continent's north. From the time of Baba Farid, Punjabi has been honed, sharpened and refined to a considerable degree of sophistication. Maanjhi is sophisticated in the sense that the poetic impulse takes easy recourse to intricate symbols and correspondences—which are the quintessence of image and metaphor—for expression that seems spontaneous and inevitable. The work of Bulleh Shah and other Punjabi mystic poets bears this out amply. Consider for example the following couplet by Baba Farid:

Farida duni wajaayi wajdi, tu'n wi wajje'n naal,
So-i jeev nah wajda jis Allah karda saar.

Strum the world, Farid, and it
Returns you a tune. You
Are in the tune you strum.
Seek refuge with
Allah if you wish to come
Out of the tune you strum.

That no serious work in the Punjabi tongue seems extant from before the time of Baba Farid is more than passing strange. Baba Farid's verse—eschewing formal modes and in straight end-rhymed couplets—and his vocabulary serve his withdrawn, contemplative tone with astonishing sensitiveness, even when the austere expression borders on baldness, when the irony is heavy, and when his symbols tend to appear naive. Indeed, Baba Farid's verse and vocabulary indicate persuasively that the Punjabi language had developed and been used for serious writing for some significant length of time before his coming.

In his work on the influence of the west on Punjabi literature[8], Mohinder Pal Kohli suggests that "the Punjabi language is basically Vedic Prakrit, modified into Vedic Apabhramsa. The origins of Punjabi literature go back to the eighth, ninth and tenth centuries—to the stalwarts of Hattha Yog Panth that flourished at the time under the leadership of Gorakh Nath (940-1031). What they wrote has not come to us in the same vocabulary. ... The advent of Islam in India had its philosophical, linguistic and literary consequences. The attempt at synthesis of Hinduism resulted in the growth of Sufi-istic traditions. (Baba Farid)... is the first Sufi poet who inaugurated the use of standard literary Punjabi".

While orientalists such as G.A. Grierson and T. Grahame Bailey, as well as later Russian scholars including Y. Smirnov and S.D. Srebryakov, agree that Punjabi is a Prakritic descendant of Sanskrit, some Pakistani scholars, like Ain-ul-Haq Faridkoti, seem to believe that Punjabi's origins are Dravidian. But Khaled Ahmad is sceptical of "Dravidian-origin" views.[9] He notes that a more in-depth study "is needed to overthrow the orientalist conclusions: yet, the 'Dravidian' view is gaining ground among Pakistan's Punjabi scholars also as a kind of chauvinistic reaction to the ancient external trespass of the Aryans. For Muslim scholars the view is attractive because Aryan civilization was subsumed by Hinduism and now represents its caste-ridden social system".

In short, Ahmad politely dismisses the "Dravidian-origin" view as absurd because it is based primarily on religion-based sectarian prejudice and local chauvinism rather than on impartial scholarly inquiry. The "ancient external trespass of Aryans" and the subsuming of Aryan civilization by Hinduism occurred many, many centuries before the coming of Prophet Mohammed and the advent of Islam.

A notable feature about Punjabi, which may have relevance especially when poetry in the language is written to be sung—as notably in the poems of Bulleh Shah and other mystic Punjabi poets—is its tonal character. Possibly, Punjabi is the only major South Asian language that has this kind of tonal character. There does seem to have been some speculation among scholars about the possible origin of Punjabi's tone-language character but without any final and convincing answer. It is doubtful if any Punjabi or other Indian scholar has commented on this aspect of the language. But Bailey[10], remarking in the introduction to his well-known English-Punjabi dictionary that "Punjabi is a tone language like Chinese", academically analyses and discerns four tones in the language:

> (1) Level tone, found in about 75 per cent of the words. It might be described as absence of tone. (2) High-falling. The syllable is begun about six or seven semi-tones above the lowest note that the speaker can reach, and falls about two semi-tones. If no pause follows the fall is in the following syllable. (3) Low- rising. The syllable is begun about a tone above the lowest note that the speaker can reach, and rises one or two semi-tones. If no pause follows, the rise is in the following syllable. (4) A combination of low-rising and high-falling, the former always coming first.

Only a phonetician and student of linguistics would perhaps comprehend easily Bailey's theoretically described modulations. To the native Punjabi speaker the rising and falling tones come naturally and unself-consciously. He is perhaps too close to the language for objective analytical discernment. But it would not be out of place to mention that the multi-tonal pronunciation of words—where change of tone may give a different meaning—characterises mainly the northern, central and eastern Punjabi dialects. It hardly applies to the south-western dialect, Saraiki. For example, gha would be read straight as 'gha' in Saraiki. But in the northern, central and eastern Punjabi dialects it would approximate to k'ha, with the 'h' a kind of glottal 'hiccup' in the larynx.

As indicated above, the tone-language factor impinges on Punjabi poetry, notably when it is written to be sung. Most of Bulleh Shah's verse is written for singing. Take this line from one of Bulleh Shah's *kafis*, frequently sung by qawwaals: *Na k'har dittha na k'harwaala dittha* ('Perceived neither the house nor the house-owner'). The author of this essay feels—instinctively or intuitively or by gut-reaction, call it what you will—that the use of the Saraiki gha in place of k'ha while saying the line in any but the Saraiki dialect would take away from it rhythm and balance. On the other hand, the rhythm and balance would seem to remain unaffected by approximating the entire line to the Saraiki: *Na ghar dittha-i na gharwaal dittha-i;* or, moving farther southward beyond Bahawalpur from Multan: *Na ghar dittho na gharwaal dittho.* It must be conceded, however, that when verse is not rigorously fastened to the metronomic beat of a traditional metre, the perception of rhythm and balance in a poem tends to depend essentially on personal ear-and-understanding: there may well be those who discern differently from the author of this essay.

Bulleh Shah's verse is written in *Maanjhi,* or 'standard' Punjabi, with words taken freely from all the dialects. Almost invariably it is in the *kafi* form. The *kafi* is a traditional form in Punjabi poetry in which "the first or the second—at times both lines together—serve as the refrain. *Kafi* is often chanted like a song. At the end of a stanza the singers sing the refrain repeatedly ... (to) build a particular mood or atmosphere. ... The *kafi* is generally sung by qawwaals, a group of singers. They get so deeply involved in the singing that they become a part of the chorus. The word *kafi* is derived from the Arabic *kafa,* which means a group".[11]

Bulleh Shah's *kafi* maintains the dialogue between music and poetry. The expression of mystic thought is not allowed to become so complex as to discourage a listening audience. Nor, at the same time, is Bulleh Shah's text such as to fade from the mind after an audience has received the oral transmission. Partly, this may be because of the *kafi* form that Bulleh Shah usually chose. But in essence it is of course the enduring significance that he imparted to his verse: every *kafi*, every *dohra*, every *siharfi* (a variation of acrostic, with the first line of every poem or stanza beginning with successive letters of the alphabet), and every other kind of poem he wrote has an authoritative inevitability about it.

The only love and worship, with its implications for personal and social discipline, that Bulleh Shah recognised were love for worship of his Master, Inayat Shah. All the rest he dismissed. This emerges plainly in his verse, where religion, ritual prayer, temples, mosques and clergy are all dismissed out of hand. For example:

Mullah'n te mashaalchi, doha'n iko chit,
Loka'n karde chaanana, aap hanere vich.

The mullah and the torch-bearer
Are of a kind in this,
They offer light to others,
Themselves in darkness.

Or consider these lines:

P'hatth namaaza'n, chikkarh roze, kalme'n phir gayi sehayi,/Bulleh nu'n shau andro'n mileya, p'huli phire lokayi.

Damn prayer, throw mud on religious fasting
Black out the kalma with ink!
I found my Love when I turned within
People search clueless.

Bulleh Shah's 'derecognition' of all restrictions but those that grew from love of and absolute faith in his Master seems to have extended even to his poetic craft and devices: therefore the flexibility of his *kafi*. He follows only loosely the prescribed prosodic structure, and seems astonishingly modern in his impatience with confinement to metronomic discipline. The base for his diction as well as metre is the speech rhythm of popular Punjabi parlance. One is led to recall T.S. Eliot's remark that "the poetry of a people takes its life from the people's speech, and in return gives life to it". Eliot also observed that "no poetry, of course, is ever exactly the same speech that the poet talks and hears; but it has to be in such a relation to the speech of his time that the listener or reader can say, 'That is how I should talk if I could talk poetry'".

Khaled Ahmad believes[12] that one reason for Bulleh Shah's all- time popularity "is his relatively modern vocabulary. But the other powerful reason is that his lines are essentially non-poetic in terms of rhythm. A non-rhythmic exclamatory quality, with a vocative usage of the proper noun 'Bullah', makes for precise assimilation in common speech. In Punjabi, personal names are declined as in Latin and there is a vocative case which creates special effect". Leaving aside the vocative usage of 'Bullah' and the special effect this creates: presumably, what Ahmad signifies by the phrase "non-poetic in terms of rhythm" is what has been described above as Bulleh Shah's "perceptible impatience with confinement to metronomic discipline".

The rhythm is based almost wholly on common speech, which makes it immediate and natural, uncontrived. But an *in-itself* "non- rhythmic exclamatory quality" is undoubtedly discernible every time in the phrase that forms the refrain in a Bulleh Shah *kafi.* The refrain becomes the focus of the *kafi's* over-all rhythm when it moves to a crescendo in repetition by qawwaal singers. Consider such *kafi* refrains as *Bullah ki jaana'n mae'n kaun* 'Bullah, what know I who I am; or *Ik nukte wich gall mukdi-e* 'The argument ends on a single point'; or *Ilmo'n bas kari'n o yaar* 'Away with scholarship, my friend'; or *Mu'n aayi baat na raehndi-e* 'What comes to the tongue will not stay unsaid'; or—about his Master, Inayat Shah—*Maula aadmi ban aaeya* God has come as a man; and so on.

The decades and centuries after Bulleh Shah's death in 1758 saw a number of well-known Punjabi mystic and secular poets. These included Mian Mohammed Baksh, author of *Safrul Ishq,* popularly known as *Saiful Malook;* Mehr Ali Shah; Ghulam Farid; Qadir Yar, author of the celebrated long poem, *Puran Bhagat;* Shah Mohammed who wrote of exploits and events in and after the time of Maharaja Ranjeet Singh; and others. In the early decades of the twentieth century the poetic gesture which had been nurtured in the work mostly of the mystic poets turned self-consciously to political and social concerns. The effect on poetic diction and metre was unavoidable. Names such as Mohan Singh Diwana, Pritam Singh Safir, Shiv Kumar Batalvi (famous in the main for *Loona,* his version of Puran Bhagat's story), Piara Singh Sahraai and Avtar Singh Azad come to mind.

A great deal of flurry is of course evident today in Punjabi literary circles in both the Indian and the Pakistani parts of Punjab. But a kind of vacuum obtains none the less. There is perceptible neither analysis worthy of socio-cultural significance, nor abiding poetic quality in most of the Punjabi verse that is being published these days. Mostly, as elsewhere, and as in the literatures of other languages, it is the media that builds myths of literary worth and eminence. Myths, that time soon enough demolishes mercilessly.

Notes

1. Quoted by Khaled Ahmad in his introduction to *Bulleh Shah—A Selection,* rendered into English verse by Taufiq Rafat, and published by Vanguard Publications, Lahore, 1982.
2. Ibid.
3. Ibid.
4. An agricultural community in the Punjab.
5. Quoted from *Punjab,* Language-Department (Punjabi), Patiala, in *Bulleh Shah* by J.R. Puri and T.R. Shangari, Radha Soami Satsang, Beas, Punjab.
6. Quoted in *Bulleh Shah* by J.R. Puri and T.R. Shangari.
7. J.R. Puri. *Guru Nanak—His Mystic Teaching* Radha Soami Satsang, Beas, Punjab.
8. Mohinder Pal Kohli, *The Influence of the West on Punjabi Literature.* Ludhiana, Punjab. Lyall Book Depot, 1969.
9. op. cit. Footnote 1.
10. T. Grahame Bailey, *An English-Punjabi Dictionary.* 1919. Reprinted in 1976 by Ess Ess Publications, Delhi.
11. J.R. Puri and T.R. Shangari, *Bulleh Shah.* Radha Soami Satsang, Beas, Punjab. Dr. Lajwanti Rama Krishna says in her *Punjabi Sufi Poets* that *kafi* is borrowed from the Persian *kafiya* and is usually "a poem on the Divine's attributes, and sometimes on different sufi beliefs". Najm Hossain Syed, in *Recurrent Patterns in Punjabi Poetry* (Lahore, 1978) says simply that the *kafi* is a "poem in (four-line) stanzas followed by a refrain".
12. op. cit. Footnote 1.

Two Kafis

by

Bulleh Shah

1

Raati'n jaage'n te shaekh sadaave'n—
Par raati'n jaagan kutte
Tetho'n utte.

Saari raat o p'haunkde raehnde,
Dine'n jaa rarha'n vich sutte
Tetho'n utte.

O dar maalik da mool na chhaddade
P'haave'n sae sae maare jutte
Tetho'n utte.

Bulleh Shah utth yaar manaa lae
Nahi'n te baazi lae gaye kutte
Tetho'n utte.

Waking of nights you would attain
Spiritual sheikh-hood.
But dogs who wake of nights
Surpass you.

They bark all night and when day breaks
They sleep in the hard open,
Surpass you.

They do not leave their Master's door
Even if they receive hundreds of shoe-beatings,
Surpass you.

Up Bulleh Shah, go please your Master
Or the dogs will triumph,
Surpass you.

2

Bullah, kih jaana'n mae'n kaun?
Na mae'n momin vich maseeta'n
Na mae'n vich kufr di reet a'n
Na mae'n paaka'n vich paleet a'n
Ma mae'n Musa na Firaun
Bullah kih jaana'n mae'n kaun?

Na mae'n vich paleeti paaki
Na vich shaadi na ghamnaaki
Na mae'n aabi na mae'n khhaaki
Na mae'n aatash na mae'n paun
Bullah kih jaana'n mae'n kaun?

Na mea'n p'het mazhao da paaeya
Na mea'n Aadam Havva jaaeya
Na kujh apna naam t' hraaeya
Na vich baetthan na vich p'haun
Bullah kih jaana'n mae kaun?

Avval aakhhir aap nu'n jaana'n
Na koi dooja hor pachhaana'n
Metho'n vadh na koi seyaana'n
Bullah o kharha ae kaun?—
Bullah kih jaana'n mae'n kaun?

Bullah, what know I who I am?
Not a believer visiting mosques
Not in the tradition of unbelief,
Not in piety and not in sinning,
Not Moses and not Pharaoh
Bullah, what know I who I am?

Not in virtue and not in evil,
Not in joy and not in sorrow,
Not in water and not in earth,
Not in fire and not in wind—
Bullah, what know I who I am?

Not learnd in the mystery of religion,
Not acquainted with Adam and Eve,
Not specific in name for myself,
Not settled and not wanderer—
Bullah, what know I who I am?

First and last I know myself
Do not recognize any other,
No one is more wise than I:
who is it, Bullah, present there?—
Bullah, what know I who I am?

MUCHKUND DUBEY

The Sadhana of Lalan Fakir

> By writing you are frustrating the fountain stream. Let it continue springing forth. Let it get lost if it will. Another spring will come forth from inside.
>
> Lalan Fakir

Lalan Shah Fakir's life spanned more than a century. During this period he composed and sang some ten thousand songs, creating a body of literature which is unparalleled in the history of folk and mystic literature in the world.

His ancestry, religion, caste, date and place of birth and even his very name are shrouded in mystery. Based on inferential evidence, Professor Mohammed Mansooriddin devoted his lifetime to collecting his songs, to construct his life story.

Born in 1774 into a Hindu family in Chapra village in the then Nadia district of Bengal, Lalan Fakir died on the 17th October 1890. Once on a pilgrimage to Murshidabad, he fell seriously ill and became unconscious. His companions threw him into the river, thinking that he was dead. After floating to a bathing ghat, he regained consciousness and cried out for help. He was saved by a Muslim family, with whom he stayed for a long time recovering from his illness. There he was initiated as a dervish by the spiritual guru of the family, Seraj Sain of Jessore. After a long interval he went back to his family and told them his story of having lived with a Muslim family—after which he was treated as a social outcast. Lalan became a Baul, devoting the rest of his life through his songs in search of the Divine.

He became quite famous during his lifetime. Two weeks after his death, a local magazine *Hitkari* published an editorial under the title *Mahatma Lalan Fakir*, reflecting the eminence acquired during his lifetime.

Baul and the River of Time, *by Arpana Caur, 1991*

> He was illiterate, but hearing his innumerable songs, one cannot but regard him as a supreme Pandit (learned man). He did not read any religious books, but in discussing religion, he displayed an extraordinary knowledge of the Shastras.

The same editorial says that at the time of his death Lalan had some ten thousand disciples. His disciples used to refer to him as *Sain*, meaning "lord"; he was subsequently addressed as "Shah", a title assumed by dervishes.

Lalan was the greatest among the Bauls, a faith which surfaced in Bengal in the second half of the seventeenth century and which fully blossomed forth in the nineteenth century—thanks to Lalan's prolifically creative *sadhana*. The Baul faith is not a religion, but a *sadhana*—just as much as Sufism is not a religion but a path of realising Allah.

Among the Bauls, there are both Hindus and Muslims. Though persons leading a family life also practised the *sadhana* of the Bauls, the hard core among them were homeless and without property. They used to wander around during the daytime with their *ektara* begging for alms, composing and singing their songs before the common people. At nightfall they would return to their *akhra*, their place for collective discussion and singing. They neither went to a mosque nor to a temple, they followed neither the Shariyat nor the Shastras. They did not go to any Pir or Swami, though they were Guruvadis: those who believe in being initiated into the faith by a guru. Unlike the Sufis, they lived with their women in the *akhras*. In fact, women were indispensable companions in their *sadhana*. However, despite living with women, they were ordained to remain childless.

The Bauls did not believe in writing down their songs. They sang as they went along, and as feelings came to them.

Baul is the Bengali version of the word "bawara" or "baula", used in North India for someone who is possessed or crazy. The verb used for this term in the Bhojpuri dialect is "baurana". The Bauls were non-conformist, as judged by the traditional norms of their time. That is why they came to be known as Bauls, or madcaps.

For nearly ten years, Lalan continued to compose and sing his songs, never stopping to correct them. No one wrote them down, and nothing was published during his life time; the work of collecting his songs started only after his death. Even now many of his songs are not published and several of them have perhaps been lost. No authoritative manuscript of Lalan's songs has yet been found. Whatever is available is either a copy or a copy's copy. One of the most eminent Bengali writers and doyen of Bengali literary figures, Shri Annada Shankar Ray, has traced and described the streams which combine to make the Baul *sadhana:* Islamic Sufism, Hindu Vaishnavism, and the Sahaja path in Buddhism. In Lalan's songs many references to Rasool, Nabi, Allah and the Divine as Nirankar or formless reflect the Sufi influence.

Pare ke jabe, nabir nauka te aay
Ki bolbo padosir kotha
Tar hasta, pada, skandh, matha nai re

Those who want to get across, should come to Nabi's boat
How shall I describe my neighbour?
He is without hands, feet, shoulder or head

The Vaishnav influence may be seen in Lalan's songs on Gora, or Chaitanya Mahaprabhu and Krishna. The Bengali synonym for Krishna—*Kalo*—occurs time and again in his songs. The following song is one of Lalan's most melodious and soulful compositions:

Amay maris ne Ma
Boli tor charan dhare
Noni churi are Korbo na

Don't beat me anymore, Ma,
I promise to hold your feet
I shall no longer steal the butter

Of these three religious streams which influenced him, the strongest has been the Sahaja path: seeing or recognising the Divine in the human being. Lalan has variously called the Divine as *Maner Manush*, 'The Man Inside', *Achin Pakki*, 'The Unrecognised Bird', *Ajana Manus*, 'The Unknown Man', and *Adhara Chand*, 'The Moon beyond my Grasp'. According to the Sahaja one can know God only by knowing oneself. One can find him only by loving humanity as a whole. Nobody proclaimed this belief more eloquently than Chandi Das:

Sunaha manush bhai
Sabar upare manush satya
Tahar upare nai

Listen Oh human brothers
Beyond all truths is the truth as human being
There is nothing beyond that

This relationship between man and god is reflected in the immortal lines:

Milan hobe koto dine
Amar manner manusher songe
Manush guru nishtha jār
Sarbo sadhan sidha hoy tār
Apanare apani chini ni

How long will it take to meet the Man of my heart?
One who is steadfast in his devotion to Man, the Guru,
Will see all his seekings fructified
You do not recognise your own self in yourself

Eyi manushe she manush acche
Koto yogi rishi char yug dhare re
Tare bedachhe khuje

In this man is the other man
And yet how many saints and savants for ages
Have been wandering around in search of Him

The contribution of Bauls as social reformers is also significant as brought out by Shri Annada Shankar Ray:

> The Bauls' *sadhana* is not religious but human. They wanted to have communion with God, but they were indifferent to other worlds. They were not anxious to go to heaven nor were they afraid of going to hell. The sphere of their songs was this body and this life of theirs, and the mortal world in which they lived.
>
> Just when the Renaissance started among the educated class in India, exactly at that time there was one more movement in the heart of the

> uneducated rural folk. History has not recorded this relationship between these two streams of Indian Renaissance. When this part of history is written, Lalan will be seen in proper perspective.

He further says that in the mind of the people of Bengal, Lalan's importance in the renaissance of Bengal is no less than that of Raja Rammohan Roy.

Lalan and other Bauls castigated religious bigotry and exploitation in the name of religion. They sang against casteism and religious divisions and saw as their task the building of bridges between Hindus and Muslims. Very few people have contributed more to the unity of Indian society than Lalan and the Bauls.

The following are memorable lines from one of Lalan's songs:

Sab loke koy Lalan ki jat sansare
Laan Bhave jater ki rup dekhlam na eyi nazare

Sab bole Lalan Fakir Hindu ki jaban
Laan bole amar ami na jani sandhan

Eyi ki ajab karkhana
Jat gelo jat gelo bole

Everybody is asking what is Lalan's caste
But Lalan has never seen with his naked eyes the form of caste

Everybody is wondering whether Lalan is a Hindu or a Muslim
But Lalan says: that he does not see any difference

This is a strange situation
For people are saying he has lost his caste

Apart from being a *sadhak*, a seeker of truth, and a social reformer, Lalan was also a great poet. No one paid him more handsome a tribute than Rabindranath Tagore:

> In the simplicity of language, in the profundity of feelings and in the painfulness of their melody, they (the Bauls) are unparalleled. In their songs are combined the essence of knowledge, the beauty of poetry and the nectar of Bhakti (devotion). I do not believe that these extraordinary qualities in folk literature can be found anywhere else.

In his writings Rabindranath Tagore often referred to Bauls, but not specifically to Lalan—yet the songs he quoted were Lalan's. In his lecture at Oxford which was later published under the title the *Religion of Man*, Tagore quotes *Kaanchar bhitar Achin Pakhi*, 'The Unrecognised Bird in the Cage', among songs by Lalan.

Tagore was the first to draw the attention of educated Bengalis to the literary value of Baul songs, and also to make an attempt at collecting them. He was again the first to publish twenty of Lalan's songs, corrected and edited in the magazine *Prabashi*.

The greatest compliment that Tagore paid to Baul songs was to see reflected in them Upanishadic philosophy. In the *Religion of Man,* he writes:

> This village poet evidently agrees with our sage of the Upanishads who says that our mind comes back baffled in its attempt to reach the unknown Being; and yet this poet like the ancient sage does not give up the adventure of the Infinite, thus implying that there is a way to it's realization.

In his foreword to M. Mansooriddin's first volume of *Haramoni,* Tagore writes:

> I remember, in my younger days, a Baul from Selaidah who came to Calcutta and sang this song with his *ektara*:
>
> "Where shall I find Him
> Who is the Man of my heart?
> Having lost that man, now for Him
> I wander around the world!"
>
> The words are very simple, but with the combination of music, its meaning gets suffused with an extraordinary light—the statement has also been heard in the language of the Upanishads:
>
> "If anyone is worth knowing, then try to know that Super Human; otherwise there will be only pain of death".
>
> I heard the same statement from someone who was not learned, in his own tune in his simple language:
>
> "He who is worth knowing more than anyone else, inflicts on you, more than anyone else, the pain of not knowing him."

> The cry of a child who cannot see its mother in the dark is what is echoed in their songs.

Shri Annada Shankar Ray comes to the conclusion that despite some common traits in their poetry the Bauls' and for that matter, Lalan's influence on Rabindranath Tagore's poetry was limited. Baul songs are esoteric in nature, and their real meaning is not easily accessible to the common man. It is revealed only to those initiated into the Baul faith, unlike Tagore's poetry.

Like the Bauls, Tagore was a firm believer in the concept of God within man. In his *Religion of Man*, he refers to the divinity of man and to the humanity of God. In *Gitanjali*, he says:

> *Roop Sagare doob diya chhi*
> *Arup ratan asha kori*
>
> I have dived into the ocean of the Manifest
> Hoping to get the gem of the Unmanifest

Although mysticism is a common feature in the poetry of both Rabindranath Tagore and the Bauls, it was not specifically the Bauls who had influenced Tagore in this respect. They both derived strands of their poetry from the common heritage of Islam,Hinduism and Buddhism.

It was in the music of his songs however, that Tagore was deeply influenced by the Bauls. In his foreword to *Haramoni,* he writes:

> I have adopted the Baul tunes for many of my songs. And in many other songs of mine, there is, either knowingly or unknowingly, a mixture of Rag-Raginis and Baul tunes. From this it can be seen that at some period of time, Bauls' tune and voice got assimilated in my mind in a natural way.

Lalangeet, or songs by Lalan have emerged as one of the most melodious folksongs of Bengal. They are truly soul-stirring and take the listeners closest to the divine. They are simple, natural, unembellished and rooted in the soil. Because of their deep and rich philosophical content, many scholars, including Shri Annada Shankar Ray, do not regard them purely as folk-songs. They put them in the category of *sadhanageet* or songs sung in the quest of the Divine or again as classical poetry. Whatever their philosophical content, there is no doubt that these songs contain folk idioms, words, images and style. Their folk root and folk characteristics are the very soul of these songs, and hence the reason Rabindranath Tagore alluded to them as folk songs. Yet there is no contradiction between these songs being categorised as both *sadhanageet* as well as folk literature, since it is their folk idiom which makes them an effective vehicle of *sadhana*.

Unlike Tagore songs or Nazrul Geeti, there is no pure or original forms of these songs. As the Bauls did not want these songs to be even written down, where was the question of giving them musical notations or *swar-lipi* to enable them to be sung by all. These songs are sung as they are heard and have been handed down from successive generations of Lalan followers. In the process they have undergone considerable changes. The singers have added their own embellishments and given them their own twists and turns to suit modern taste and make them more pleasing to modern ears. Even during Lalan's time these songs were reportedly sung in different tunes. Those who lived in the *akhra* sang in one tune while those who lived in families sang differently. Despite this diversity the distinctive character of Lalangeeti comes out very clearly even in today's rendering.

The Baul faith of Bengal was not a separate social or spiritual movement. It was part of similar such movements elsewhere in India. The influence of the Sufis, the Vaishnavites and the Sahajias has already been discussed. The Bauls were also close to the saint poets of North India like Kabir, Nanak and Dadu. There is a lot of similarity in the essence, idiom, style and the apparent and hidden meanings of Baul poetry with those of the saint poets of North India. At the same time there are interesting differences. In this context, a comparison between Lalan and Kabir can be very revealing and interesting..

The birth and religion of both Lalan and Kabir remain a mystery. However, it is generally believed that both were born Hindu, but were brought up by Muslim families. The poetry of both was a means of seeking the Divine and as an instrument of social reform. Both of them emphatically declared the oneness of humanity and the inseparability of the human and the divine. Several citations from Lalan to illustrate this point have been given. There is an apt citation from Kabir to illustrate this unity:

Lali mere lalki, jit dekhon tit lal
Lali dekhan main gayi main bhi ho gayi lal

The glow of my Beloved—wherever I see it glows
I went to see His glow; and in the process I also started glowing.

In castigating religious bigotry, superstition and social evils, both Lalan and Kabir effectively use the language of sarcasm. In castigating Hindu superstition Kabir says:

Pahan puje Hari mile to main pujun pahar
Usase to chakki bhali, pis khaye sansar.

If one can attain God by worshipping a stone, then I would rather worship a mountain. Better still is to worship a stone-mill which gives livelihood to the people

Against Muslim rituals, Kabir says:

Kankar pathar jorke, masjid layi banay
Ta chadhi mulla bang de, kya behra houa Khuday

Putting stone and mortar together, they have built a mosque
Climbing on top of that, the mullah shouts in the name of God. Has he become deaf?

And Lalan has this to say against Muslim and Hindu rituals:

Sunnat dile hoy Mosalman.
narir ki hoy bidhan
Brahman chine poita pore
Brahminir kemon chini re

If by circumcision one becomes a Muslim,
Then how does one identify a Muslim woman?
If a Brahmin can be recognised by his sacred thread
Then how does one recognise a Brahmin woman?

There are, however, very significant differences in the poetry of Lalan and Kabir. Kabir's couplets are precise, short, carefully constructed and hence immediately effective. Lalan did not believe in writing down his songs—he composed as he went along. His songs therefore tend to be repetitive and somewhat diffused. Lalan was primarily singing to an audience—his songs are thus conversational in style and sometimes highly dramatic. He is also often addressing himself. Many of his songs start with a question:

Samanye ki tar morm jana jay?
Eyi manab janam ki are hobe?

Can anyone easily know His essence?
Will I be born a human being again?

Lalan's songs moreover are suffused with *bhakti* not found even in mystic poets like Kabir. As the practice of many bhakti poets of India, such as Tulsidas or Surdas, Lalan frequently repents for his sins, asking for forgiveness from God, and totally surrendering to Him. Some examples are:

Akarmer phol bhoge Lalan
Cheerdin kupathe gaman
Khama kore he aporadh amar, eyi bhaha karagare

Lalan is paying for his wrong deeds
I have forever walked on the wrong path
Forgive my offences committed in this wordly prison

Lalan like many other great bhakti poets and philosophers, recognised the futility of *gyanamarg*, the path of knowledge, and he opted for total surrender:

You are wasting valuable time by indulging in all kinds of logic....
You must close your mind to bad logic.

Lalan's life story demonstrates that despite a person's humble and obscure origin, with courage of conviction and the power of faith one can defy outdated, unjust and exploitative social practices and norms. A person's voice can hence be heard not only by his own generation, but also by generations to come. Time and again such persons have appeared on Indian soil, have drawn mass followings and have been venerated and deified by their countrymen during their life time. Gandhiji was one such example in our generation, and again in the Bengal of the nineteenth century, when Lalan Shah Fakir composed and sang his songs.

Lalan's poetry and music, a priceless heritage, thus belong not only to India but to all the three countries of the subcontinent. The message conveyed through Lalangeet is of great relevance today. At a time when an unprecedented revival of communalism and casteism is gnawing at the very roots of Indian unity and democracy, Lalan's message of pure human love, compassion and brotherhood should lead one to reflect more on our heritage of tolerance and compassion.

SUMANTA BANERJEE

Look What They've done to My Song!

Ray Charles, the renowned jazz musician and gospel singer, in one of his songs bemoans the sad fate of folk music brought about by the peddlers of tinsel. "Look what they've done to my song, Ma! (They've) put it in a plastic bag!"

This fear of contamination and commercialisation of what was respected as the clear waters of folk culture is shared by folk-singers all over the world—whether in the developed or the developing countries. It is more so in the latter, where the oral tradition of folk culture is the only exclusive property that the poor and the illiterate can claim as their own.

In the subcontinent of India, Pakistan and Bangladesh, our folk culture had grown out of the community rites and collective festivals of a rural society. Even romantic folk songs developed from within the framework of these rites and festivities. They were passed down from one generation to another, each folk poet and singer adding something new to them and quietly retreating into anonymity. Folk songs are the poor man's stalagmite in world culture—growing up from the ground in a variety of shapes, formed by the steady dripping of beliefs and ideas from the roof-top of an unbroken tradition.

But can folk culture, like stalagmites which are found only inside caves, continue to develop within the cloistered confines of a rural society—deriving sap from the soil below and irrigating itself with ideas from the ancient ceiling of the same society? Can folk artists adapt their traditional art forms to the new opportunities offered by the commercial media—recording studios, radio, film, television? How are they to respond to the waves of political conflicts that shake their society, or to the state's programmes of development?

These pressures had beset folk traditions in other parts of the world during periods of political and economic transition. Yet in the subcontinent they assumed complex dimensions peculiar to this area, due to certain historical developments. The partition of the subcontinent in August 1947 split a folk culture that was created and shared by generations of artists, composers, singers and their audience over centuries. The abrupt axing of the territory unleashed a reign of communal terror that became a traumatic experience for millions of Hindus and Muslims who lost their lives, their near ones and their homes during those dark months of 1947. It also left a bewildered and helpless generation of folk artists both in India and Pakistan who suddenly found themselves estranged from each other, denied access to that common tradition of shared social and cultural art genres that had been built up through the ages.

The disruption in the continuity of the folk traditions brought about by the Partition of 1947 hit hard at two linguistic groups: the Punjabi-speaking Hindus and Muslims spread across the Indo-Pak border in the north, and their Bengali-speaking counterparts in the east, straddling West Bengal and today's Bangladesh. The tragedy that accompanied Independence and its continuing repercussions have left an indelible mark on the development of folk-culture in India and Pakistan. The folk singers are torn between a sense of nostalgia for the common cultural heritage shared in the past and the new challenges faced during the last fifty years in their respective states.

In style and content, the traditional oral culture both in West Bengal and Bangladesh have much in common, particularly in folk songs reflecting the joys, the ecstasies, the ordeals and the agonies which form the themes of these songs. Their melodic curves, their rhythm and the performers' intonations on which these songs float all derive directly from the sound and pulse of the Bengali language and its dialects.

Although folk songs cannot and should not be divided into water- tight compartments, for the sake of easier comprehension, they may here be grouped into broad categories. Borders dividing West Bengal and Bangladesh being porous however, these songs can easily float from one group to another. *Gambhira* songs, for instance, give one a good idea of how seasonal songs, associated with certain agricultural rites, often merge into songs of social protest. *Gambhiras* were once popular all over the countryside of undivided Bengal from Dinajpur, Rangpur, Rajshahi in Bangladesh to Maldah and Murshidabad in West Bengal. Sung in the months of April-May, they formed part of a religious festival associated with the worship of Shiva and his consort Parvati. Although the songs usually began with a homage to Shiva, over the years they evolved into an effective musical medium for an annual stock-taking of the major events in the village. These included economic hardships, social scandals, natural calamities, political developments—all of which were reported to Shiva with a view to seeking his divine mediation.

This built-in penchant in the *gambhiras* for social criticism has enabled folk singers in post-Independent decades to express their views on contemporary political developments in most imaginative ways—an instance of innovative acculturation marking the continuity and changing idiom of Bengali folk culture.

In the years immediately following Partition and Independence, folk poets and singers such as the Sufi master Gopal Das, Gobinda Mandal, Fajlur Rahman and others, from the then East Pakistan, chose the *gambhira* to lampoon black marketeers, corrupt politicians, inept bureaucrats, and dishonest social and religious leaders. These songs were popular enough to be perceived as a threat by the Pakistani government, and at one stage *gambhiras* were banned in East Pakistan.[1]

In West Bengal too, the *gambhira* emerged as a medium of protest for folk singers who found soon enough that the new rulers who had taken over from the British were no better than their counterparts in East Pakistan. Typical are the words from the following songs, where the *gambhira* singer, after pleading with Shiva to wake up and set right the economy, complains:

Baro sadher sadhinata, rath chalaley deshey,
Gareeb dukhee dal shara holo chakar taley pishey hey

Ganotantrer ashol rupta besh uthechhey phutey,
Maramari, katakati, narir dharam lutey hey,
Ghush, gherao, gundabaji, hartal, electric, pulish lathi,
Gas, guli aar boma - ey shab Ram Rajotter goyna...[2]

Oh, our long-cherished Freedom! You are driving your chariot
over the country, pounding the suffering
poor under your wheels...

> Democracy is showing itself in its true colours.
> Fightings and killings, raping of women, bribery,
> workers laying siege to factories, thuggery, strikes,
> police cudgels and tear gas shells and bomb-explosions
> these are the ornaments of 'Ram'Rajatya' (Rama's regime)...

This is the picture of post-Independence West Bengal as perceived by a folk poet, who thoroughly disenchanted with the fruits of 'Freedom', indicts every one—from state authorities such as the police and corrupt and criminal elements in society, to even workers who go on strike and besiege factories! The *gambhira* singer shared the age-old rustic scepticism about the political concepts expounded by the urban intelligentsia—particularly terms such as 'ganatantra' or democracy. Any one suspected of making use of such concepts to further his or her own interests in the unprincipled morality reflected in the newly won 'Freedom was the butt of ridicule. As in the former East Pakistan, so also in West Bengal, *gambhira* poets and singers such as groups led by Mator Babu (Jogendranath Choudhury) and Gopinath Seth had to face attacks from political powers whom they lampooned in their songs.[3]

Another category of Bengali folk songs which continues to enjoy enduring popularity in both Bengals is the *bhatiali*, songs sung by boatmen while rowing across the rivers that criss-cross the Eastern subcontinent. Composed in the dialect of the riverine people of East Bengal, these songs usually convey a mood of yearning or nostalgia—for home, for a pretty girl seen on the banks of a river, for a distant lover. The *bhatiali* songs are still improvised by these boatmen in a loosely-knit language, while rowing or resting along some obscure banks, or meandering through far-flung villages. While singing they allow their voices to rise and fall, almost echoing the movement of the waves of the river which toss their boat.

During the last fifty years of Independence, however the melodic structure of the *bhatiali*, as well as tunes from a number of other genres of Bengali folk culture such as Baul, Bhadu, or Bhaoaiya, underwent a change— through commercial exploitation by a variety of urban interests.

Among those who use this medium over the radio in Calcutta and Dhaka are musicians and singers who present *palligeeti,* literally 'songs from villages'. The film industries in both parts of the Eastern subcontinent use the melodious strains of these songs to compose the sentimental songs for their romantic scenes. Government departments use them to spread messages of development such as family planning, adult literacy, etc. Politically committed cultural activists base themselves on these songs to compose the *ganasangeet*, or songs used in both regions for persuading the rural poor to join the struggle for a socio-economic change. Listening to these ersatz versions of traditional songs—the music twisted by gyrating orchestras of commercial studios or the declamatory tone of the political *apparatchiks*—rural folk poets and singers must have wondered, like Ray Charles, whether their songs were not being put in plastic bags.[4]

One genre of folk culture in Bengal which to some extent escaped commercial and political exploitation was the repertory of tribal songs. This may be due partly to the different linguistic origins and melodic styles of these songs which make them stand apart from the mainstream Bengali cultural tradition, and partly because of the exclusiveness of the rites and customs of respective tribal communities from where these songs originated.

Among the main tribal groups straddling the frontiers of West Bengal and Bangladesh are the Santhals, Oraons and Mundas who inhabit upper parts of Bangladesh and large tracts of West Bengal; and the Chakmas, Kochhs and Rajbangshis who inhabit the northern areas of both the countries. Their songs provide a fascinating insight into the resilience of a socio-cultural tradition, hardly affected if at all, by the political and economic intrusions of modernization over the last fifty years. A quote from one particular song for instance expresses the continuity of tribal loyalty to agricultural gods, as also the erotic longing for women.

The song quoted below was part of an agricultural ritual traditionally followed by Rajbangshis in the northern parts of the Bengali subcontinent. The ritual was observed by women alone during the Bengali month of chaitra (March and April) which preceded the onset of the monsoon and was performed to please *Huduma*, the god of rain. The women, who assembled on a dark night, in an uncultivated field with plough and seeds, shed all their clothes, untied their hair and danced wildly, singing hymns to *Huduma*. No man was allowed to watch the performances, the belief being that if a male stole a look at the nude dancers, no rain would ever fall.[5]

Some seventy years ago, a British official claimed to have secretly witnessed the Rajbanshi rain dance in a village in Cooch-behar (now part of West Bengal), and left an account of it.[6] That the ritual continues to be followed by Rajbangshi women is evident from the following *Huduma Geet*, collected some years ago from a village in Rangpur in Bangladesh. Unabashed erotic impulses merge with the parched earth's desire for rain.

Hil hilase komarta mor
Shir shirase mor gao,
Konthe kena geley ela
Huduma dekha pao.
Patani khani paresey khasia
Aaola hoieyesey khopaata mor
Hudum dekha deogo aasia.
Aasek re Huduma deoa rasia rasia
Tor padey moi aase re basia.
Dingsali dingsali komarta
Tateo nai mor bhatarta
Karo ki moi kaiba koy
Konthe gela dekha hoy
Dekha haley dehata juraya.[7]

My loins are stirring, my body is trembling,
Where should I go to meet my beloved *Huduma?*
Now I've shed my clothes, my hair is hanging loose.
Huduma, come and bare yourself. Come and satisfy me.
I'm awaiting your arrival. My loins are stirring.
But my man is away. To whom shall I complain?
Where can I go to meet *Huduma?*
Once I meet him, my body will cool down.

A vast repertory of Bengali folk religious songs exist in the Baul songs, based on popular syncretist beliefs shaped both by the Bhakti and Sufi traditions. The Baul today has acquired international fame, thanks to the festivals organised abroad—due more, one suspects, to the colourful attire and soulful singing style of the Baul performers than to the deeply spiritual humanitarian messages conveyed by their songs.

These mendicant minstrels do not follow any orthodox divisions based on caste or religion, and express in their songs a healthy contempt for all bigotry - whether Hindu or Muslim. To them, temples and mosques are hindrances to the realization of the *moner manush* or the 'man-within'—the divine essence that resides within the human body awaiting discovery by its owner.[8] The human body therefore becomes a major motif in their songs; and the theory of *dehatattva*, "of the body", is variously used as a symbol of the fate of human life, or of the abode of the Supreme Being as a primordial concept in their beliefs. The style is often marked by *double entendre*, allusions to various parts of the body in the innocuous garb of place names or characters.[9] A typical example is the following verse from a Baul song:

Dhaka hotey aami korechhilam asha
Bhojbo Hari boley karo kholsha
Achhey Rangpurer tamaasa ta dekhey holo nesha
Shei hotey durdashaye nilo ghiriye.
Shoyda bajarey shoyda hobey ki?
Chhoyjon gant-kata khelchhey phanki
Shei phankitey holam phanki...[10]

Frankly speaking, I hope to worship Hari from Dhaka.
But I got hooked on the revelries of Rangpur.
Since then I've been in a wretched state. How can I trade in the market?
Six pickpockets are playing tricks on all, and
I've also become a victim of their tricks...

The hidden meaning here needs to be deciphered. Dhaka, the name of the capital of Bangladesh also means in Bengali 'hidden' or 'covered'. In this song the reference is to the sexual organs, which are 'covered', and therefore 'concealed' The devotee who sings the song implies that he tried to worship the god Hari through esoteric sexual practices, which are part of the Sahajiya-Tantrik religious tradition. But in the process, he lost his way, enamoured by the attractions of the flesh. The song describes the 'revelries of Rangpur'— Rangpur being the name of a town in Bangladesh—and the word 'rang' or 'ranga' meaning fun or frolic. When the singer arrives at the 'marketplace', a metaphor for the judgement place in the 'final reckoning', he finds himself deprived of everything by six pickpockets— the six passions, being lust, anger, greed, addiction to drinks, infatuation and envy. Thus the devotee is left with nothing and is unable to offer anything to god.

The Baul singers continue to maintain their tradition, moving from one place to another, dressed in saffron gowns and strumming on a one-stringed instrument called the *ektara,* singing at marketplaces, in trains, or on village roads. They congregate at festivals on two main occasions. In Bangladesh they gather once a year in a village in Kushthia district to pay homage to the memory of the famous Baul philosopher and composer Lalan Shah, born there in the late 18th century. In West Bengal, they come from different parts of the state in early January every year to coverge in a village called Kenduli in Birbhum.

Despite Partition, its bitter memories, and a succession of communal riots in both parts of the eastern subcontinent, the popularity of these folk singers still cuts across borders and religious differences. They still move, sometimes freely, sometimes surreptitiously, from West Bengal to Bangladesh and vice versa.

While on a trip to a village in Nadia in West Bengal bordering Bangladesh some years ago, a distinguished Bengali scholar and collector of folk songs heard the story of a Baul singer, Sadananda Khyapa, who gave a moving account of his experiences in Bangladesh. Sadananda recounted how he had crossed over without legal travel documents. Being a Baul, he went there wanting to visit Kushthia, the birth place of Lalan Shah. Sadananda was arrested by the Bangladesh police soon after he crossed the border, and was taken to the nearby police station. The police inspector there, a Muslim called Nasiruddin, sprang a pleasant surprise on a petrified Sadananda with a strange request. Nasiruddin asked him to sing a kirtan—a Bengali devotional song in praise of the love of Radha and Krishna.

Sadananda sang for hours, with a totally absorbed Nasiruddin listening with his eyes closed. At the end, the police inspector opened his eyes, and exclaimed: *Jay Gaur*!—"All praise to Gaur"— the traditional form of greeting among Bengali Vaishnavites. The greeting invokes the name of the sixteenth century reformer Chaitanya, who patronised and popularised the kirtans on Radha and Krishna[11]. He then turned to Sadananda, and addressing him as 'gonsai' the colloquial Bengali term, used for Vaishnavite followers of Chaitanya, said: "Can you imagine for how many years I haven't heard a kirtan, gonsai? Ever since you people left for Hindustan, we lost our chance to listen to kirtans."[12] This story suggests the dilemma of a divided community which looks back nostalgically to its shared heritage of the past.

Folk singers, on both sides of the border, have refused to be bogged down by memories of the past. During the last fifty years, folk music in this part of the subcontinent has travelled a precipitious road: from the early days of despondent outpourings about Partition and the loss of roots[13], to present day political satire and songs of protest. Thus in 1967, when a coalition of political parties formed a United Front government in West Bengal and within a year began to crack up, each party accusing the other, a gambhira singer invented the word *dalatantra* (partycracy) and sang:

Toder dalatantrai holo shaar
Deshbashi shudhu korley hahakaar
Ashtamashey Ashtarambha juktafranter upohaar! [14]

All that you produced was 'partycracy'.
The people of the country only cried in distress.
In eight months, the United Front
could give us only eight bananas! (a big hoax)

At around the same time, across the border in East Pakistan, one could hear this hilarious ditty about a politician who swindled people out of their share of rations:

Shone re kangal chacha, Barisaler khabor khasha!
Food committeer Prisidingre jotar mala
Galaye diya ghuraichhe raastaye.
Abar notun khabor paoa gechhey,
O tar ration card galaye baindhya
Chini ettu hatey diya, kerasin dae mathaye,
Abar notun kapor diya galaye
Tainya beray rastae rastae...[15]

Listen, O my poor uncle, there is good news from Barisal!
The people have tied a garland of shoes
around the neck of the President of the Food Committee,
and taken him through the streets. Still more news!
They have hung his ration card down his chest as a medal, put a bit
of sugar in his hands, and have poured kerosene
on his head. Tying him with a piece of a new cloth,
they have dragged him along the streets...

Folk music of the subcontinent continues to be fascinating and powerful because of its ability to say many things to many people—appealing to different layers of human sensitivity. The following lines from an old folk song are illustrative:

Aami shei gharer malik noi,
Parer jomin, porer jayega,
Ghar banaiya aami roi.
Ghar khana kar jomidari,
Aami pai na jomindarer dekha,
Moner dukhho kare koi?
Aami khajnapati shab-i dilem, bhola mon,
Tobu amar jomi hoy go nilem...[16]

I'm not the owner of the house.
It is another person's land
where I have built this house.
I have not been able to set my eyes
on the landlord who owns this land.
To whom shall I complain? My poor soul,
though I paid my rent and all other dues,
the land is auctioned off...

At one level, the song can be interpreted as the simple complaint of a poor peasant deprived of his home. At another level, it is an allegorical description of the human condition, the unseen landlord being God and the auctioned land the human body.

Without ceasing to be itself and without losing its melodic and rhythmic specificity, Bengali folk music has organically evolved since 1947—finding its way into the heart of every human situation from common-place situations to pondering on age-old truths. It survives like a tunnel raging beneath the subcontinent's turbulent history of the last fifty years—a tunnel that keeps alive much that religious fundamentalism, political chicanery and social immorality have long since destroyed above ground.

Notes

1. Mustafa Nurul Islam (ed.), *Abahaman Bangla*, Dhaka, 1993. pp.36–37
2. Dr Pradyot Ghosh, *Loka Sanskriti: Gambhira*, Calcutta: Pustak Bipani, 1982. p.110.
3. Ibid. p.71
4. To give an example of how official propaganda sticks out like a scarecrow from such songs set to the tunes of folk melody, consider the following: *Sustho bhabey banchte holey dushon-mukto poribesh chai. Gachh lagiye shei poribesh dushon-mukto korbo shabai.* (To live healthily, we need a pollution-free environment. We shall all clean the environment by growing trees). Quoted from *Birbhum Zilla Sakshaarata Samiti*, ed. Madal, Birbhum, 1991. p 35.

   In the genre of *ganasangeet* (manufactured by both Rightist and Leftist cultural *apparatchiks*), there have been occasionally fruitful and creative innovations through collaboration of middle class political composers and village folk singers, one of the most oustanding examples of which is the unforgettable satire 'Mountbaton Mangal-kavya, (composed by the veteran Communist singer, the late Hemanga Biswas, immediately after Independence). It drew upon a variety of traditional folk tunes to make fun of the concept of 'transfer of power' described as 'Independence' by Lord Mountbatten to the Indian leaders. It reflected the typical sceptical suspicions nurtured by the common people about political deals manipulated above their heads—suspicions which, ironically have come out to be true during the last fifty years!
5. Abdus Sattar, *Tribal Culture in Bangladesh*, Dhaka: Muktadhara, 1975. p.144.
6. Augustus Somerville, *Crime and Religious Belief in India*, Calcutta: Thacker Spink and Co. Ltd., 1966., pp. 183-84.
7. Abdus Sattar, 'Tribal Folklore of Bangladesh' in Mustafa Zaman Abbasi, ed. *Folkloric Bangladesh*, Dhaka: Bangladesh Folklore Parishad, 1979, p.41.
8. The Baul spirit is summed up in the following verse: *Karim, Rahim, Radha-Kali, E bul o bul jatoi boli, Shabdobhede thelatheli hoitechhe sangsare, Manobdehe theke swaong ek-i shakti dhare.* (Words are shoving and jostling each other in our society. But however much you may swear by words like Karim, Rahim, or Radha and Kali, it is from the human body that one derives the common strength.) Quoted in Sudhir Chakraavarty, ed. *Bangla Dehatattver Gan*, Calcutta: Pragnya Prakashan, 1990, p. 34.
9. Cf. "... when the poor and the deprived can have no access to, and possess any external commodity, they cling to their bodies as the sole essence of existence. It is in the body that they discover and try to realise deeply all the truths of existence" (Ashok Sen in Baromash, April, 1987).
10. Composed by Gour Gonsai. Quoted in Sudhir Chakravaraty, Ibid. p.21.

11. Vaishnavism, as preached by Chaitanya, was embraced both by Hindus and Muslims during his life time, giving rise to a large number of Muslim Vaishnavite composers of kirtans, which could explain the abiding popularity of the musical tradition of kirtan among Bengali villagers of all religious hues even in Bangladesh.
12. Sudhir Chakravarty, *Panchagramer Karcha,* Calcutta:Pratikshan Publications Pvt. Ltd., 1995., pp.54–55.
13. A typical example of the nostalgic longings of the years immediately after the Partition of 1947, is the following verse from a *gambhira* song: *Hindu-Mochholman ek-i jaat, bhai. Ek-i deher duida haaat, keu karu noy shottur, re bhai, dui-e dui-e mittir hoy. Roj shakale ajaan gaan, aar Berambhoner montar paath, sand-hyakale nemaj pore, kulanaree peerdum dae, ek sathete roichhi mora, ek sathete korchhi khela, ek-i shongey cholchhi phirchhi, Ekhon kane bhinno bhab?* (Hindus and Muslims are the same people. They are like the two hands of one body. One is not the enemy of the other; the two are friends. Every morning begins with the call of the azaan by the muezzin and the chantings of the Brahmins. The evening ends with the namaaz and the lighting of the lamp by the housewife. We have been living together, playing together, moving together. Why then this segregation today?) Quoted in Dr. Barun Kumar Chakravarty, *Loka Sanskriti: Nana Prasanga,* Calcutta: Book Trust, 1980, p.17.
14. Ibid. p.25
15. Shankar Sen Gupta "Banglar Lokasanskriti O Prachar Madhyam' in West Bengal Government Information and Public Relations Department, *Paschim Banger Lokasanskriti,* Calcutta, 1970, p.55.
16. Collected from an anonymous folk singer.

NABANEETA DEV SEN

Rewriting the Ramayana: Chandrabati and Molla

We shall discuss the retelling of the Ramayana by two sixteenth-century women poets. Molla was a potter's daughter from a small south Indian town in Andhra Pradesh, familiar with the regional court culture of her day. Chandrabati was an impoverished Brahmin woman from a small village of Bengal, in eastern India, who had never been exposed to urban culture. We shall try to see how similar these two contemporaries were in their own cloistered cultures, and why one text is regarded as a major success while the other is considered a dismal failure by scholars of literature. To find an answer, we have to sift through questions of gender roles, silenced voices and the tensions between social versus individual priorities.

Just as Chandrabati was the first woman poet of medieval Bengal, Molla was the first woman poet of medieval Telugu literature. Both were devotees of Shiva; yet they wrote about Rama, an avatar of Vishnu. Both women remained unmarried and earned a living writing poetry—a pretty tough task even in twentieth-century India. More importantly, Chandrabati had written a short Ramayana in her mother tongue, Bengali; Molla had written one in hers, Telugu. Both women moved away from tradition by discarding the literary language, Sanskrit, in favour of the regional. For Chandrabati, choosing Bengali as the language of her poetry had no larger significance, as her knowledge of Sanskrit was minimal. But for Molla, the choice of Telugu was a conscious and subversive decision.

Having fallen prey to the literary charms of Chandrabati, I was utterly thrilled with the prospect of getting acquainted with yet another sixteenth-century woman poet who rewrote the Ramayana. I soon discovered that Molla had not been translated into English. Irrespective of the endless references to her Ramayana the text itself was not available in translation. So I set out to find her myself in Andhra Pradesh, her homeland, and finally did manage to get hold of a tattered copy of a Hindi-Telugu bilingual edition of the Molla Ramayana, long out of print. This happens to be the only available translation of the text in any language. And as I studied Molla—I discovered that this poet wasn't like Chandrabati at all. There were more differences between the two women re-writers of the epic than the few superficial similarities.

Molla's Ramayana is regarded as one of the classical Ramayanas in Telugu, ranked after the two other medieval Telugu Ramayanas by Ranganatha and Bhaskara. Molla's Ramayana is still widely available in Telugu—thin paperbacks in cheap newsprint, with a shiny colourful picture of a beautiful young Molla lost in meditation on the cover.

Hardly anyone knows about Chandrabati's Ramayana, except for researchers of medieval Bengali literature. Even then, it is known only as a notoriously weak attempt at retelling the Ramayana. Thus, no one generally cares to read it. I wouldn't have, either, had I not felt an unholy urge to see just how bad this Ramayana was. That's when I came to know Chandrabati, in 1989. You will find Chandrabati's Ramayana either in D.C. Sen's collection, *Maimansingh Geetika,* volume IV (1916), or in K.C. Moulik's *Purva Banga Geetika,* volume VII (1976). Both scholarly editions are out of print, and therefore rare. Only the most exhaustive libraries may have them.

There is one uniform opinion in the sparse literature on Chandrabati's Ramayana: that it is her worst piece of work. Not only is Chandrabati's Ramayana regarded as incomplete, it is also labelled structurally and stylistically weak. Even D.C. Sen, who was full of praise for two of Chandrabati's other works, agrees. Sukumar Sen has ripped the text apart, and believes it to be fake. In fact, he believes the whole of the Maimansingh ballad collection poems to be fake!

Although her Ramayana is rejected by critics, Chandrabati herself commands some respect as the first woman poet in Bengali literature. And two of her ballads—*Sundari Molua* and *Dasyu Kenaram*—are rightly regarded as gems of the Maimansingh collection. They are taught in literature curricula both in Bangladesh and in India's West Bengal. However, the text of her Ramayan a is not included, since it doesn't measure up to the language and style of the ballads.

Molla's father, Atukuri Kesan Setty, was a potter, a devotee of Shiva. They lived in the village Gopavaram, near Nellore, in Andhra Pradesh. It is widely believed that his talented young daughter, a rare beauty, was the concubine of King Krishnadeva Raya. Molla was well versed in classical literature and Sanskrit poetics. Her mastery is reflected in her work. Her Ramayana is brief, but it is praised for its comprehensive use of the rasas, not just *bhakti* and *karuna*, the two most often associated with women writers. She is very good at using the rasas considered typically masculine: *shringara, veera, raudra, bhayanaka, adbhuta* and *bibhatsa*. Her emphasis is only natural, since the *Yuddhakanda* is her longest chapter. In Valmiki's classical Ramayana too, the *Yuddhakanda* is the longest, since the epic battle is at the core of every heroic epic.

To the contrary, Chandrabati ignores the war and describes it only through a *Baromaasi*, a woman's song about her everyday sorrows, narrated by Sita herself. Sita devotes only two couplets to the epic battle because she saw it only in a dream. It is not surprising, therefore, that Chandrabati's retelling of the Ramayana, with its disregard for epic conventions, was quickly labelled as all wrong.

Molla, however, would have pleased Bengali critics greatly. Her pen has run dry singing Rama's praises, and establishing the kingdom of Rama. She has dealt with the first four books in 245 stanzas; whereas the fifth book of *Sundarakanda* alone, leading to the war and dealing with the burning of Lanka, takes up 249 stanzas. And the Book of War? It consists of 351 stanzas—a full 102 stanzas more than even *Sundarakanda!* But she totally omits the post-war *Uttarakanda,* dealing with the unfair rejection and banishment of Sita. Still, that doesn't prevent this Ramayana from being respected as a classic. It follows the structure and conventions of an epic, complete with the formal introductions and ritual dedications, in a judicious mixture of prose and verse—and infused with reverence, for Rama, the ultimate God-King.

To whom does Molla pay her respects at the very beginning of her text? To *Mahagunashali dayavan Sri Rama Chandra* who, if pleased, will protect his subjects. The ensuing shlokas beg the blessings of the divine trinity, then she moves on to other gods and goddesses, and finally arrives at Saraswati, praying for her power over words and meaning. (One can't but be reminded of Kalidasa's homage to word and meaning at the beginning of *Raghuvamsam*, a Sanskrit classic). That done, she runs through the whole list of classical Sanskrit poets, from Valmiki and Vyasa through Kalidasa and Bhababhuti, right up to Telugu poet Tikkanna. It does not matter whether her father was a potter or a trader. That Molla was a pundit in classical literature is evident from the structure of her epic, her similes and metaphors, her control over rhetoric and the variation of metres. Her Ramayana is a superbly crafted praise-book of Rama, and wisely dedicated to him, too. By being dedicated not to any mortal king but to the king of kings, the text smoothly steered clear of political complications. It was self-consciously created in the "Great Tradition".

That Chandrabati's Ramayana is not comparable to Molla's is evident from the prologue itself. Chandrabati's attitude is very different, as is her diction and her style. Her father, Dwija Bansi Das, a wandering minstrel, lived in Kishorganj, Maimansingh (now in Bangladesh). He was an impoverished Brahmin who worshipped the snake goddess Manasa. Evidently Chandrabati was not interested in creating sophisticated urban literature as Molla was. Nor did she want her Ramayana to be a part of either the court tradition, or the devotional Bhakti tradition. Not once has she paid her respects to Rama—her Ramayana doesn't contain even a cursory dedication to the epic hero at the beginning or at the end! Nor does she mention the spiritual advantages of listening to the sacred Ramayana, as does Molla. Chandrabati's Ramayana begins humbly by mentioning the little river in her village, immediately making it clear that her work stands outside the so-called "Great Tradition".

Introducing first the poverty-stricken family of her grandparents, she dedicates her poem to the snake goddess Manasa, by the grace of whom they had escaped starvation. Then she pays her respects to her parents—her father who had taught her the Puranas and her mother who had shown her the world. She pays homage to Shiva and Parvati, and, in the same breath, shows her gratitude to the kind river Phuleshwari "who is always there to quench my thirst." She isn't concerned with the army of Sanskrit poets or the entire gamut of gods and goddesses, but is happy expressing her gratitude to her immediate family and the little river which is the lifeline of the village. In contrast, we don't know who Molla's family members were or what her financial status was. Molla's ornate poem is all dressed up in dazzling silk, ready for a visit to the king's court. And Chandrabati's poem? It is in a comfortable everyday cotton sari, with no ornaments at all, ready to husk the rice in the yard.

Although her Ramayana is no longer read or even known, Chandrabati herself is all remembered fairly well for her tragic love with Jayananda. Even after 400 years, the love story, as told by Nayanchand Ghose, holds our interest, like the story of Tristan and Isolde, or Laila and Majnu. Chandrabati, a historic character, has thus turned into a legend, and lives on in ballads herself. But in these ballads, Chandrabati the poet and the writer of the Ramayana is hardly given any importance, it is simply the sad tale of a young woman, and her lost love.

The story is that Chandrabati and her childhood sweetheart Jayananda are engaged to be married. On the wedding day she learns that Jayananda has converted to Islam and married the daugher of the Kazi, the local governor. Chandrabati's life falls apart. She asks for her father's permission to remain single and devote her life to Shiva. Her father permits her to act according to her own will, but he tells her, "Write the Ramayana". That is probably why Chandrabati in her introduction states that— "Chandra sings the Ramayana at the insistence of her father," whereas Molla declares in her introduction. "I am writing the Ramayan at the behest of Rama". One night a repentant Jayananda returns to Chandrabati when she is deep in meditation within her temple. A great storm rages outside and Jayananda's piteous appeals do not reach her ears. In the morning as Chandrabati steps out of her temple, on the door, she finds the words: "Just came to say good-bye". She goes to the river and is stunned to find his lifeless body floating in the water.

Unfortunately, while discussing Nayanchand's melodramatic ballad of Chandrabati, some literary historians tend to treat it merely as the story of a woman who took the oath of virginity. That the ballad also describes how this brave woman chose a life of intellectual fulfillment and produced a Ramayana is irrelevant to even respected scholars like Sukumar Sen. ("She remained a virgin all her life, that is the sum total of the ballad," he writes.) This I would regard as part of a denial of Chandrabati's identity as an epic writer, the same tactic that made Chandrabati's

Ramayana, written from the woman's point of view, a silenced text.

Not so with Molla. Although she had a glamorous lover—probably the most famous of all Telugu kings—nobody discusses her love life. Her work is greatly appreciated although the epic was never read in court, because it was a Shudra kavya, a poem written by a non-Brahmin. Molla is doubly barred—she is also a woman. Anything she writes is bound to fall short of the court proprieties. Critics are not surprised that she didn't have her day in court. But quite overlooking the fact that Molla was very likely the concubine of the king, they are astounded by her grasp over the erotic. "How could a virgin know so much about erotic details?" We find this earnest question in the translator's introduction to the Molla Ramayana published in 1977. (It is revealing that these male historians of classical literature display such an interest in the virginity of Chandrabati and Molla. The sexual status of male writers has not, however, sparked such lively speculation in our scholars!)

Although Molla chose a classical genre, her preferred language was her mother tongue. She believed she was translating Valmiki into Telugu. Unlike Chandrabati, who just plunges into her tale of Sita without setting her work within any literary tradition, Molla makes some very interesting comments on the importance of regional language literature—how it should stand on its own strength and not lean too much on Sanskrit.

But ironically Molla begins her poetic commentary with a disclaimer. She exhaustively lists the things she professes not to be aware of. She is not familiar with Telugu or Sanskrit, she claims; she cannot play the sophisticated games of grammar, has no knowledge of the sentiments, of rhetoric or of prosody, is incapable of a style of her own, cannot fashion literary conceits or poetic ornaments nor coin words of her own; she is ignorant of alphabets and scripts, verbs and nouns.... One wonders how she could have written up to this point. The writer ends with an all-too-humble confession: everything poor Molla has come to know she has learnt thanks to Lord Shiva in her home town, Gopavaram.

By the time we come to the end of the long declaration we know that educating Molla was not the job of any country Shiva lingam but most certainly that of a court pundit. Her Ramayana was clearly meant for the court. Literary pundits cannot reject it—it fits too perfectly within its chosen genre—but the court pundits could, and did. It was praised and banned from the court at the same time. As a result, the courtiers missed out on some exquisite erotic imagery! Over and over again she brings in the image of youthful vigour and erotic power to describe various aspects of life where *shringara* rasa is not exactly called for. She portrays the strong urban nature of Ayodhya by telling us how everything is brimming with sexual energy—from the strapping horses to the wily prostitutes. There is nothing that these fabulous courtesans cannot achieve: "with their honeyed words they can snatch the loin cloth away from the greatest hermit". When Molla's Surpanakha describes Sita to her brother Ravana in order to incite his lust, she uses such sensual language that it would make anyone lust after Sita.

Chandrabati, on the other hand, has no interest in eroticism. Chandrabati's main concern is singing Sita's sorrows—she describes love, longing, the pain of separation, but the erotic details of a fecund world full of sexual energy has no place in her text.

Also, Molla describes Ayodhya as a strong business centre, paying a lot of attention to commercial matters, which are of no interest to Chandrabati. Besides, there are those unladylike but truly epic details of the battlefield that Molla is so engrossed in. She has it all—the single combats, the special weapons, the catalogue of armies, council of kings, gory scenes, mutilation of bodies. Displaying a typical classical temperament, Molla seems to take as much pleasure in the details of war as in the details of the erotic. In Chandrabati, war and erotica are as absent as are the sacred spirit of homage to Rama and the courtly fineries of language found in Molla.

Molla has little poetic interest in Sita, except in her beautiful body. She makes Sita quite insignificant—her birth is not mentioned, and she is barely mentioned even in her own *swayamvara*—a ceremony that by definition should revolve around the bride.

Chandrabati couldn't care less about Sita's physical charms. As unconventional as ever, she begins her Ramayana with the story of Sita's miraculous birth. Chandrabati presents Sita, rather than Rama, as the one born to destroy Ravana and devotes six sections to it. The remaining two sections fit in the birth of Rama, his three brothers and one sister with remarkable ease. That takes care of the first book, *Janmaleela.*

In the second part of Chandrabati's epic, she does something even more drastic: she brings in Sita herself as the narrator. It is presented as a flashback. The war is over, Sita is back in Ayodhya, with her girlfriends in the palace. Chandrabati gives us the whole story through a *Baromaasi.* A *Baromaasi* is usually a women's song, belonging to the folk genre, describing the hardship of a woman all through the twelve months of a year. These are specifically songs of misery, related either to poverty or to emotional turmoil. Chandrabati chooses this vehicle to tell the story of the Ramayana. This *Baromaasi* takes us from *Balakanda* to *Yuddhakanda*. All six books are pressed into this one song—and by dint of the genre itself. Chandrabati's Ramayana becomes the song of Sita's sorrows.

And whenever Rama's heroic deeds need to be mentioned, a dream is conveniently introduced. How else would Sita know? She wasn't there! Chandrabati is meticulous in her narrative logic. Sita takes her time telling us about her own experiences from childhood to marriage and the idyllic camp life in the forest with Rama, the abduction, the separation and the rescue. The great epic battle is gently referred to in an incidental manner—after all it had to happen—"and then Rama killed Ravana in a single combat." This is really getting as far away from the Great Tradition as you can. It is using not only the folk tradition, but specifically the women's folk tradition. Epic themes like war are replaced by essentially female concerns. For instance, in the Janmaleela sections, Chandrabati carefully describes the pregnancies of Mandodari, who gives birth to Sita, and Kaushalya, who delivers Rama to the world.

Twice mediated by a feminine sensibility—first by the narrator-poet Chandrabati herself, and then by the second narrator, Sita—what remains of the epic is anything but heroic. Both in her selection of episodes and choice of poetic form, Chandrabati seems to spurn the mainstream tradition, unlike Molla. Elsewhere

I have argued that Chandrabati's Ramayana was rejected not because it was incompetently crafted or incomplete, but because it was not a traditional text. It is a woman's text, an atypical retelling of the Rama tale in which Rama is first marginalised and then criticised from a woman's point of view. In fact, Chandrabati's Ramayana was never even properly read for what it actually was: the story of Sita's journey from birth to death. Instead of praising Rama, Chandrabati often intrudes into the narrative to comment on Rama's foolishness, to advise and guide him and to accuse him of the devastation that awaits Ayodhya. It is clearly not a devotional text, but a secular one; the story is presented as a plain human drama and not as divine mystery.

After reading Molla, Chandrabati's Ramayana becomes even clearer as a text. Chandrabati wasn't aligning herself with the written tradition at all, but following the oral tradition. Clearly, she was writing not for the court, but for the women folk, as is evident from her refrain: "Suno sakhijana" (listen my girl friends) and not the usual "Suno sabhajana" (listen, members of the court). Chandrabati's Ramayana was composed by a woman, singing about a woman, meant for other women. Unlike Molla's Ramayana, which, following the classical tradition, praises the exploits of a god-man, for the godly men of the court, but only happens to be authored by a woman. Chandrabati's aims and Molla's were different, hence so were their styles.

According to Molla's own claims, she wrote the Ramayana for 'self improvement'. To the discerning reader, however, her writing is clearly that of an upwardly mobile poet, her poem cleverly marketed as a devotional text. Here was a low-caste daughter of a potter, but she wrote a traditional Ramayana, appropriating a male Brahmin's job. On the other hand, Chandrabati, the daughter of a Brahmin poet, was capable of writing excellent ballads in the mainstream tradition. Yet she chose to write her Ramayana in a form that is not used by professional poets, but by illiterate village women. Why did she make this choice? To express her own sorrow and anger perhaps, and also to voice the collective tragedy of the typically unrewarded virtue of Indian women.

It is clear from its obvious silences that Chandrabati's Ramayana is a woman's text. Chandrabati is silent about Rama's valour, silent about Rama's goodness, silent about Rama's battle skills, silent about Rama's wisdom. The only aspect of Rama that we find stressed here is as a lover. But he turns out to be a traitor in love, unjustly banishing his pregnant wife. We find Chandrabati's Rama to be a poor king, a poor elder brother who bullies his loyal younger brother into acting against his own conscience, a poor father who does not carry out his parental responsibilities. He is most of all a poor husband—sending Sita into exile partly as a result of his jealousy of Ravana. The description of the jealous Rama runs like this:

> Unmatta pagal pray hoilen Ram
> Raktajaba ankhi Ramer go
> shire rakta uthe
> Nashikay agnishwash go brahmarandhra phute
>
> Rama becomes nearly insane
> His eyes are blood-red hibiscus, boiling blood rushes up to his head
> His nostrils flare with breath like fire, his head is about to explode.

Chandrabati keeps stepping into the narrative to pass uncomplimentary comments on Rama, thus not merely narrating the Ramayana, but also judging and criticising a flawed man. Her Rama is thus a far cry from the balanced, moderate, *sthitadhi* image of Rama that Molla—following the dominant male tradition—presents. Also, Molla's literary personality never enters the text. Molla's voice does not represent herself, hers is the disembodied objective consciousness of the classical epic tradition. Clearly the two women poets have widely divergent aims. Molla wants to be recognised as the equal of the major Telugu poets. Chandrabati wants to give voice to the silent suffering of women. To suit their own purpose, one identified with the literary lineage of the male Brahminical tradition, whereas the other found her voice in the folkloristic world of a women's oral tradition.

When I finally made it to Bangladesh, to Chandrabati's village Patuari, in Maimansingh, I discovered to my horror that though her temple still stands, the river has dried up, and so has her Ramayana. Nobody knows it. Though people still know her ballads, minstrels don't sing her Ramayana anymore. Besides, ordinary women no longer sing the Ramayana; professional singers do. These happen to be men. "What do you sing then?" I asked the village women. "Oh, just wedding songs and lullabies!" they answered. Could they sing some of the those songs for me? "Sure!" And what do I hear? A song about Sita's wedding; a song about Sita's birth; one on Sita giving childbirth; one on Sita's banishment to the forest; some on Sita and Rama playing a game of dice; some about young Sita bathing before her wedding; and long ballad imitating a *Baromaasi* recounting the story of Sita's life, from her birth to her banishment. These women, in short, were singing the Ramayana, or rather, the Sitayana, as the episodes were all taken from Sita's life.

I recognised that many of these songs were in fact by Chandrabati. Of course, in the oral tradition, songs don't remain exactly the same, but here they were singing Chandrabati's Ramayana, though all but in fragments. The narrative was the same. The themes were the same, the formulas recognizable. As I listened, I couldn't tell whether I was in Bangladesh, Bengal, Bihar, Andhra Pradesh or Maharashtra. Having worked on women's Ramayana songs in Maithili, Telugu and Marathi, the regions seemed to merge in my head. The words sounded similar, the sentiments were the same. The choice of episodes, remarkably were identical.

In the Bangladeshi women's songs I collected from Kendua, Netrakona, and Kishorganj, the narrative is the same as that of Chandrabati: Sita is Mandodari's daughter conceived from poison, found on the seashore at Janaka's land. We also find Kukuya here—the evil sister-in-law, the one responsible for sending Sita off to the forest. The songs often use harsh words about Rama like *tobuo papishthi Ramer puri dekha jaay:* Rama the "saviour of the fallen"; *patita pavana* is himself referred to as *papishtha* "the sinner". In another song Rama is described as *pashanda* "stone-hearted", not an usual epithet for one known as *Karunasindhu,* the "ocean of compassion" (*Panchamasher garbha Sitar Chilo rajdhame/ Pashanda hoia Ram sita dilo bane*).

I had asked a professional male Ramayana singer, Khetra Pal, whether he would use such words in connection with Rama. He bit his tongue, touched his ears and shut his eyes, saying only illiterate, ignorant women could utter such blasphemous words. Well, women don't find it difficult in Bengal to criticise Rama, Chandrabati had started the tradition early enough.

However, these women singing songs that more often than not echoed Chandrabati's text, denied any knowledge of her Ramayana. I first assumed that Chandrabati had become so much a part of their cultural tradition that they didn't even know whose songs they were singing. Authorship was no longer relevant. But then, one puzzling question remained. Why didn't the women sing those sections in which Chandrabati interrupts the narrative to give Rama a piece of her mind?

Once back from Bangladesh I reread the Chandrabati along with the women's Rama songs from Bangladesh, determined to finally solve this enigma of Chandrabati's Ramayana—an enigma that is represented in a series of seemingly unrelated questions. Why did the women from Chandrabati's homeland leave out the parts in which Chandrabati comments in her own name? Why was Chandrabati's style in the Ramayana so different from the polished grace of her other ballads? What accounted for the distance of Chandrabati's Ramayana from the classical texts and its affinity to the Jaina and tribal Ramayanas? And, finally, why did the village women who sing her songs vehemently deny that the songs are hers?

Could it be that Chandra Kumar Dey, the first collector of Maimansingh ballads, was not the first one after all? Could it have been Chandrabati herself who collected some of the songs floating around and then strung them together under the epic title of "Ramayana"? The echo in the contemporary songs came from sharing the same formulae. Chandrabati had made use of the repertoire that the village women used in her times, and her vocabulary is still in use today among the women of Maimansingh. The common use of only a small number of traditional themes and fixed formulas is typical of the oral tradition. That probably also explains why no manuscript of Chandrabati's Ramayana has been found.

And finally, this would also explain the perceived "weakness" of style in Chandrabati's Ramayana. She was not trying to be original. She was using the oral repertoire. And repetitions are not only natural but essential in oral compositions. One cannot apply the literary standards of classical epics to judge a folk oral composition. These are two entirely different genres. Chandrabati tried to lend the rural women's voice a larger identity by calling the work a "Ramayana," and by adding her own anxious and caustic comments to it under her own signature.

One cannot truly blame the literary critics for rejecting Chandrabati's Ramayana. If it calls itself a Ramayana, it is expected to follow the classical rules. An epic, according to Dandin, should possess, among other qualities, "a noble and clever hero." Chandrabati clearly accuses her Rama of having lost his mind; and the way she describes his weaknesses makes him look far from noble. Another crucial criterion for an epic—"the final triumph of the hero"—is also not fulfilled by Chandrabati. She holds Rama responsible for the fall of Ayodhya.

Molla, however, clearly fulfills each and every requirement of Dandin.

Chandrabati does none of this. Rereading Chandrabati in the light of Molla, however, revealed that her Ramayana was never meant to be an epic poem in the mainstream tradition but a collection of Sita songs in the women's oral tradition. Now we can understand why the critics termed it incomplete and incompetently crafted. According to the rules of the canon, it is both. In the women's oral tradition, however, it is neither. Chandrabati's Ramayana touches upon all the major events and experiences of Sita and the associated sentiments, turning her, rather than Rama, into the protagonist. Chandrabati's Ramayana is, in fact, an oral Sitayana. Deliberately choosing women's songs to compose an epic, Chandrabati also challenges the conventional hero's nobility and intelligence, and charges Rama with being responsible for the destruction of his land. However, Chandrabati adheres to the crucial theme of Indian epics—indeed of all epics—the battle between good and evil. Only, while in a patriarchal system this eternal struggle is represented by the male characters, in her Ramayana it is represented by the women: Lakshmi versus Alakshmi and Sita versus Kukuya. Thus, Chandrabati subverted the male epic tradition both in content and in form.

Molla, too, effectively challenged the male epic tradition, but from within, by strictly following the rules in an impeccable, superior style. Writing a perfect epic as a woman, and a lower-caste woman at that, was an undeniably subversive act.

A closer look at these two audacious, single women rewriting the Ramayana in two separate parts of sixteenth-century India, shows how the mechanics of silencing change through time. Although Molla is very popular today, she was silenced in her time, her Ramayana barred from the king's court. The potter's daughter, turned classical poet, was rejected because of her caste and gender. Literary excellence was not enough to win the recognition of the court.

Today, with the framework of literary criticism changed, when extra-textual elements like caste and gender are no longer part of the criteria to judge literary works, Molla reigns supreme for her poetic excellence. Although aware of the women's simple poetic tradition in Telugu, she had chosen not to follow it. What a Brahmin man could do, she must have felt, she could do better. Molla rewrote the Ramayana in her mother tongue, summoning all the sophistication of a classical language. In her own way, by following the mainstream poetic tradition so closely, Molla too was a rebel who challenged the patriarchal system.

Chandrabati's case is different. In her own time she was not silenced. In fact, she was so popular that she became a legend after her death. She was writing in two folk traditions: in the more polished balladic tradition of her father, and in the much more humble women's oral tradition (of her mother?). She was accepted in both. It was only much later, when the literary canons had changed once again that Chandrabati's posthumous silencing began. Bengali literary historians of the twentieth century were baffled with the problem of evaluating her work, especially determining how her Ramayana would fit into the epic genre. In terms of its form, its style, its diction or even its contents, it clearly could not measure up to the traditional epics. But her ballads conformed nicely with the balladic tradition and fulfilled the criteria of the genre perfectly.

It is time to judge Chandrabati's Ramayana for what it is—a long poem composed in the oral tradition, drawing heavily on available rural women's songs on Sita. She strung the songs together, added her own outraged comments on Rama, and gave them a single corporate identity under the name "Ramayana". In one way however, Chandrabati did accommodate the dominant ideology in her poem: in the figure of her main character and narrator Sita. Sita never rebels. In Chandrabati's text we hear two voices—one rebellious and sharp, which is her own, and the other, conventional and soothing, the voice of Sita. Molla, on the other hand, writing in the male tradition, speaks in a single authoritative voice all through. We hear neither her own voice, nor Sita's. It is a faceless, disembodied poet's persona that she makes use of. A male voice, if any. Ultimately, both Molla and Chandrabati were sisters in sorrow who rebelled against the orthodoxy of their times through their art, but each woman poet chose a very different path from the other to voice her resistance. One was silenced in her lifetime, the other four centuries later.

In the Ramayana songs sung by Marathi women, we often hear lines like *Sitecha dukha baiyanu tumi batun ghiya* ("Women, share Sita's grief among yourselves" or, "Sita distributed her sorrow among us all when she walked to the forest".) The meaning of this became clear to me when in Bangladesh. I was recording a song by a woman, 79 years of age, whom everyone calls Pishima; she once owned the largest water reservoir in Kishorganj town, Paramanik Dighi, and much landed property around it. When her family moved to India she refused to accompany her sons and stayed on in her home town, all alone. Since then, the tank and all the property have changed hands, she has no roof over her head and takes turns in staying with different families. Pishima was singing the song of Sita's exile *Kichu kichu jaay re Sita pichu pichu chaay/tathapi papishthi Ramer puri dekha jaay re puri dekha jaay* ("Sita goes a few steps and looks back a few times/ the palace of the sinner Rama still rises high"). In the middle of the song she broke down, wiped a tear, and muttered to herself, "what is my grief, compared to Sita's?" This fleeting comment on my tape more than proved the point of the Marathi songs. Even to this day Sita provides a voice to our silent, suffering women. We are all sisters in sorrow, be it in India or in Bangladesh...

Tum aaye ho na shabe intzar guzri hai
Talash me he sahar baar baar guzri hai

Verse by Faiz Ahmad Faiz. Calligraphic drawing by Ameena Ahmad Ahuja

BINDU CHAWLA

The River of Hindustani Music

The word Hindustani originates in the word 'sindhu' which possesses layers of meaning. Referring to the Great Indus River that seems to run like a lifeline through this vast peninsula, 'sindhu' literally means divider, but not necessarily separator. Metaphorically, there is a deeper meaning: keeper of the two parts of one whole.

The *Hindustaniyat* of Hindustani music is the story of these two parts when, in village after village, kasbah after kasbah, the cultures on both sides of the Indus mingled, and merged with each other. This culture was given the name of *ganga-jamni*, as a flowing and fusing culture of the Hindustani north.

This tradition began with the Sufis. Mystics from Baghdad and Khorasan, they came to India at the same time as Mohammad Ghori entered India in the eleventh and twelfth centuries. With their penance and austerities and their everyday miracles, they sought neither to colonise the local people nor preach down at them like missionaries. The people flocked to them, from both sides of the Indus, and the subcontinent came to belong to the pirs and fakirs who in the final analysis, were neither Hindu nor Muslim.

Through centuries the spiritual mindset of the people was already attuned to the Jogi; the wondering mendicant and seer. When the Sufis came, in their own special way, they simply reaffirmed the existing patterns of the collective psyche. Though men of great learning, their way was to sing and dance in the love of the divine. The Sufis settled in and around Lahore and Multan, as well as Delhi and Ajmer, into a land whose spiritual mindset was the same. The Sufis belonged.... they had merely come home.

In the same eleventh century as the Sufis arrived in India, the Nath Jogis travelled from Hindustan outwards: from Peshawar out to Central Asia and Iran, carrying their *ektaras* or one- stringed instruments with which they sang songs of mystic love and union.

They were the disciples of Baba Gorakhnath, the initiator of one of the most celebrated of jogi paramparas. The jogis belonged to a bardic tradition which is centuries old. To this day versions of the *ektara,*called *yak taro* in the Sindh of olden times, the *tun-tuni,* the *gopi yantra,* and the *hudka* are found all over the countryside. The *ektara* is the ancestor of the latter-day *tamboora* which first with its six and now its four strings, has come to symbolise the astral reach. To this day it is referred to in whispers as 'guru ki deh', the 'spiritual body' of the guru.

The Sufi fakirs and the Nath Jogis roamed up and down absorbing the folk melodies and songs of the soil through which they passed. As their movements widened, they finally created several orders and paramparas. Thus came both the early as well as the later mystic poets of Hindustan: from the Chishtis and Suhrawardis, to the Vaishnav poets of the fifteenth and sixteenth centuries, and the Bauls—whose poetry would provide the single most important inspiration for musical forms in the coming centuries.

The most noteworthy among these was the khayal. It was the mystics who taught the people about the unknown, for the life of the spirit was not yet lived through the letter; so the people believed what they actually saw and felt. *Main kahun ankhan dekhi tu kahe pustak lekhi* is one of the favourite sayings of the masters of those times, meaning: "I speak of what I see, you speak of what is written." And no wonder, for the holy books that came to be read later by the educated classes would one day become holier than life itself. This is why few can understand that the tradition of Hindustani music is a peasant tradition and no less the truer for it.

When religions came to base themselves more and more on the letter of the holy books, there arose the concept of morality and the concepts of good and bad. And the world came to be divided between those who followed the letter and those who did not. Those who followed the letter were socially safe and went to the mosque and the temple, and those who did not had no place in the social systems of the world.

It is to those who had no place in the social systems of the world that Hindustani music truly belonged. To this day the great masters of the khayal scoff at institutionalised religion. In our times, the story goes that once some friends of a petty musician tried to make a fool of him by making him sing during Muharram. The fellow went up all the way to Ustad Amir Khan and lamented that he had been made to do it unawares. The great Ustad laughed, and to pacify him, said, tongue-in-cheek. *'Abe koordh, sur men gaana mana hai'*. (You fool, singing *in tune* is prohibited.) And with that he had jibed both at the *koordh* (gharana parlance for a person with a false understanding of music) as well as at a ban that did not sanction singing 'in tune' during Muharram! This is not to say that Khan Saheb had not observed the honour (*maryada*, as would be said) of the sanctions, or lack of them, in his own lifetime. But the comment was from a great Ustad, known for the deeply mystical quality of his music.

Both Ustad Amir Khan Saheb and his major disciple, Pandit Amarnath were Sufis, their gharana the Indore gharana. While Ustad Amir Khan established the *vilambit* or slow style of singing in Hindustani music, Pandit Amarnath is celebrated for the mystic poetry he wrote for the khayal. In one composition for the raga Gunkali he writes:-

Tab paar Bramha paye,
Jab hi naad sadhe.
Naad hi to aadi roop avinashi dhare,
Ved gyan, dev dhyan,
Miturang sab paache.

By *sadhana* of the *naad* (or mystic sound) is attained the state of Ultimate, or Parabramha. For *naad* is itself the primordial state of the Undestroyed. The Vedas and the worship of gods come after.

Perhaps the path of true non-fundamentalism has been the mystic path. Hindustani music came into its own due to its very inability to identify completely with the Vedic or the Islamic, the Muslim or the Hindu.

That is why with the coming of the Arabs and the Iranians into the subcontinent there came a great renaissance for the music of the ragas. The Sufis brought with them their *qauls,* their musical instruments like the *taoos,* the Persian name for the *israj* or the *dilruba,* and their system of melodic categorisation known as the *maqam.* Even before the two peoples interacted by speaking

Verse by Mirza Asadullah Khan Ghalib. Calligraphic drawing by Ameena Ahmad Ahuja

Na karda gunahon ki bhi hasrat ki mile daad
Ya rab agar in karda gunahon ki saza hai

together, they interacted by singing and playing their instruments together, using mnemonic syllables in place of language to communicate their emotions in melody. To this day forms such as the *tarana* contain dummy words or phonemes which tell the story of these early times—*neem tadeem tadiya tadare dani.*

Music was an essential part of *ibadat* or prayerful meditation in the Sufi *khanqahs* everywhere in Hindustan; and it is here that mystic poetry found itself being sung. It was the celebrated Sufi, Sheikh Suhrawardy (pir of the Sufi saint Bahauddin Zachariah, who conceived of the raga Multani), who said that music did not produce anything in the listener that was not already there—thereby meaning that the *khumar* or mystic intoxication of the musician was an inspiration which would lead the listener to the same experience as well.

This is why, though king after king invaded the lands of Hindustan, the real conversions took place at the hands of the Sufis, who united the seemingly disparate cultures as no other force at that time. The quwwals would sing at the *dargahs* to the accompaniment of the dholak, and the jogis would sing their bhajans, also to the accompaniment of the dholak. The *rababiye,* players of the rabab, were a community of musicians who were neither Hindu nor Muslim nor Sikh, and several of their musicians travelled everywhere with Guru Nanak to serve his spiritual court.

The Sufi sheikhs may have found Hindu idol-worship not in keeping with their path; but they bowed to the mystic visions and visitations by Rama and Krishna—which can happen to saints regardless of birth. Almost until the British came to India, the Vaishnavite *bairagi* and the Sufi pir had followers from all faiths.

So it was that the Muslim musicians would sing of the goddess Saraswati, and the Hindu musicians would write verses about Allah. It was this living together that also brought the local 'Hindawi' dialects which included also Braj and Bhojpuri into contact with Persian and Arabic. Together they formed what finally came to evolve as the 'Hindustani' language—the true language of Hindustan, and to this day the only language for the Hindustani khayal. For one does not hear of khayals in Marathi and Bengali, though one hears of khayals in Punjabi. But of Punjabi later.

One of the first musicians who perfectly symbolised this union of cultures—the first Hindustani poet-musician was Amir Khusrau. Court poet to eleven emperors in Delhi, he was the well-known disciple of Sheikh Nizamuddin Auliya of the Chishti parampara—and known as the father of the Hindustani khayal parampara. Khusrau was the first to define and categorise mystic poetry sung at the dargahs into form types, and in that process he came to define the khayal type from amongst the many types of quwwali that were being sung—among them *naat, gul, khamsa, kafiya* and so on. With Khusrau categorising the khayal type sung by the quwwals, the form became more and more of a specialised art—finally making its evolution from a poetry-based form to a raga-based form, which is its speciality today. However, today's chota or drut or fast khayal is still poetry-based, still very close to the quwwali; and today's *vilambit* or slow khayal has become the great art of the raga.

The Iranians brought with them to India their music and the mystic poetry of Sanai, Hafiz, Nizami, Attar, Rumi and Sadi. With the settling down of the Chishtis in Ajmer Sharif (Sheikh Auliya was from Chisht in modern Afghanistan), and especially after Khusrau, there would begin the khayal *silsila* in Hindustani music. From the same order would bloom the tradition of the Punjabi Sufi poets, beginning with Baba Farid. As is well-known, Baba Farid, disciple of Bakhtiar Kaki who was himself the disciple of Nizamuddin Auliya, wrote poetry. From him followed the tradition of poets like Sheikh Hussain, Inayat Shah, his disciple Bulleh Shah, as well as Waris Shah and Shah Karim.

The traditional music of Punjab is full of the *kafis* of these poets, *kafi* being a beautiful song-form sung in these parts. The word itself comes from the Persian *kaifiyat*, meaning *haal chad-hana*— the complete release from the idea of the world, to an intoxication with the divine. It is interesting that Ustad Amir Khan Saheb, who traced his musical ancestry to the Quwwal Bachche gharana of Hindustani music (the first gharana ever initiated by Khusrau), found a disciple in a Sufi from Punjab also known for his renderings of *kafis*. He was born in Jhang, to the north of Sindh in the Pakistan of today, the town known by the legendary Heer. According to Richard F. Burton, celebrated traveller of these parts who wrote a much-loved book on Sindh, Jhang was famous for its 'mystics and lovers'. By lovers Burton meant the likes of Heer and Ranjha. Pandit Amarnath's *bandishes* or lyrics for the khayal too are a landmark in mystic love poetry.

While Waris Shah celebrated the love of Heer and Ranjha, Shah Karim wrote of Sassi-Punnu and Sohni-Mahiwal. The beloved's lover and the lover's beloved, are known as *meet* in the *bandishes* of the khayal. *Meet* or *mitwa*, meaning friend, is another powerful image to have emerged in this genre of poetry and music in the centuries gone by—an image after the image of the jogi, a take-off from the Sufi concept of the Lord appearing as the beloved, the 'yaar'. And here perhaps lies the only difference between the Sufi fakir and the Vedantin jogi—the former unlike the latter takes on the metaphor of love while on the Way.

For the Vedantin, 'jog' or union with the divine cannot have any reference to worldly love. For the Sufi, on the other hand, worldly love is merely a pretext for spiritual love. *Milna te rab noon hai tera ishq bahana hai.* (I have to meet the Lord, after all, your love is an excuse). So for the Sufi it is not the beloved who is the Lord. It is the Lord who is the beloved, the yaar, and therefore love is immortal. And so the Sufi says to the jogi, *"Are O re jogi, preet na bhogi?"* (Oh Jogi, so did you not taste the fruit of love?) Ultimately of course, whether through love or through austerities alone, the common goal to be achieved is the transcendance of duality.

Khayal poetry, whose two major images have been the jogi and the *mitwa,* has never absorbed lyrics from contemporary Hindu poetry which are not mystic in nature. While it has absorbed the work of Guru Nanak, Meera, Tulsi, Surdas, Ras Khan, and most importantly Kabir, whose lyrics of bhakti are in a sense no different from Sufi poetry, it remains immune to Hindi as a language. For the Hindustani musician there is a sea of difference between the two. Formal Hindi has its roots in a political culture not without its doctrinal overtones. For this reason it is sad that some young musicians in our times have seen traditional khayal poetry as dated—it is not. For even as it takes up the themes of everyday life in traditional India, it merely camouflages their mystic import.

To put it simply, the music of Hindustan, whether classical or semi-classical or folk, is characterised by mystic art forms, with the khayal as its most important vehicle today.

There have been no gharanas exclusively for Muslims or Hindus, nor ragas sung only by Hindus or Muslims, in the past. For music the only ism is the raga—and even ragism is ultimately not an ism. The raga for both Hindus and Muslims ragas is like the mandala: it transforms. The deeper the musician reaches into the inner states of purity and non-duality, the higher is the level of the raga he renders. The same with taal; the same with *bandish*. The slightest conditioning of the mind and the raga begins to turn technical and is reduced in grace.

Yes, the raga sung correctly, is an active force whose mystic touch will not be understood rationally.

Contemporary times have fast destroyed this energy. The biggest loss to Hindustani music are sama gatherings. Sama is from *sam,* which in essence refers to a complete 'equipose', when the inner and outer are at a point of equilibrium. The excessive commercialisation of music has been a fall from its own state of transcendance of the world, and one hardly hears any more a comment made barely a few years back from the mouth of a connoisseur to a musician—*Kya sama baandh diya aapne* "What a deep spiritual state you took your listeners to!"

Today Hindustani music industry is a colonised industry, colonised by the missionaries known as the patrons of music. Today in India a Sufi Punjab is overlaid by the smoke of post-terrorist times. In Pakistan the Sindh of legendary lovers has been torn by riots. For an art that has been free for centuries, practised for the love of the seen and the unseen alike, for the love of humanity and the love of the divine, these are fallen times.

It is the past that is laughing at us all the time—at our concepts of nationhood and our concepts of religion. The past has scored over the future.

Drawing in pen and red ink by Qamrul Hasan, Dhaka

IV
NATIONALISM AND ACTIVISM

ENAMUL HAQUE

Reflections on the Early Art of Bengal

Not much has been written about the state of artistic activity in Bengal from early times. This essay attempts briefly to re-evaluate a few of the existing ideas concerning the development of sculptural art in Bengal, particularly in its initial phase, as manifested through the medium of terracotta. The 19th century in India was dominated by the study of architecture with three savants on centre stage: James Fergusson, Alexander Cunningham, and James Burgess. Despite their pioneering initiatives and investigating enterprises, they appear to have been unable to cope with sculptural art. If at all, sculpture was an auxiliary subject for them. Also in their scholarship there was hardly any separate existence for Bengal, and obviously, none for the art of Bengal. The study of architecture was considered as primary because it was regarded by the Indians as the most important of the visual arts. Therefore, for the pioneers, it was the earliest of the arts which received careful and analytic treatment. In these studies, Bengal's presence was negligible, for there was very little evidence available till then, of surviving worthwhile architecture. Mahasthangarh, Paharpur, Bangarh, Chandraketugarh, Mainamati, Rajabadidanga and other sites were yet to be excavated by the archaeologists.

The transition to the twentieth century saw not much difference until about the second decade. A new spurt of enthusiasm was visible in the collection of ancient relics, mainly sculptures, under the aegis of the newly established museums at Dhaka and Rajshahi. Not that the older Indian Museum at Calcutta was idle, but that had become the grand storehouse of objects from the whole of India and even beyond. The sculptures from Bengal, though not unimpressive in number, were relegated to being considered second rate items as compared to those from Bharhut, Gandhara, Mathura, Sarnath, Amaravati and Bodhgaya.

Within a span of half a dozen years, exactly between 1928 and 1933, there appeared a sudden flurry of publications related to Bengal art, all of which focused on sculpture. These were outstanding works and remain so till today, even after the passage of such a long time and even though, naturally, many of their observations and conclusions have been superseded. J.C. French (1928), N.K. Bhattasali (1929), Stella Kramrisch (1930) and R.D. Banerji (1933), together introduced a plethora of publications on sculpture from eastern India, treating the subject from the standpoint of historical development. Among them, N.K. Bhattasali specifically dealt with iconography, breaking altogether new grounds.

The most noticeable and common feature of these publications was that, in the absence of an appreciable corpus of art material from the early period, the principal preoccupation of these authors had been the sculptures from Bihar and Bengal. These were the specimens in stone and bronzes found in various public and private collections, belonging to a period of political pre-eminence of the Pala and Sena dynasties from the eighth to twelfth centuries. It was even considered that this was the only period of art activity in Bengal, before the Muslim conquest. The above authors, except N.K. Bhattasali, were committed to pursuing the dynastic art of the Palas and Senas, disregarding any territorial differences between Bengal and Bihar. Obviously, there was no harm in trying to establish other dynastic art idioms in India beside those of the Maurya, Sunga, Kushan, Gupta and later eras. Dynastic periodisation was their essential preoccupation, taking precedence over geographic affinities.

The impact of these works was further enhanced by S.K. Saraswati: first, by his three reports of four tours undertaken in the districts of north Bengal (1932, 1936), and subsequently, by his pioneering brochure on pre-Pala sculpture (1938). In this latter publication, Saraswati left out the art of the terracotta "as this branch of art, being particularly the art of Bengal, should justly be reserved for a separate treatment". Years later, in 1962, Saraswati redeemed his promise when he brought out an enlarged second edition of this brochure as a full-fledged book, incorporating most of the terracotta materials discovered in Bengal. Here was a definite attempt to identify a distinct place for Bengal sculpture out of the corpus of the more extensive and numerous "Pala-Sena" sculpture.

The importance of Bengal art, both sculpture and architecture, rose at once to a new level of significance when the piecemeal reports of the excavations at Paharpur were presented in a single volume by its excavator K.N. Dikshit (1938). Besides the architectural importance of the site, never before had so large a number of stone and terracotta sculptures *in situ* been unearthed in the whole of the sub-continent. The former dependence on Pala-Sena stone sculpture to evaluate the art of Bengal were now supplemented with voluminous terracotta material adorning the colossal brick temple at the centre of Paharpur monastery. The continuous bands of terracotta plaques, set in recessed panels around the basement and the walls of the circumambulatory passages in the upper terraces, represented 'a local and indigenous trend, popular in inspiration and imagination, as well as in appeal'.[1]

Three other works on Bengal sculptures, basically three University dissertations done almost simultaneously, not only augmented knowledge on the subject but demonstrated some new trends in methodology and comprehension. The publications by Frederick Asher (1971), Susan L. Huntington (1972) and Enamul Haque (1973) presented together a large number of hitherto unnoticed images. Asher and Huntington, pursuing micro-level investigation, primarily dealt with the development of styles during 300–800 and 800–1200 A.D. respectively. Later their works were published in 1980 and 1984, after substantially adding fresh knowledge based on further field trips to Bihar and Bengal. Whereas the two authors covered the geographical eastern India, the work of the present author, published in 1992, specifically concerned sculptures from Bengal alone. For the first time, a quantitative assessment was presented of the iconography of Hindu sculptures from Bengal up to the mid-thirteenth century, based on the analysis of an unprecedented number of 1860 images, located in different private and public collections.

In all the works cited so far, the general preoccupation of the authors were to deal with stone and bronze sculptures, mainly from the Gupta period onwards. A handful of pre-Gupta specimens were hardly enough to engage them into a special investigation of the early plastic art of Bengal, particularly in the pre-Christian centuries. However, sporadic explorations and excavations in different sites of Bengal between 1930s and 1960s brought about astonishing changes in prevailing opinions. The surface finds, followed by excavations at Mahasthangarh, Bangarh and Chandraketugarh, and a few other places, unearthed a host of early terracotta materials—at once confirming large scale art activities in north, west and south Bengal. Thus S.S. Biswas got a welcome opportunity for presenting in a single volume in 1981 a selection from these terracotta figures.

However considering the number and variety of material, it must be said that a full-scale study of the terracotta art from Bengal is yet to be undertaken. All the excavated objects from Chandraketugarh art (CKGR) numbering several thousands according to the brief annual reports published in the pages of *Indian Archaeology: A Review*, are placed in the Ashutosh Museum of Indian Art at Calcutta University. It is a pity that no initiative has been taken as yet to study or evaluate this indispensable wealth of early Bengal art, since the closure of the excavations in 1967. Not even a consolidated excavation report for the years 1955–67 has been published as yet. Recently, the present author has made an attempt to summarise the excavation results from CKGR, based on the excerpts published earlier in the IAR.[2] But this is not, and cannot be, a substitute for a regular excavation report by the actual excavators.

The situation has become more acute. During the last decade, the western art markets were literally flooded with materials from CKGR area, collected from surface explorations and from clandestine excavations by treasure hunters. These transactions might have begun during the last two or three decades. One believes that this outward flow of antiquities remains unabated as is evidenced by the demands of the museums and individual collectors. Needless to say, they fetch amounts that were inconceivable only a few years ago. When I was in the U.S.A. in 1992–93, I spent considerable amount of time, deviating from my set course of research, in gathering information about these objects. I had the privilege of examining the holdings of a few museums, dealers and private collectors. With the permission and encouragement of the owners, I felt tempted to study nearly five hundred of such specimens, almost entirely unknown to the Indian scholars. The result is awaiting publication soon.

Terracotta plaque, from Chandraketugarh, courtesy: Dr Enamul Haque

This fresh evidence has brought to life the hitherto unknown early history and culture of Bengal. It has revealed an ancient horizon, particularly of early art, indeed unveiling a panorama of life comparable to any matured civilisation of the ancient world. Among the new discoveries, the terracotta artefact has surpassed the other associated materials. This is a befitting tribute to the geographical traditions of the alluvial plain of Bengal, criss-crossed by innumerable rivers and streams.

The early terracottas of Bengal offer an extraordinary variety of themes and subjects. They not only represent manifold affairs of social life that the artists could see around them, but often scenes conceived with imagination. They are conveniently classified as individual male and female figures often described as *Yakshas, Yakshis, Apsaras, Kinnaras* etc., animals, birds, toys of animal figures, some of which were recognised as emblems of cults, narrative plaques representing legends, mythology, erotic motifs, decorated pottery, and seals and sealings. The individual female figures have been identified by many to be representing some form of the ancient cult of the mother goddess like those found in many other countries. In spite of inadequacy in knowledge about these early sculptures, no doubt they will ultimately, illustrate the history and culture of Bengal. Human figures in terracotta from the early period have been found in large number in various other sites of India, but apparently fewer in number than from Bengal. These are yet to be definitely identified either as divinities or mortals.

At this stage we may take a fresh look at the traditionally accepted views about the well-known dynastic sway over Bengal, or parts of it, by the Mauryas, Sungas and Kushanas. It is known that the Ashokan pillars with their animal capitals were widely dispersed along the well-travelled pilgrimage and trade routes. Whether they attest to the movement of the finished works of art from one single manufacturing centre to various sites, or to the movement of artists themselves along these routes, it is disappointing to note that not a single Ashokan column has been discovered in Bengal. The Magadhan connection to Tamralipti or to Pundravardhana, for commercial or administrative purposes is, rather well known and not difficult to imagine. Bengal, as is today, must have been then the most populous region of the subcontinent. But still no royal edict appears to have been issued for the people of the region. It is therefore, not totally unreasonable to doubt, that the northern and the southwestern parts of Bengal were ever within the bounds of the Ashokan empire.

This is not to say that the movements of artistic ideas stopped at the Bihar-Bengal border. Whatever may have been the political status, the discovery of the much-noted Brahmi inscription of the 2nd 1st century B.C. at Mahastangarh, and the legend of Ashoka's visit to the port city of Tamralipti, suggest connections. On the contrary, a set of common Gangetic valley patterns and motifs, at least in the cases of terracotta objects, appear over an extensive area along the Ganges, providing insights into the movement of cultural boundaries. Allowance must be made for the fact that since the sites and regions in Bengal in particular and eastern India in general, during the ancient period, were not insular, local traditions alone could not account for the development of stylistic trends in a given locality.

Similarly, it is not accurately known as to how much of Bengal was under the actual rule of the Sungas, or the Kushans or for that matter, or whether the region was at all ruled by these dynasties. However obscure the political details of Bengal in the pre-Gupta period, we have not insignificant evidence to link the art of Bengal with the north. Therefore, until we have satisfactorily developed a separate yardstick of periodisation for the early art of Bengal, we have to continue with the use of the dynastic appellations on an all-Indian scale, such as the Mauryan, Sunga and Kushan?

Although excavations have revealed that the earliest phase of occupation at CKGR goes back to the pre-Mauryan age, excavators did not mention the find of any terracotta figurines from this level. They identified such material from subsequent phases, covering the Maurya to the Gupta period. Truly speaking, the terracottas from the Mauryan occupational levels were extremely rare from the excavations at CKGR. Notable among them were two female heads with elaborate coiffures, one wearing a bicornate head-dress and the other with circular medallions and precious ornaments, all shown in applique technique. A few more specimens from this epoch are known from the surface finds.

The next phase is dominated by the abundance of archaeological materials with a set of distinct characteristics. These are terracotta plaques of an idiom bearing the name of the Sunga dynasty. In fact, the style was strong and persistent, substantially remaining effective even after the fall of the dynasty in about 75

B.C. The Sunga decades played a significant role in the formative stages of the development of Bengal art. The most revolutionary achievement of the short-lived Sunga period was the introduction of the mould technique in place of modelling. This helped to speed up the production of the terracotta pieces to meet the demands of an expanding clientele. An increased use of the mould helped the transition from the round figures of the early period to the composition of the flat relief.

During the Kushan period, a more intense contact appears to have existed between the Hellenistic world and deltaic Bengal. Sensitive local artists could not have missed the visiting aliens, with their strong and distinctive features and costumes. These immigrants would soon be in the forefront of commercial activities in and through Bengal, even introducing their own imported Kharosti scripts into the daily transactions. Naturally, they found their place on the terracotta plaques in large numbers.[3] Regarding the themes and subjects, the repertoire of the Kushan artists was as varied as in the immediate preceding period. The plastic medium, now much influenced by the vigorous physical form, would further be transformed by the emphasis on nudity. The low relief of the Sunga period would develop into plaques with bold and high features, almost conveying a sense of three-dimensional effect. With their characteristic roundness of feature in the later Kushan phase, these figurines usually stand in extremely flexible positions, demonstrating an unprecedented pliability of the figure, that accentuates beauty of the human form. Thus the terracotta art of early Bengal reached its zenith during the Sunga-Kushan epochs.

Bengal appears to have missed a fresh stimulus in technology at this juncture as compared with the neighbouring middle Gangetic valley. There, besides probable foreign technical hands, some of the terracotta artists were engaged in the newly- introduced art of stone carving. The new medium was a challenge to them, and their new productions lack the lustre and refinement of the skilled professionals. It is therefore difficult to sustain the previously held opinion of some scholars that the stone edifices of Bharhut Bodhgaya and Sanchi were earlier in date than 'skilled terracotta modelling of the profusely ornamented female figures.[4] The comparatively heavy and static features of human form with hardly any suggestion of volume on

Terracotta plaque from Chandraketugarh, courtesy: Dr Enamul Haque

the stone surface were not necessarily earlier than the vibrant Sunga-Kushan phase of the terracotta art. Rather, they were either contemporary or even later in time—from the hands of the same terracotta artists who had been introduced only recently to the new medium of stone.

In early terracotta art the dominant majority represent women. In a recent study of the previously unpublished pieces from CKGR alone, the author found 226 individual female against 110 male figures. As many as 176 plaques, both complete and fragmentary, depict a standing two-armed lady bedecked with rich details of ornamentation all over the body, elaborate head-dresses and designed costumes, reminding us of the outstanding Yakshi piece from Tamluk, now preserved at Oxford. Scholars have broadly classified them as *Yakshas and Yakshis,* due to their similarity with the iconography of sculptured specimens often with identifying labels at Bharhut, Bodhgaya, Sanchi, Patna, Parkham and other places. These *Yakshas* and *Yakshis* were attributed with supernatural powers and "were it not for the names inscribed upon them... ... would be taken for princely donors or rich merchants and their wives..."[5]

It is to be noted that while the artists and their patrons in Bengal were satisfied with terracotta plaques of tiny format, and with comparatively fewer three-dimensional figures, also in terracotta, there were stone figures of various dimensions, even larger than life-size, in contemporary and nearby Bihar. Monumentality and impressiveness are not determined by size alone. The females in these plaques, in spite of their diminutive size, demonstrate no less brightness in conception and monumental effect than the renowned larger than life-size Yakshi from Didarganj. The CKGR ladies cannot be denied to have achieved a real effect of majesty. The heavily jewelled lady survives as a record of the physical and psychological experience of the people, as well as their thoughts and aspirations.

At CKGR, most terracottas possess an almost complete standardization of costumes. Ornaments, decoration, with the general pose and expression of the body. This leads us to believe that the artists were duty-bound to translate into clay some sort of convention sanctioned by long usage. The discovery of pieces with almost identical features, even though with different styles, at so many distant places along the Gangetic valley, only strengthens this assumption. Yet, we cannot be sure as to whether the terracotta images were enshrined or worshipped. Most probably not. Their vast numbers suggests that they were popular household items. It is a plain truth that the so-called *Yakshi* figurines of CKGR represent the natural charm and ethereal grace of feminine beauty. The society that patronised such items were amply bestowed with an aesthetics capable of sustaining the creative expressions of its own people. A few scholars have identified *vyantara devatas* in the terracotta plagues from CKGR such as Lakshmi, Surya, Indra, Agni, Kubera etc. in their preliminary stages of iconographic appearances. The number of such pieces are few, and such conclusions are at best tentative. Also, there are some doubtful depiction of the Jatakas. Strikingly, the epics and the emerging puranas had almost no sway over the artists at CKGR. There is a general consensus that religion had been the primary source of art at every age. Terracotta art in early Bengal clearly demonstrates that the case can be, at least partially and substantially, different.

With the decline of urban cities and the rise of the new feudal culture under the domination of the landed gentry, the character of Bengal terracotta also changed. This was the time when terracotta themes started transforming from largely secular to religious themes. Soon elaborate images from the Buddhist, Brahmanical and Jain pantheon, or iconography, overtake the entire spectrum of art activities. Terracotta art did not die altogether, but went through a new transformation. It now emerged as a part of surface embellishment on the walls of the brick temples of stupas. Besides being used as mouldings of different shapes and designs, they were now manufactured as panels depicting a variety of themes, both religious and secular. But the religious themes, newly introduced, required inscribed labelling of an elementary nature for the ordinary population, urban or rural. The artists or their patrons were conscious about the unfamiliarity of the masses with even the principal characters of epics such as the Ramayana. This happened with the recently discovered terracotta panels from Saralpur and Palashbari, villages on the outskirts of Mahasthangarh, the ancient capital city of Pundravardhana, enjoying uninterrupted urban status since at least the Maurya period.[5]

The labelling of sculptures at Bharhut, Mathura and elsewhere may suggest that the figures depicted were not well-known previously, or there was no tradition, perhaps, for picturisation of well-known religious stories. The particular religion must have been introduced in that locality only recently. Significantly, the innumerable plaques from CKGR have not produced a single piece with any label, indicating that the depicted figures must have been fairly popular to the community for a considerable period of time. Numerous seals with cryptic writings have been discovered. It is likely that these labelled art materials from Saralpur and Palashbari, the first of its kind from Bengal, and that also in terracotta, probably were made at a comparatively initial stage of the introduction of this Brahmanical epic in the region. The terracotta artists of the previous centuries were not accustomed to make panels of such religious significance, or perhaps there were no proper patrons.

This supposition appears most likely to be a valid one, at least on the basis of available archaeological finds. It is a well-known fact that only two pieces of stone sculptures have so far been found from the pre-Gupta Bengal, with definite Kushan idiom. A solitary fragmentary figure in mottled red sandstone has been found from CKGR, depicting the head and bust of a Buddha-Bodhisattva which has been recognised to have "distinct affinities with Kushana art idiom".[6] It has been surmised that this stone image was "made at a Mathura workshop and exported".[7] The other piece is the headless standing figure in non-local red stone, tentatively identified as Karttikeya, from the outskirts of Mahasthangarh in Bogra district. Even though "The figure is close enough in overall composition to a fine Kusana Karttikeya from Mathura now in the Mathura Museum, and to several other Kusana Mathura images of this deity now in the State Museum, Lucknow, to have been modeled on this type of figure", it has been concluded that the "sculpture is clearly a provincial production".[8] This conclusive opinion lacks adequate support or evidence, and the statement quoted itself suggests that the piece was an imported one.

During the Maurya through the Kushan eras, the terracotta artists in Bengal, and for that matter, the artist community in general, were mainly engaged in the production of objects in terracotta and a few other mediums, but excluding stone. The two stone images referred to above, representing the well established Buddhist and Brahmanical faiths, were not manufactured locally and, perhaps, were meant for non-local residents.

Terracotta plaque, from Chandraketugarh, courtesy: Dr Enamul Haque

This gives us ground to suppose that the expansion of Aryanisation in Bengal was rather slow as compared to the mid-east Gangetic valley. Progress in the principal religions in those regions required the production of anthropomorphic deities to satisfy their votaries. But the people of the lower Gangetic delta did not appear to have accepted the classic religions to such an extent. Consequently, they were not required to produce such religious deities, although they were prolific, in producing terracotta figures of various themes, either secular or of their own belief, or an unknown denomination.

The early art of Bengal, like every other art, is to be understood in its own circumstances, and history. The combined perusal of the limited number of excavated materials, and those found through clandestine methods, reveal that the impetus for the manufacturing of art objects in large number grew towards the close of the Maurya era—when contact between the region and the Hellenistic lands gathered momentum. At about the same time, the discovery of the monsoon wind by Hippalus brought a boost to maritime trade between Bengal and the West. The resultant economic factor cannot be ignored. The *Javaṇi* woman might have inspired the delicate and sensitive modelling of the *Yakshi* or the *Apsaras*. When Graeco-Roman art was enriching the Gandhar countries of northwest India in stone and stucco and the Mathura idioms were consolidating the foundation of the indigenous art on the middle Ganges valley, Bengal was vibrating with a prolific production in terracotta. It was indeed a cultural upheaval of unprecedented dimension. The inspiration and yearnings of the artists remained satisfied with delicate and sensitive terracottas of small dimension, displaying superb power and dexterity. Indeed, the creativity of the Bengal art found its best expression, at least during the early centuries of its emergence, in these terracottas.

Notes

1. S.K. Saraswati, 1962, p.108
2. Enamul Haque, 1996, pp.39-75.
3. B.N. Mukherjee, 1990, pp.9-73.
4. Niharranjan Ray, 1993, p.646
5. J.C. Harle, 1987. p.29.
6. G. Bhattacharya, 1987, pp.1043-66

7. S.K. Saraswati, 1962, p.11.
8. F.M. Asher, 1980, p.10

Bibliography

Frederick M. Asher, *The Sixth-Through-Eighth-Century Sculptures of Bihar.* Ph.D. dissertation, University of Chicago, 1971.

———, *The Art of Eastern India, 300-800 A.D.*, Minneapolis: University of Minnesota Press, 1980.

R.D. Banerji, *Eastern Indian School of Mediaeval Sculpture*, Archaeological Survey of India, Delhi, 1933.

G. Bhattacharya, "Early Ramayana Illustration from Bangladesh", *South Asian Archaeology 1987*, Rome, 1043-66, 1987.

N.K. Bhattasali, *Iconography of Buddhist and Brahmanical Sculptures in the Dacca Museum*, Dhaka, 1929.

S.S. Biswas, *Terracotta Art of Bengal*, Delhi, 1981.

K.N. Dikshit, *Excavations Paharpur, Bengal*, Delhi, 1938.

J.C. French, *The Art of the Pal Empire of Bengal*, London, 1928.

Enamul, Haque, *Iconography of the Hindu Sculptures of Bengal: up to c. 1250 A.D.* D.Phil. dissertation, Oxford University, 1973.

———, *Bengal Sculptures: Hindu Iconography up to c. 1250 A.D.*, Bangladesh National Museum, Dhaka, 1992.

———, "Chandraketugarh: A Resume of Excavation Reports (1956-67)", *Journal of Bengal Art*, Volume I, 39-75, 1996.

———, (Forthcoming), *Chandraketugarh: The Treasure-house of Bengal Terracottas.*

J.C. Harle, *The Art and Architecture of the Indian Subcontinent*, Pelican Books, Harmondsworth. Pelican Book, 1987.

Susan L., Huntington, *The Origin and Development Sculptures in Bihar and Bengal, ca. 8th-12th Centuries.* Ph.D. dissertation, Los Angeles: University of California, Angeles, 1972.

———, The *"Pala-Sena" School of Sculpture*, Leiden: E.J. Brill, 1984.

Susan L. Huntington, and John C. Huntington, *Leaves from the Bodhi Tree: The Art of Pala India (9th-12th centuries) and its International legacy*, Dayton, 1990.

Stella Kramrisch, "Pala and Sena Sculpture", *Rupam* XL, 107-26, 1929.

Debala Mitra, *Bronzes from Bangladesh: A Study of Buddhist images from District Chittagong*, Delhi, 1982.

B.N. Mukherjee, "Kharoshti and Kharoshti-Brahmi inscriptions in West Bengal (India)", *Indian Museum Bulletin*, Vol. XXV, Calcutta, 1990.

N.R. Ray, *Bangalir Itihas*, Revised edition, Calcutta, 1983.

S.K. Saraswati, "Notes on Two Tours in the Districts of Maldah and Dinajpur", *JPASB*, XXVIII, 173-83, 1932.

———, "Notes on a Third Tour in the District of Dinajpur", *JPASB*, XXVIII, 185-95, 1932.

———, "Notes on a Fourth Tour in the District of Dinajpur", *JRASBL* II, 9-19, 1936.

———, "Early Sculpture of Bengal", *Journal of the Department of Letters, University of Calcutta*, XXX, 1-85, 1938.

———, *Early Sculpture of Bengal*, 2nd ed., Calcutta, 1962.

KAZI KHALEED ASHRAF AND
JAMES BELLUARDO

Building the Nation: The Architecture of Achyut Kanvinde and Muzharul Islam

The 1940s and '50s were both a turbulent and optimistic time for the subcontinent. The period spanned the end of colonial rule and witnessed the granting of independence to India and Pakistan. With Independence also came Partition—not only a political one but also the breakup of a civilizational unity.

Yet at the same time there was a vision, an optimism, and a faith in the radical transformation of society for a collective well-being and common good. Science, rationalism and secularism became the most visible medium and expression of this idealism. Chandigarh, and the partnership of Nehru and Le Corbusier make a most compelling example. Modernism was proposed as an alternative civilizational unity in a fractious time. Achyut Purushottam Kanvinde in India and Muzharul Islam then in East Pakistan and later Bangladesh, shared a critical time in the history of the subcontinent.

Kanvinde began his architectural practice in 1947 after returning from the U.S., while Muzharul Islam's practice began in 1953. In their respective countries, both were the earliest proponents of an architecture of modernism; and both engaged in their work the issue of nation-building with a social purpose.

Even today, despite the gradual weakening of social idealism and the faltering stature of modernism, Kanvinde and Islam have remained more or less steadfast in their commitment to a rationalist rigour and a modernist vocabulary. They have continued to define modernism not only as a formal creation but in its ethical and existential dimensions, to articulate the exigency of time but often to counter the tyranny of tradition.

The Modern Movement in architecture spread rapidly throughout the world in the years immediately following the Second World War. Its intellectual approach was functionalism and its aim was to make architecture accessible to all. As a style, it dominated architecture in Europe, North and South America, Australia and Japan from the late 1940s until the 1970s. Using modern technology the movement allowed for rapid rebuilding of the industrialised nations devastated by the War's destruction .

The Movement offered India the possibility of meeting its needs and participating along with the industrialised nations in a common future that would restore India's greatness. However, it met with strong opposition by some in India, including Claude Batley at the J.J. School in Bombay. Moreover there was pressure in the mid-1950s for legislation that would have meant that India adopt a national policy for architecture—similar to what was adopted in the Soviet Union and China. Proponents advocated an architecture that would make use of traditional Indian motifs, so that an easily understood Indian identity could be given to all buildings. Even Nehru, who strongly believed in the present, appreciated art and architecture as belonging to the past. Chandigarh was seen as part of his programme for a twentieth century India, respected for its efficiency and challenge to the past, but not for the greatness of its architecture. While Nehru was not concerned with modern art or architecture, he was an enlightened leader and open to ideas.

A group of modernist architects were well aware of the proposed mandate for a national policy on architecture, and they were disturbed. One of them arranged a meeting with Nehru to convey his strong opposition to such action. At a seminar on architecture convened at the Lalit Kala Akademi in New Delhi, the opening remarks appealed directly to the Prime Minister:

> Our problems concerning architecture have changed entirely from the past age because of our changing cultural outlook, namely the political institutions, scientific and technological development, our knowledge about human sciences, and our new ideas of aesthetics which developed as a result of the visual arts. Almost all past periods of architecture came into being as a result of desire for glorification, as an expression of the vanity of the ruling class and the dominant religious sentiments. Thus the architecture of the past was essentially feudalistic in approach. Contrary to this, the present political institutions are democratic in their approach where the stress is on the economic and social values related to the common man.[1]

Nehru's inaugural address was his only direct reply and statement to the architects.

> You cannot isolate architecture from the age, from the social conditions, from the thinking, from the objectives and ideals of that particular age. In an age which is rapidly changing, like our present age, in fact since the industrial revolution came, that necessarily has a powerful effect on architecture.[2]

To those who favoured the use of historical elements, Nehru pointed out that the past was good when it was the present, but that it cannot be brought forward when the world had entered a technological era.[3] Nehru was firmly aligned with those who supported modernism—in the ultimate analysis he felt that a thing that fits with its function is beautiful.[4] He saw modern architecture as a way to bring India into the contemporary world. The Prime Minister expressed confidence that India's young profession of architecture would be able to meet the needs of its time in providing new forms. India would not have a national policy of architecture.

The architect who met with Nehru, convened the seminar and delivered the opening remarks was Achyut Purushottam Kanvinde. Born in 1916, the son of a landscape painter, in a small coastal village, south of Bombay, Kanvinde enrolled in the J.J. School in 1937. Under the direction of Claude Batley, the J.J. School provided training in Beaux-Arts principles with decorative elements that relied on Indian motifs extracted from measured drawings of historic buildings.

In 1945, Kanvinde was sent by the government to study architecture at the Harvard Graduate School of Design, which was headed by Walter Gropius. Here he absorbed the design principles inherited from the 'Bauhaus' which were based on an aesthetic that was in revolt against the past. Gropius proclaimed that a *breach has been made with the past, which allows us to envisage a new aspect of architecture corresponding to the technical civilization of the age we live in; the morphology of dead styles has been destroyed; and we are returning to honesty of thought and feeling.*[5] *He defined the New Architecture as simply the inevitable consequential product of the intellectual, social and technical conditions of our age.*[6] For the young Kanvinde, these remarks were aimed directly at his lessons from the J.J. School, which he now jettisoned. Like many of his generation, and especially those who passed through the Graduate

Achyut Kanvinde, Balkrishna Harivallabhdas Residence, Ahmedabad, 1962

Achyut Kanvinde, Balkrishna National Science Centre New Delhi, 1986

School of Design, his course was set. He had found a direction for architecture which would serve him for a lifetime. After graduating from Harvard, Kanvinde came back to India in September 1947—barely a month after independence.

Under obligation to work five years for the Council of Scientific and Industrial Research, he based himself in Ahmedabad. With few architects available in India at the time, he was immediately assigned such major commissions as the Ahmedabad Textile Industry's Research Association (ATIRA) and the Physical Research Laboratory. It was here that Kanvinde made important contacts with the powerful and enlightened textile millowners who would, with Kanvinde's guidance, become important patrons of modern architecture along with its social concerns. Leaders like Vikram Sarabhai and Kasturbhai Lalbhai would consult Kanvinde on such matters as the merit of inviting Le Corbusier and Louis Kahn to Ahmedabad.

A great deal had to be built within a short period of time; there was a sense of urgency and little time for debate, or to set a theoretical basis for Indian architecture after Independence. Modern architecture gave India a vision of the future based on a functionalist language that was free of colonial reference, and easily understood by the technocrats who made decisions for the state, which prioritized industry, commerce and science. Traditional ways of building could not meet the needs of a nation anxious to participate in a new world which was rapidly industrializing. The manual trade of building would have to be transformed into an organised industry.

Well equipped with the language of functionalism, Kanvinde legitimized the modern movement in India years before the arrival of Le Corbusier and Kahn. His buildings during his tenure with the Council of Scientific and Industrial Research were typically long slab structures, each an object in itself set on an open site, and the logical result of an individual idea which embodied the universal language. Kanvinde firmly believed that buildings were an expression of their time, and that modern technology presented new possibilities that architects should exploit.

In 1955, released from his government contract, Kanvinde entered into private practice in New Delhi with Sahukat Rai and Morad Chowdhury. He organised their private professional office into a discipline driven by modern technology. Most of their commissions were for projects of large scale on tight schedule, that address India's industrial possibilities. They required an organised construction industry similar to the construction process throughout the industrialized world.

Their first major commission was for the Indian Institute of Technology at Kanpur in 1960. While the overall layout of this campus makes reference to Gropius' planning principles, and in particular to the Graduate Center at Harvard University, the buildings themselves represent a significant departure. Kanvinde's superior handling of local red brick within a concrete frame acknowledges not only Le Corbusier's and Kahn's work at that time and the first buildings of the New Brutalists in England, but also recalls several large projects, including St. Stephen's College (1938) in New Delhi, designed by Walter Sykes George.

Kanvinde's involvement with the National Dairy Development Board began in 1968 with the construction of their campus at Anand. This cooperative was set up by the government to allow small dairy farmers, mostly those with less than four cows, to sell their milk to a collective so that it could be processed into powder, ghee, cheese, and other dairy products that required substantial facilities with highly regulated sanitary standards that these farmers could not provide for themselves. This is an example of how a large scale industrial project, dependent upon modern technology, has been able to help sustain a traditional way of life for small farmers by guaranteeing them a market for their production and a steady income. Here two very different Indias, appearing to contradict each other, find themselves in mutual support.

In the 1970s there was a global questioning of "progress", and of architecture which had made use of advanced technology. Kanvinde, as one of India's foremost modernist architects, found himself out of fashion. In India, the presence of Le Corbusier and Kahn made the Bauhaus principles seem obsolete to many. The newly found interest in contextualism became a call for an architecture with a specific Indian identity.

Kanvinde remained true to his search for an architectural expression that responded to new ideas transforming if not all, a prominent segment of India. He saw modernism as a way to advance social goals, that were not part of India's past; he believed in the concept of modern democratic India, and Nehru's egalitarian and socialist policies. Modernism, solidly rooted in the present, was still relevant.

In an effort to popularize India's great investment in science, the government commissioned two major museums. These we to display not only scientific discoveries, but also enable a scientific understanding of all India and its vast natural resources, and make these accessible to a larger public. Visitors were to be involved as active participators in a series of experiments and especially young students were to be encouraged to pursue a career in the sciences. These museums have proved highly successful in attracting a large number of visitors from all strata of Indian society.

In 1976, Kanvinde was asked to design the Nehru Science Centre in Bombay and in 1986, the National Science Centre in New Delhi. Free from his functionalist training at Harvard, he considered these projects an exercise in providing visual excitement through volumes which could be used to create abstract patterns. The repetition of multidimensional hexagonal modules juxtaposed to create a dynamic space maintains a unifying structural system. Columns act as shafts that utilize roof fans to blow and extract air on all levels, and project beyond the roof to give the centre its distinctive profile.

Both museums, strongly identifying with science, rely on a powerful geometry to give them architectural clarity and strength. Unlike Kahn, who also utilized a forceful geometry, Kanvinde does not monumentalize his architecture. Instead, he searches for ways to scale even his large buildings to the human dimensions. Yet he does this without making the work look timid. As part of an historic precinct in New Delhi, and mediating between the trade fair grounds and the adjacent fortress of Purana Qila, the National Science Museum asserts itself as a strong modern building that can stand next to the powerful architecture of the past—with more credibility than one which relies on historic images.

For most Asian societies, modernism is conveniently seen as the perpetrator of a disruption, set against a 'pre-modern' condition: tradition. It is necessary to rethink this demonization characterizing most contemporary criticisms. A different claim may be presented: that Muzharul Islam, in his

Muzharul Islam, College of Arts & Crafts, Dhaka, 1953

work and thinking, adopts the principles of modernity in order to *overcome* what has been perceived as *colonialist* rupture. Modernism, in this sense, becomes an attempt to "return home".

The idea of modernity in Bangladesh—by extension the ideology of Muzharul Islam—can best be understood by that broad sweep of cultural and intellectual upheaval ushered in Bengal by the "Bengal Renaissance" movement. It was a complex intertwining of resistance and acceptance; a resistance to both the traumatic results of colonialism and to the tyranny of tradition. The condition of acceptance was also two-fold: it involved embracing from a global repository anything that assured new degrees of social and intellectual liberation—as for example, what the scientific and progressive institutions of European Enlightenment seem to promise; and an inward journey, a conscious "archaeological" excavation of one's own taken-for-granted cultural strata.[7]

Self-awareness however is double-edged: while it is a moment of self-discovery, it is also a moment of distancing from the familiar. Self-discovery presupposes a sense of alienation and remoteness from tradition and does not happen so long as "we *unreflectively* live under its domination, or fail to see the novel present as it actually is and claims us."[8] Both Charulata and Bimala, characters from two of Rabindranath's novels, portray this. At the moment of their self-awareness, when they become conscious of their *own* identity, the familiar is made foreign; one is made a stranger to the comfort of habitual setting. And, yet, it is within this condition, *where tradition is no longer available unreflectively*, that the idea of identity—gender, cultural or national—arises.[9]

What is the historic root of this alienation from "home"? The colonial experience still remains the point of departure for understanding contemporary conditions. For Muzharul Islam, the idea of return emerges through interpreting colonialism as a "rupture", a fatal and irreversible condition created by its disruptive mechanisms. In Bengal, as in the rest of India, the "rupture" was experienced as conflicts between pre-colonial and colonial conditions. In the context of Bangladesh, especially after 1947, the aggressive Islamic ideology of Pakistan introduced a second and a more deadly wedge. Religion was used, often deviously, to undermine Bengali cultural consciousness.

The events of the 1971 War of Independence marked a violent form of Pakistani intervention and a critical moment of Bengali resistance. Bengali culture faced a trichotomy with European traditions and Pakistani-Islamic ideology.[10] It is in the context of these various disruptions—from political to psychological and spiritual—that Muzharul Islam speaks of *mone-prane-karmokande khati Bangali houa*, that is, to be a 'true' Bengali in mind, spirit and praxis. The metaphor of "return" assumes that one is displaced from where one was once *mone-prane-karmokande Bangali*, and the return there is prior to any ethical and creative behaviour.

Modernity, for Muzharul Islam is as much a returning as going away. It is a going away from the immediate colonial past, and a returning to an "essentialist" condition, free from exclusivist religious ideologies, traumatic inheritances, propagandist symbolisms and pretentious iconographies. As much avowed to a Bengali political identity, he would not immediately translate this iconographically by adopting traditional motifs and other such tell-tale signs. Architectural modernism seemed to be a convincing way of arriving at an essentialist condition. It is this move which is not to go away further but towards an essentialist condition, encircling both the past and the present that may be understood as the metaphor of "return".

It is apparent though that one can now only return to a transformed or constructed locus. Once self-awareness begins, one is forever fated to a "re-construction". But what distinguishes this from the facile method of instant traditionalism? What might give it a greater degree of authenticity?

Muzharul Islam's position is dialogic. Although it is hinged to a specific place, it does not falter in engaging in a "world dialogue", that is, in recognising "the mode of existence of present-day man, who has his sojourn in a region where civilizations, cultures and and religions touch each other, where times and places flow together"; it is also not daunted that this might necessitate a different or new way of making. Muzharul Islam wants to operate within the nexus of a cultural particularness and the humanist idea of "the-world-as-my- village". This is what brings him close to a Rabindrik ethos.

In Bengal, "aesthetics" and the idea of the nation have historically formed a kinship. It was through the Bengal School movement, constituted primarily by the writings of E.B. Havell, the famous art educator, and the paintings of Abanindranath Tagore that art becomes a site for nationalist discourse. The development of 'modern' Indian art becomes the most vivid record of the triangular tension of traditions, nationalism, and modernity.[12]

The attempt for "aesthetic and national recovery" was countered by another camp which was critical of the pretentious "Indianness" of the ideal and spiritual art as envisioned by Havell, Coomaraswamy and Abanindranath. A group of younger Calcutta artists emerged who declared in their manifesto that the "Bengal School paintings lacked vitality and that the false sense of Indian art and the propaganda for the eastern art should be resisted." They argued that the so-called "traditionalists", in their attempt to confront the colonizer, took refuge in a 'recovered' pre-colonial past—or more correctly, in a fabricated past, never questioning which or whose past was being recovered and whose past was being suppressed. This invariably lead to sentimental spiritualising which eulogized "a pre-capitalist social order" ignoring "the grim realities of a people striving under sub-human conditions."[13]

An important figure in this debate is Rabindranath Tagore. Although he appears like his nephew Abanindranath disengaged from social realities, and actually comes close to the idea of the spiritual artistic persona, he is sharply critical of the "narrow-mindedness" of an 'Indian' art:

> I strongly urge our artists vehemently to deny their obligation carefully to produce something that can be labelled as Indian Art by conforming to some old world mannerisms.

The debate focuses on the one hand on the figure of the truly artistic persona such as Rabindranath and the architect Louis Kahn, who are suspicious of political rhetorics, and, on the other, on the impossibility of political aloofness particularly in nations like Bangladesh. Political ideology and architecture enter an impasse. While political consciousness, in the nation- building context, is about drawing boundaries whereby nations are articulated, architecture cannot be contained within political perimeters.

Although these two strands—commitment to the idea of a nation, and to the realm of architecture—are tied up in Muzharul Islam's thinking, his architecture remains adequately distanced from nationalistic polemics. He understands that nationalistic posturing does not automatically lead to the spirit of architecture. Yet, through political engagement he is gradually lead to the confirmation that architectural form is inadequate in addressing immediate social problems and therefore he himself moves towards the realm of politics.[14] While he adheres to a Rabindrik idea of a Bengali cosmopolitan spirit, he remains, in the light of Marxian materialistic rigour, suspicious of talks on artistic spirituality.

In his 1944 essay *Our Heritage*, Humayun Kabir notes that "in all modern manifestations of Indian art, the one form which is absent is architecture". If literature, painting, and somewhat later, cinema, were thematically confronting the existential question of 'what it means to be a Bengali in the twentieth century', architecture remained far behind as a mere activity of construction. An architectural discourse was clearly missing from the "Renaissance" movement, despite the stimulating debates on aesthetics.

It was in this imbalanced situation that in 1953 Muzharul Islam began his career. After training in engineering at Calcutta University, he went to Oregon University in the United States from where he received an architectural degree in 1952 and later a master's degree under Paul Rudolph at Yale in 1981. As a thirty-year old and the only formally trained architect working in Dhaka, he began with an enormous task: an architectural production which involved, at one level, a challenge to the entrenched practice of the engineers, and, at another level, the making of a Bengali building paradigm.

From the very first projects, his work raised a two-fold concern: the question of the house and the question of the city. Throughout the 1950s and most of the 1960s, Muzharul Islam experimented with a number of house types, compositional configurations and construction methods. The early houses, in articulating the paradigm of the pavilion in modern bungalows, incorporated the spatial and planar dimensions of the classic houses of early modernism.

The idea of the 'pavilion' was also behind large buildings, from the Public Library and the Science Laboratory to the NIPA building at Dhaka University. The Public Library (1953) was organised in a clearly Corbusian mode, but for Dhaka it was a fresh approach to urbanism. The NIPA building at Dhaka University (1967) signified the pavilion with its array of concrete piers girdling the building, the 'usable' space being recessed behind. The hovering plane of the roof as a *chattri* (parasol) completed the imagery.

The Art College, designed at the same time as the Public Library, stands apart. It comes closer to mediating with the sensorial conditions of place. Sprawling, low building volumes, the use of exposed fired brick which always has such a magical resonance with the "greenness" of Bengal, the natural garden setting on an urban site—all went to form the atmosphere of a campus ideal for the contemplation and learning of the arts. More importantly, it indicated a spatial environment evoking the architectural poetics of the land.

The 1960s remain his most prolific period of building in a practice affected by many discontinuities. He was involved in the development of the Institute of Architects, and influential in drafting its constitution, for which he is still well remembered by architects in Pakistan.[15] Besides his own contribution to architecture culture, he was also instrumental in bringing Louis Kahn, Paul Rudolph and Stanley Tigerman to Bangladesh.

His early projects from the 1950s upto works like NIPA and his own house in the '60s owe much to Frank Lloyd Wright, Le Corbusier and Paul Rudolph. This is evident, in varying degrees, in the basic skeletal configuration of the works, in the innovation of climate control; in the sculpturesqueness made by varying reliefs, deep shadows and juxtaposition of materials; in the spatial composition; and, finally, in the manner the buildings confront the landscape with an assertive stance.

His later phase—the late '60s—saw the commissioning of two university projects, involving large-scale organisation. While the theme, as in Jahangirnagar University (1967-71) and the housing for Jaipurhat Limestone Factory (1979), is an *a priori* geometry, the concern is to generate an 'urbanized' order by the formation of spatial enclosures, streets and continuous facades. The buildings are constructions in brick, where spaces and voids seem to

Muzharul Islam, National Institute of Public Administration (N.I.P.A.), Dhaka, 1989

Muzharul Islam, Students' Dormitory Jahangirnagar University, Dhaka

be carved out of masonry solids, and which, despite their often curious geometrical purity and unlike the skeletal nature of earlier projects, form a more earth-hugging ambience.

The shift in architectonic configuration is most explicit in the National Library project undertaken in 1978. Gone is the stark clarity of his earlier skeletal work; there is now a ponderous presence accentuated both by the centralised form and the use of brick-mass. The building presents a convincing response to the neighbouring ensemble by Kahn, which has by now formed an important context in the north of Dhaka. While geometric abstraction and a consummate skill for crafting constitute a continuity in all his work, the iconography of the National Library is a world removed from the Public Library of 1955. The National Library is a surreptitious triumph, almost against Muzharul Islam's own rational rigour, of the accidental over the planned, and of the *a posteriori* over the *a priori*.

The plans for Jahangirnagar University and Jaipurhat Housing are also Muzharul Islam's closest effort to move away from the conventional morphology of either the city or the country. Muzharul Islam has arrived at a kind of 'alternative' city—collectivised, yet receptacles in sun, light and air—after a Marxian reading of the difference between the city and .so-called rural hinterland as social disparity. Here a Marxian perspective comes to agreement with a Rabindrik vision. Finding the difference unacceptable, and, echoing Rabindranath's 1928 essay "City and Village", he believes that "old ideas of society divided into haves and have-nots are no longer valid.... The world has advanced sufficiently in science and technology to help remove the difference between the city and the so-called rural hinterland.[16] While the vision of this city has a strong moral and economic underpinning, Muzharul Islam recognizes that "the cities should provide the environment for civilized life within the context of our own culture". Moreover

> the city can develop only as a part of the physical environment of the country—with the ultimate aim of abolishing all differences between the city and the rural areas. The traditional relationship with nature (still existing to a certain extent in the villages of Bangladesh) should be continued in the cities.

Notes

1. *Seminar on Architecture,* March 1959, Lalit Kala Akademi. Jaipur House, New Delhi, 1959. p. 12
2. *Ibid.* p. 5.
3. *Ibid.* p. 7.
4. *Ibid.* p. 9.
5. Walter Gropius, *The Scope of Total Architecture,* New York: Collier Books, 1962. p. 59.
6. Walter Gropius, *The New Architecture and the Bauhaus,* (trans. P.M. Shand and F. Pick). Cambridge, Mass: The MIT Press 1965.
7. Tapan Raychaudhuri, in *Europe Reconsidered: Perceptions of the West in Nineteenth Century Bengal,* writes about the perceptions of the West among the Bengali intelligentsia, whose productions, mostly literary, affected and continue to affect the thinking of the larger public. "All responses to the West in colonial India were not within the two polar limits of slavish admiration and xenophobic rejection. There is an extensive area of rational and scholarly assessment untouched by hang-ups of one sort or another", p.5.
8. J.L. Mehta, "World Civilisation: The Possibility of Dialogue", on *Heidegger, Hermeneutics and Indian Tradition,* edited by William J. Jackson, E.J. Brill, Leiden: New York 1992.
9. Tapan Raychaudhuri calls this an "anxious and neurotic effort at cultural self-assertion", a major trait of the late nineteenth century milieu in Bengal. In *Europe Reconsidered,* p.11.
10. This antagonism, between a Bengali Islam and a pan-Islamic ideology, has older roots. Pakistan, in the context of Bangladesh, tapped this as a major political instrument. Much literature exists on this, but for a synoptic view, see Rafiuddin Ahmad, "Conflicts and Contradictions in Bengali Islam: Problems of Change and Adjustment," in *Shariat and Ambiguity in South Asian Islam,* University of California Press (1988).
11. Interview in *Sthapatya O Nirman,* January-March 1992.
12. A number of recent studies treat this important period in Bengali cultural history: Tapati Guha-Thakurta, *The Making of a New 'Indian' Art: Artists, Aesthetics and Nationalism in Bengal,* c.1850-1920, Cambridge University Press 1922, and Ratnabali Chatterjee, *From the Karkhana to the Studio,* Books, and Books, 1990.
13. R. Chatterjee, *From the Karkhana to the Studio.*
14. From the mid-1960s, Muzharul Islam became increasingly involved in matters political, accelerated in 1970-71 by the Bangladesh liberation movement, and formalized by the mid-70s by his joining of political organisations.
15. Zaigham S. Jaffrey's comments at the Aga Khan Award for Architecture seminar "Regionalism in Architecture," Dhaka, 1985.
16. From Muzharul Islam's unpublished essay, "Re-Designing and Re-Building of Cities".

RANABIR SAMADDAR

Interpretations of the Bangladesh War

In the year of the twenty-fifth anniversary of the nation, Bangladesh still does not have an authoritative and exhaustive history of the Liberation War. Some have argued that documentation is still insufficient; some say it is a problem of classification of the documents. To others it remains a problem of historiography: namely, how to write a political history which frees the liberation struggle from the inevitable militarist interpretation in the aftermath of 14 years of military rule in Bangladesh.

The problem also is how to investigate the earlier years leading to the cataclysmic event. The war of 1971 should appear in history as the logical outcome of the previous two decades, and not as a sudden episode. Historians now suggest that oral and local accounts have to be collected, and autobiographies and memoirs given greater importance in constructing 1971. For the politics of the nation "an authoritative and comprehensive" history of the liberation war has become imperative.[1]

The history of 1971 is complicated by the many histories imbricated into it. The right chronology, or the right history of events leading up to 1971, is to be retrieved along with the roles of political actors over two decades in united Pakistan, and the struggle for cultural and political autonomy. One obvious problem is how to merge the two "peculiar times" in the same historical time-frame of 1971. These two histories are the times of the growth of left-radical sentiments in Bangladesh through the '50s and most of the '60s, when a peasant leader like Maulana Bhasani could lead Bengal in the upsurge against Ayub while Sheikh Mujib was in jail.[2] Flags of independence could be seen flying in rallies and assemblies without the sanction of the Awami League leadership. The other is the sudden and phenomenal popularity of the Awami League, erasing all earlier conflicting histories of the country.

The dilemma is: if we were to periodise 1971 working backwards, the other times are erased; or else, the faultlines grow so much into visible cracks that 1971 becomes, of necessity, a matter of destiny, a history of separate articulations. A single history of 1971 remains, perhaps, an impossibility.

It is not that as though the historians of Bangladesh engaged in writing the birth of the nation state are unaware of these complications. Their efforts to straighten out these complications are intended to achieve a single and uniform history of 1971. Historians believe that if they can answer certain fundamental questions, they will be able to achieve a comprehensive "history" of the liberation war. These questions relate to the nature of the liberation war, the leadership of the war, the political and military organisation of the war, strategy and tactics, differences in responses of the Left organisations to the liberation war, the widespread phenomenon of traitors and collaborators, the response and reactions of the super powers, India's role, the role of non-resident Bengalis, and finally the response of the world community.[3]

Besides their intrinsic importance, these questions reveal the dilemmas inherent in the historiography of 1971. Most of these questions have differential traces, they overlap, they cross each other's path—in short, they make a history leading to 1971 impossible. One historian asks, where should we begin this history, that classic moment of 'break' from when the specific narrative of 1971 might begin? Prof. Salahuddin Ahmed suggests that this date might be 1905, with the first partition of Bengal; others have their doubts, since this first partition was undone in 1911.[4] Still others suggest this history begins from the Lahore Resolution of 1940; this also is an uncertain journey since the second partition of Bengal in 1947 was contradictory to the Lahore Resolution of many Pakistans. Fazlul Haque's proposal of more than one Pakistan was not liked by Hossain Shaheed Suhrawardy, who piloted the resolution in 1946 to amend the earlier proposal—to the effect that there should be only one Pakistan. Ironically, only a year later, on 27 April, 1947, Suhrawardy himself proposed a sovereign united Bengal!

The agenda of 1971 was not introduced in the three major charters of the preceding twenty years: the 21 point charter of 1954, the 6 point charter of 1966, and the 11 point of 1969. While these were all charters of autonomy, full independence did not occur in any of them. The Kagmari Conference of 6-10 February in 1957 was the first occasion for such a parting call, and this came from Maulana Bhasani's Asalamu Alaikum. But we know that the

Kagmari Conference was not endorsed by the dominant leadership of the Awami League. Maulana Bhasani had to part ways soon, and the Conference left in its trail bitterness and recrimination. After that, radical politics in East Pakistan remained a movement always ensconced as "environmental opposition"—never to grow into an "organisation" capable of leading a nation to liberation.[5] The anti-Ayub upsurge poses a similar problem in terms of historiography. Immediately after Sheikh Mujib was released and elections were declared, the radical movement was sidelined—although in the odd meetings of the radicals, slogans of full independence would continue to be raised.

One way of dealing with the inbuilt contradictions around 1971 would be to sidestep proper historical writings, and enter the world of political memoirs. There, without the bindings and the imperatives of formal history, another history is recorded by the actors. But can a comprehensive history be written on the basis of these memoirs? For, the authors of these memoirs, justifying their political life, determine the genealogy of 1971 in the structure of their own political activities. Therefore, when they look back, do they perceive any moment of break? Abul Mansur Ahmed, one such actor, is found rescuing Shaheed Suhrawardy, the leader of forties and fifties, from the latter's trapeze acts of mid-fifties—for he cannot tear himself away from the moment of genesis in 1940 (*Amar Dekha Rajnitir Panchash Bachar,* 1974). Similarly, Tofazzal Hossain Mian has to exorcise the moments of break, and therefore to criticise strayers from the mainstream (*Pakistani Rajnitir Bish Bachar,* 1981): Ali Ahad's account (*Jatiyo Rajniti 1945-1975*) registers another kind of self-torment: that 1971 must represent a continuity.

In August 1977 the Government of Bangladesh took the initiative of forming a Commission for writing the history of the liberation war. The Commission undertook the task of collecting various documents around the world, and particularly within the country, pertaining to the liberation war. They appointed a Committee of experts for the authentication and credential work. Work started in 1978 January, and by 1985 June fifteen volumes of documents were published under the title *Bangladesher Swadhinata Juddha Dalilpatra.* Each volume contains an editorial introduction. The editor declared in the introduction to the first volume (Dhaka, 1982,pp 3-12), that it was difficult to avoid subjectivity in historical writings on a momentous event like 1971. Therefore the primary task has been to collect and publish documents. "The main consideration was to have correct documents for correct events. We do not have any comment, we point towards nothing, we offer no explanation, no analysis of our own."[6]

A few thousand questionnaires were distributed among various classes and sections of people, with "no appreciable response". Many had "no sense of history", many did not want to part with documents in the hope of "greater reward in future", some died, and most important, there was no government ordinance to support the collection and preservation of necessary documents. Yet the published documents ran into almost 14,000 pages, and the editor said that the Committee had in its possession almost three and half lakh pages of documents.[7]

The first two of these fifteen volumes deal with the background which starts from 1905, the first Partition of Bengal. The next four are on "Mujibnagar", the government in exile, and the activities of Bengalis in exile, the campaign over the radio, and other mass media reports like reports of war correspondents, writings in local and small newspapers and journals. The seventh volume deals with Pakistani documents, official and non-official. The eighth volume is on mass slaughter, exodus and refugee camps. The next three volumes are on the armed struggle. The twelfth volume is on the Indian reaction, and the next one is on reactions from the United Nations and other countries. The fourteenth volume reports world public opinion. The last volume is a collection of interviews.

Despite this immense corpus of work being completed, the complaint of not having a proper, authentic history of 1971 has persisted. Although documentation is important for writing a comprehensive history book on 1971, this is not the critical element. Documents are there, but the question is how to link them, find their differential traces, consider the moments of break, so that 1971 itself becomes the moment of break for the post 1971 history of Bangladesh.[8] A comprehensive history thus has to rely ironically, on fragmentary experiences. The question of historicizing 1971 lies in those experiences.

Experiences as fragments mean, however, more because they do get dissolved into the monolithic project of national history. We can take the collection of writings by the radical historian Badruddin Umar, *Juddhopurbo Bangladesh* (1976), written as features in a newspaper on events of 1970. Written from the viewpoint of the radical Left, these were critical of Mujib, sometimes of Bhasani, sometimes of all political forces—criticisms as only the fringe Left can do. The historian made that self- admission in his preface to the collection in 1976. Yet we have in the these essays experiences which cannot be denied. The Sheikh tries to control the radical upswing in the popular mood, the Left gets exasperated with the dominant nationalist leadership, the cyclone leaves thousands dead and lakhs homeless... The Sheikh warns the radicals, the workers' unrest becomes acute. Nationalism is about to be redefined through being suffused with rising popular expectations, various class demands and an uncompromising mood of the society.[9] Though given little credence in professional, academic history-writing, the history of the previous twenty five years abounds with such experiences in Bangladesh.

The multi-volume document of *Bangladesher Swadhinata Juddha Dalilpatra* full of half-suppressed, subaltern voices provides us again with such instances. The first volume has the engaging two-page deposition of Ila Mitra at the Rajshahi Court in 1950. She was arrested and tortured by the police, who were deployed in heavy numbers for suppressing the Nachol peasant revolt led by Matla Sardar. The deposition was distributed throughout Bengal (pp 150-151). We do not know if the nationalist movement building up at that time took cognizance of the peasant revolt at Nachol. Again, we have the speech of Ataur Rehman Khan on 27 April 1952, at the all-party council meeting convened on the demand for the status of national language for Bengali ending with the words, *Rashtrabhasha Bangla Chai, Bandider Mukti Chai, Pakistan Zindabad.*

Now when exactly did Pakistan Zindabad give way to a different cry? Do we locate this in those acrimonious words of Fazlul Huq in his letter to Liaquat Ali Khan (8 September, 1941, pp 5-7), which spoke for "33 millions in Bengal" and "Muslim India" in the same breath? Here we may locate the end of praja politics, already drowned in the "phantasm" of "Muslim India"—

as also the parting of ways between the peasants and the nationalists of Muslim Bengal. The voice of the Nachol revolt is not to be heard any more in the ensuing "history". The volume certainly reverts back to the subaltern presence through those documents that relate to the Kagmari Sammelan (pp 591-615) and the events of food crisis, flood and eviction. But by now, the documents have entered a pattern, an "order".[10]

The history of 1971 appears in the popular mind as a representation of his or her experiences. One example readily coming to mind would be *Swadhinata Amar Raktajhara Din* "My Bloody Days of Independence", written by Begum Mushtari Shafi whose husband and brother perished in the battle. In her memoirs, 1971 appears not as a story of the government in exile, nor of military engagements and guerrilla struggles, but as the travails of countless mothers who, having lost sons and husbands, move from one place to another in search of shelter, greeting the day with a vacant mind, surviving to the day when independence would be finally achieved.[11]

It was certainly no accident that a poet, Hasan Hafizur Rehman, was entrusted with the work of Bangladesh *Swadhinata Juddha Itihash Prakalpo.* Literature has been to Bangladesh what history has been to India in the project of nation-making. If historical writings have aroused the imagination here, in Bangladesh historical writings themselves have been the product of the literary imagination which are products of particular historical circumstances but end up as contra-history. How else is one to see in this context the writings of Jahanara Imama *Ekattarer Dinlipi*, Mushtari Shafi *Swadhinata Amar Raktajhara Din*, Basanti Guha Thakurta *Ekattarer Smriti* or of Panna Kaiser *Smritir Bhelaya* or Hamida Rehman *Jiban Smriti*? This holds true of earlier writings of the '40s and '50s like Abul Fazal's *Rekha Chitra*, or Abul Zafar Shamsuddin's *Atmasmriti.* These writings have a fictional time that makes a mockery of the chronological time on which the "authoritative" history of 1971 has to be based.

There is thus more to the relation between literature and the history of 1971. While the history of 1971 will appear by its nature as a single narrative, its literature by the nature of its function of storytelling will pluralize this. These stories refashion the event, produce differing, at times opposing, commentaries, even programmes for action. There is one more subtle point in this whole problem. They are not just stories, memoirs, biographic accounts, dramas, paintings, novels. Hence for an "objective" history of 1971, they are an embarrassment. Yet they cannot be wished away—for the post-1971 developments have already futurized the liberation war. Thus these literary writings will become another history, the "other" of any formal history—ready to be summoned in a futurized account of the past.

Ironically it is literature that suffuses 1971 with ethicality, with desire, with possibilities that an event or an epoch can exceed or transcend itself. Literature, then, does not do away with the history of 1971, and it cannot do so; but the historicity of 1971 requires its presence as the "other" in its history.

The desire to produce a political history of 1971 is of course crucial; because such a desire is born from the fifteen year long military rule in Bangladesh. That period has seen glorification of the military in the liberation war, the exaltation of the role of the soldiers, and the "downgrading" of the civilian leadership of the war. In the militarist version, 1971 was principally a military conflict with Pakistan. Most of the civilian political leadership which fled to India, was politically inefficient and corrupt; and the country won liberation not because of the civilian political leadership, but in spite of them. This militarist version attained dominance. Official accounts invariably tend to stress the military part of the war, ignoring the political nature of popular participation in various forms. Therefore to counter such a militarist history of 1971, oral history of the liberation war has to be emphasized. Without such a "new history" and "new ethnography" of the time, the crucial role of the civilian is lost.

Yet, we would be mistaken to assume that a shift away to "oral history" can retrieve and restore the political nature of 1971. The efficacy of such a shift is suspect. First, one does not create oral history, it is there. There are powerful reminiscences of military accounts which reinforce the point that the contradictory politics of 1971 could be resolved only by sudden military interventions. Therefore 1971 itself lends to a military reading. In some of the accounts, we are told how the Indian intervention became a deliberate strategy to preempt the advance and subsequent victory of the liberationist forces of Bangladesh—when the former found that the guerrilla fighters of Bangladesh were about to achieve victory on their own. And thus the liberation war became a victim of the super power rivalry and the cold war. Also, if we peruse the documents in the three volumes of the *Bangladesh*

Swadhinata Juddha Dalilpatra (Vols 9-11) we cannot but be struck by one feature of the situation, namely the absence of any "central command", the relative isolation of the military from the political mass, the necessity of a military solution, the impending militarist climax of December.

In short, the point is driven home that in the ultimate analysis the freedom struggle was a militarist solution. Second, an oral history of 1971 will all the more decentre the narrative, thereby making the project of retrieving the political nature of 1971 through a comprehensive history of the war a non-starter. Possibly, behind the legitimate complaint against a militarist reading of 1971 remains the dominant question: on what type of history is this discourse to build itself—an Awami League history or a BNP history—these being the two major mainstream parties.

However, the history of 1971 refuses to be trapped in that bind. Like all cataclysmic events unplanned, very much contingent on a set of historical circumstances, 1971 has remained a "participatory" episode or event. Thus there is a deluge of memoirs, local chronicles, oral accounts, reports that refuse to get historicised in a single frame. These narratives have stepped on the stage of history not with a recognizable cast, but as participants in a continuing carnival scene, refusing the anonymity that the playwright and the prompter may have wished to impose on them.

Therefore if the text of the history of the liberation war in Bangladesh eschews the problem and opts to become a text of "new history" that is, a polyphonic text, (assuming one agrees to use the phrase "new history"), then the contribution of 1971 to the power of the nationalist discourse in Bangladesh needs to be examined; as also how 1971 transcends the frame of contemporary nationalism. In short, 1971 no longer remains a containable text.

Notes

1. Unpublished lecture by Prof. Salahuddin Ahmed, an eminent historian of Bangladesh, at the Maulana Abdul Kalam Azad Institute of Asian Studies on 18 April 1996, on the historiography of the liberation war.

2. On the activities of the Maulana during the anti-Ayub upsurge, see Syed Abul Maksud, *Maulana Abdul Hamid Khan Bhasani*, Dhaka: Bangla Academy, 1994, pp 313-354.
3. Syed Anwar Hossain, "Bangladesher Bis Bachar: Muktijuddher Itihash Charcha" in Abu Md. Delwar Hossain (ed.), *Muktijuddher Itihash Charcha*, Dhaka: Arani Prakashani, 1993, p.30.
4. Shah Ahmad Reza, "Swadhinata Juddher Itihash Rachana Shamashyar Kotipoy Dik" in *Muktijuddher Itihash Charcha*, p.7. The *Bangladesher Swadhinata Juddha Dalilpatra* (hereafter BSJD), a 15 volume collection of documents pertaining to the liberation war and published by the Government of Bangladesh (Dhaka, 1982-85), begins with the order announcing the partition of Bengal in 1905. However, it does not state why it begins with the first partition, as it does not and possibly cannot produce any document as evidence of some public activity demanding a separate Bengal for the Bengali Muslims. Thus the BSJD (Vol. 1) opens with the government order of 1905 and then makes a jump to 1940, i.e., the year of the Lahore and Resolution.
5. On the Kagmari Conference, see Abu Jafar Shamsuddin, "Kagmari Sanskritik Sammelan, 1957—Smriticharan", *Dainik Sambad*, 7 February, 1982; Haider Akbar Khan Rono, "Byatikramdharmi Neta Bhasani: in *Maulana Bhasani* (Chattogram: Ganotrantik Forum, 1992).
6. BSJD, preface, p.v. In fact, in the preface, it was further remarked, "The thousands of trees and plants around the giant ones make up the forest. To know the forest, one has to know the whole."
7. BSJD Vol.1, preface, p viii.
8. In fact, many will argue that what happened to Bangladesh in the years following 1971 leading to a long spell of military rule did not "negate" 1971, but followed from it. And, hence, the history of 1971 has to be studied afresh from the vantage point of post-1971 developments, i.e., there is a need to write a truly genealogical history of 1971.
9. Badruddin Umar, *Juddhopurbo Bangladesh* (Dhaka: Muktadhara, 1976). The book is dedicated to the Left activists who died in the liberation war. The mood described by Badruddin Umar is corroborated in Jahanara Imam's immortal portrayal, *Ekattarer Dinlipi* (Dhaka: Sandhani Prakashani, 1994). The mood is captured in some of the pages of the first volume of the BSJD also, which *document the thesis* of the *Purbo Bangla Sramik Andolan*, later known as the Sarbahara Party. Siraj Sikdar, its leader, was killed during Awami League rule after 1972. These pages also record the extremely militant mood of the student community, the *Sangrami Chatra Samaj*. (pp 377-392).
10. That order is revealed through the document—the attack by the Dainik Azad on the Kagmari Conference on 12 February, 1957 (BSJD, Vol 1, p 599) and also the desperate appeal of Bhasani in his speech to the Conference that the Awami League must take lessons from the failure of the Muslim League. (pp 593-597).
11. Begum Mushtari Shafi, *Swadhinata Amar Raktajhara Din* (3rd edition, Dhaka: Anupam Prakashani, 1992), pp 276-290.

Pendulum, *etching by Laila Rehman*

SALIMA HASHMI

An Intelligent Rebellion: Women Artists of Pakistan

During the inauguration of the Pakistan National Exhibition in Lahore in 1983, major women artists attending the seminar drafted a Manifesto for themselves which began thus:

> We, the Women Artists of Pakistan, having noted with concern the decline in the status and condition of the life of Pakistani women, and having noted the effects of the anti-reason, anti-arts environment on the quality of life in our homeland, and having noted the significant contribution which the pioneering women artists have made to the cause of arts and art education in Pakistan, and believing as we do in the basic rights of all men, women and children to a life free from want and enriched by the joys of fruitful labour and cultural self-realisation and our commitment as practitioners and teachers of the arts to the noblest ideals of a free, rational and civilised existence, affirm the following principles to guide us in our struggle for the cultural development of our people to serve as the manifesto of the women artists of Pakistan.......

The manifesto was signed by fifteen artists, present at its drafting, five of whom are represented in my paper. This document was never made public but the act of getting together was a symbolic gesture that suggests that women artists had grown conscious for some time of the political and social oppression imposed by the regime of General Zia-ul-Haq. Although this applied to all sections of society it was directed especially towards women.

The responses of women to this reality found expression in their activism, their writing, their poetry and their art. Pakistan thus presents an intriguing landscape in the domain of contemporary art and culture—a scenario in which women artists, writers, social scientists and activists have played a crucial role in developing a liberal ethos. They have dominated almost all areas of creative and cultural expression either as individuals or through the institutions which they pioneered and nurtured. This pivotal role in the art and culture of Pakistan becomes even more curious when viewed in the context of the Islamic Republic which came into being in 1947. Pakistan's chequered social and political history has had an ambiguous attitude towards women's status and development.

Ayesha Jalal, the political historian, makes a compelling statement about this era during Zia's time:

> The relationship between women and the State in Pakistan has been both compelling and paradoxical. After nearly a decade of State-sponsored attempts at stifling women's voices in the public arenas and pushing back the boundaries of their social visibility, Pakistan became the first state in the Muslim world to have a woman Prime Minister.

Ayesha goes on to quote from the Report of the Pakistan Commission on the Status of Women of 1986, a document prepared in Zia's rule by a committee of women nominated by the Government!

> The average rural woman of Pakistan is born in near slavery, leads a life of drudgery and dies invariably in oblivion.

The paradox of the invisibility and the visibility, and the potency of women became most acute during the Zia years; but its roots go much further back. One must go back at least to 1947 when the State of Pakistan was carved out of the subcontinent. The political upheaval of 1947 was marked by a tragic bloodbath as well as by one of the greatest population migrations of the 20th century. Muslims coming from India brought with them vestiges of the urban court traditions. The women were accepted practitioners of the art of music, poetry and the arts and crafts within the home. A more rural form of arts and crafts already existed in the woman's domain in the geographical boundaries of what was to become Pakistan.

There were only two formal centres of 'art education' in 1947, both in Lahore. The oldest, the Mayo School of Arts, established by the British in 1876 as a traditional "arts and crafts school", was entirely male, both in its faculty and student body.

The Fine Arts Department of the Punjab University was the second such Centre, set up in 1940 and headed by a woman, and admitting *only* female students. This policy was not adopted to create a gender balance in art education, or to give special opportunities to women. As Anna Molka Ahmed, the pioneering head of the Fine Arts Department has said, "The Vice-Chancellor of the University didn't want women to 'clutter up' the more 'serious' Departments of Physics and Chemistry"!

In 1940 the British Raj obviously had a clear cut idea of its priorities vis-a-vis the education of women. The fact that art was considered a peripheral activity to be relegated to the realm of women was therefore a policy which continued even after 1947. Neither women, nor art were of immediate social or political significance. The setting up of a Fine Arts Department at the University, for whatever convenient reason, created an opportunity for the training of women artists and art educationists. This became an important venue for exhibitions, discussions and other forms of cultural expression.

The first Head of the Department, Anna Molka, was from Britain and from a European Jewish emigre family. She had trained at the Royal College of Art in London, where she had also met her future husband Sheikh Ahmed, and had come to the subcontinent, making Lahore her home for the rest of her life. By her own description, Anna Molka (who died in April 1994) was a passionate expressionist painter of vigour working in heavy impasto oils. Anna Molka's work, although academic in its European genres of still-life portraits and landscapes, also incorporated social, historical and mythological themes of her adopted country.

Her dynamic personality made her a major force in the setting up of the Fine Arts Department, and in persuading women to take up art as a career, but even more so in the teaching of art as a profession. Until 1954 this department of the University was exclusively meant for women, and it trained a large number of teachers who set up a network of art departments in universities and colleges all over Pakistan. Many of them went abroad to well known art schools and academies in the US, Britain, France and Spain.

Esmat Rahim was the 'unknown painter', the 'neglected voice', amidst her peers. Her presence was forgotten because she happened to be the wife of one of Pakistan's most illustrious career diplomats, later the Foreign Minister of Pakistan. Known only as "Rahim's wife", Esmet or Esther developed quietly into a painter of maturity and significance in her later years, a fact known only to a few friends and the family. She began painting in the early '30s and died in Spain in 1963. Owing a great deal to an understanding of the aesthetics of the subcontinent, her adopted milieu, she synthesized it with her studies at Dusseldorf and Paris. A friend of the great painter Amrita Shergill, Esmet concentrated on themes to do with women. Later her own inner fantasies and fears were reflected in her last, compelling surrealistic works.

Another painter of significance who began her career in the 1940s was Zubaida Agha, who initially had not trained as a painter. In the early forties she took private lessons in Lahore from an Italian prisoner-of-war, Mario Perlingieri—a pupil of Picasso's. She was already an abstractionist when she went to study at St. Martins in London and to the Ecole des Beaux Arts in Paris in the early fifties. Today, Zubaida Agha continues to dominate the art scene in Pakistan. She is a colorist with a strong affinity for the lyrical with occasional motifs which suggest the floral. The architectural and figurative do make an appearance in her canvases; but the dominant interplay is between the octaves of colour, and forms remain subservient.

Zubaida was also responsible for setting up Pakistan's first private art gallery. While Anna Molka and her band of women students were establishing the climate which made painting and sculpture a valid activity in the north of Pakistan, the women artist from India were mostly concentrated in and around Karachi. Sughra Rababi, Hajira and Rabia Zuberi began the first art institutions in the city. By the late sixties there were flourishing art centres both in Lahore and Karachi. Traditionalists like Hajira Mansur worked in the turn-of-century watercolour-wash technique of Bengal. Drawing on a certain nostalgia for the past, her work reflected the 'sentimental literary tradition' in painting.

Harking back to a nostalgic 'glorious' past, perceived through post-colonial eyes, can be both alluring and reassuring. Contemporising the past raises disturbing questions of the effects of colonialism on painters of today—mimicking the male gaze by women artists. It is not surprising that into the late '70s, the work of women painters could be termed as a faithful echo of their male counterparts. Women pursued the well-trodden genres in colonial art education—with predictable post-colonial reactions.

Mussarat Mirza is a painter who works in the western style, her work being strongly affected by her immediate environment. She heads the Fine Art Department of the University of Sind of Jamshoro, a small dusty desert town near the old city of Hyderabad. Her isolation from the main stream of art activity in Lahore, Karachi and Islamabad has contributed to her continuing to work in the manner which she does. But yet her introspection, delving into Sufi thought and mysticism, has suffused these works with a sense of timelessness and withdrawal which echoes the physical and spiritual state of where she is situated.

Ironically, it was the trauma of Pakistan's third coup d'etat in 1977 and the overthrow of Z.A. Bhutto's civil government by General Zia-ul-Haq which set the stage for the surprising development and maturing of the work of Pakistan's women artists.

The dual colonisation first by the British, and then by men came to be recognised (often quite unconsciously) by women as straitjackets for both content and form.

The eighties witnessed the entrenchment of an official art policy in Pakistan. It was created by patronage if not by dictate, and consisted of a non-figurative, 'pseudo-Islamic' expression. Painters were encouraged to give up their own genres and adopt Islamic calligraphy, or else the safe territory of 'landscape painting'. The argument provided by state-sponsored cultural bodies was that calligraphy should be the "natural" artistic expression, since it fulfilled the requirements of General Zia's 'Islamic' dictate, as well as being both traditional and abstract. It was implied that artists need not go beyond the parameters provided by the calligraphic tradition. They could conveniently forge an identity for their work which was both 'Pakistani' and 'Islamic'. Large commissions became available for artists who were willing to make calligraphic works for public places. Figurative work, although not forbidden, was only acceptable if it consisted of portraits of sanctioned public figures.

A significant aspect of this time was the refusal of women painters to change their themes or genres. Not a single female painter adopted calligraphy, while very well established male painters took up public commissions in response to the Government policy.

Meher Afroze, Qudsia Nasir and Nahid Raza, all from Karachi, were among other women who established their artistic reputations during this decade. All three artists stood their ground in a milieu which did not encourage the kind of sensibilities which nurtured their work. They differed in their idiom, yet all of them shared a common interest in the exploration of surface and materials with an affinity for tradition in a convincing, humanist manner. All three worked on paper, which is itself a rejection of the Euro-centric tradition of oil on canvas.

Meher Afroze came to Pakistan from India in 1971, being part of the third wave of migrants. Trained at the Lucknow School of Art, she began her career in Karachi as a printmaker. In her work there are reverberations of images from folk-art, from wall textures, and from urban surfaces. Qudsia Nisar works in water colour; playful, gestural and diminutive. The last attribute is not suggested as a "feminine" quality, since the miniature in scale implies both rigour and an exacting focus in the practice of one's art. This is unlike the Western tradition where the 'heroic' scale is taken very seriously. Nahid Raza is the most articulate of this trio, in her feminist concerns in paint. Her work deliberately takes up her cause: the imagery is alternatively symbolic and explicit. Working primarily on paper, she uses acrylic mixed with pigment, graphite and other mediums. The paintings are heavily textured, gestural and strongly hued, in deep reds and Indian yellows.

The social and legal climate during the '80s began to permeate women's consciousness in a more direct manner. The infamous police attack in Lahore on February 12, 1983, against a peaceful demonstration by women against the proposed Law of Evidence, became symbolic of what was at stake. The insistence that women should wear the chaadar in public forums, educational institutions and the media became a focal point for rebellion for artists like myself. Dance was forbidden, but it could not be suppressed while there was Nahid Siddiqui and while one could paint her. The 'chaadar' became a symbol of constraint, and tearing it apart became an act of defiance for artists like Naazish Ataullah.

While remaining in representational art, women artists had imitated a reality described and delineated by male artists. When they liberated their vision, bringing it closer to their own aesthetics—the aesthetics of an ancient reservoir of cultural experience and art production—these women began "speaking in many tongues". They began to evolve a personalized vocabulary which the history of male art had denied to them. The flirtation with tradition is a temptation for all artists, male and female in a post-colonial world. The choice is either this or capitulation to the modernist market place. In the struggle for cultural identity it becomes a problem to avoid retreating into the nostalgia of a self-conscious ethnicity.

The increasing mobility of our times has found Pakistani women artists living and working abroad and grappling exactly with these problems. Mansoora Hassan, Sylvat Aziz, and Lubna Agha are painters who return home frequently, consciously nurturing ties and entering into dialogues with their counterparts in Lahore, Karachi and other places. They experience the harshness of the geopolitic reality from afar and find themselves caught between several worlds and many timewarps. Summaya Durrani and Nilofer Akmut comment very differently on current and past history. Summaya looks at the destruction of the Gulf War with anger and sorrow—dark doorways leading nowhere. Nilofer looks at the partition of 1947 with its untold stories, and silent sagas.

Delving into the problem of relevant imagery in a male-dominated traditionalist society, women find that conventional approaches, hallowed by centuries of practice, look redundant. For example, the representation of the female body in men's art has an established pattern of interpretation. In a Muslim society like Pakistan, the nude, while officially frowned upon is an acceptable feature in the work of male painters—their images being predictable as objects of desire and ornament. Women painters, on the other hand, have taken up the female nude as a symbol of rebellion, social oppression and political dissent. The change in context is reflected in Sabina Gillanis' work while she worked in

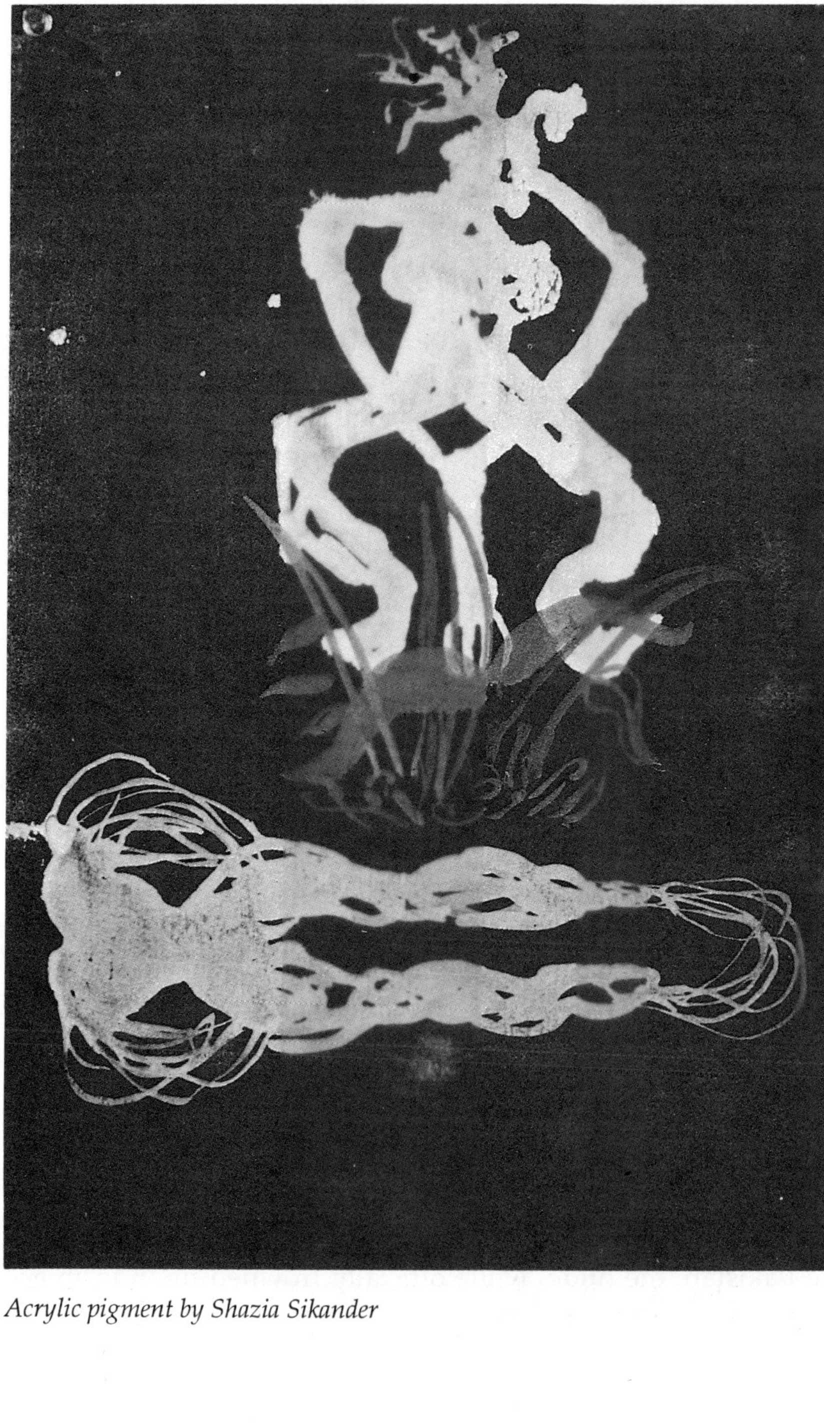

Acrylic pigment by Shazia Sikander

Pakistan, and now that she is living in Europe and Canada. Similar concerns appear, modified in the works of younger artists newly emerging on the scene.

Samina Mansuri addresses both the physical and spiritual, as do Laila Rehman, Asma Mahmud and others. Women painters in Pakistan, are rejecting the entire western premise of 'High Art', by attempting to widen the context of art production. They are looking for inspiration in the traditional folk-crafts as well as the popular urban art forms, often crafted by women in their homes, and are attempting to build bridges and assimilate ideas from unlikely sources. Shazia Sikandar is a traditional miniature painter who attempts to contemporize these skills to express her experiences of today. Younger painters are following suit, turning to diverse sources such as the popular 'truck painting' tradition, the skills of crochet and embroidery, ceramics and photography, and bringing them into painting, into multi-media installations and performance art.

The growing interest among women artists to give a new meaning to their art, has its effect on the institutions which train them. Art Schools and Colleges have mushroomed all over Pakistan, a majority of them being headed and staffed by women artists. They address several problems from the colonial, male-biased approaches to art education, the rural-urban dichotomy, as well as regional inequalities and many other questions that have appeared on the horizon.

It is ironical that the desire in 1947 to impose reservations on women's learning and their acquisition of knowledge, by relegating women to the pursuit of art—as a 'peripheral' activity—has now been turned around by women! Art has been made into a forum from which women question the whole social and political order.

Notes

1. Ayesha Jalal, "The Convenience of Subservience: Women and the State of Pakistan", *Women Islam and the State"*, Philadelphia, Temple University Press: 1991.
2. 'Report of the Pakistan Commission on the Status of Women', Government of Pakistan, 1986.
3. 'A Selection of Contemporary Paintings from Pakistan' Exhibition Catalogue. Pacific Asia Museum, Pasadena California 1994.
4. Marcella Nelson Sirhindi, *Contemporary Painting in Pakistan,* Lahore: Ferozesons, 1992.
5. Ijaz-ul-Hassan. *Painting in Pakistan*, Lahore: Ferozesons, 1991.

Gulf war series by Summaya Durrani

MEGHNA GUHATHAKURTA

Gender Politics in Theatre

> We don't know what women's vision is. What do women's eyes see? How do they carve, invent, decipher the world, I don't know—I know my own vision, the vision of one woman, but the world seen through the eyes of others. I only know what men's eyes see[1].
>
> Vivianne Forrester

The above quote constitutes part of a critique of French cinema on the silencing of the woman's voice. Forrester contends that we cannot know how women view the world, since in most representations the feminine voice has been repressed. In other words, she feels that women's vision is not to be discovered solely in history (as has been the case of much Anglo-American criticism) but in the unconscious—in that aspect of the human psyche which is denied expression. Women are placed in the domain of the silenced.

What Forrester has to say about French cinema can easily hold true for mainstream theatre and film in any part of the world. Given the fact that the visual media is specially prone to male voyeurism and male ways of viewing the world, and given the historical domination of men in the industries which produce such images, it is not surprising that most representations of women in such media are fabricated by men and projected onto an entirely androcentric world.

It would be easy to argue that contemporary Bengali theatre is no different and give evidence in support of such a view. This paper seeks to show how Dhaka Podatik's *Bishad Sindhu* (The Sea of Sorrow) explores ways in which women are represented and to see whether the play challenges, in any meaningful manner, established notions of gender relations and sexuality.

The play needs to be situated within the evolving tradition of contemporary theatre in Bangladesh. It needs to be examined in the light of current politics of resistance, as well as in terms of a nascent critique and practice of feminism in Bangladesh. The director and the playwright seek to represent women characters in this play with different emphasis.

Bengali theatre in its modern form originated during colonial times.[2] It started its journey in 1795 with the staging of a Bengali translation of two English plays, *The Disguised* and *Love is the Best Doctor.* Tarachand Shikdar's *Bhadrarjun* was the first original play in Bengali to be staged in Calcutta, in 1852. Modern theatre in Bengal thus began by initiating both the form and style of the European stage, as imitation; for this reason it did not easily become part of mainstream Bengali culture.

It was only with the rise of the class of the Bengali bhadrolok that Bengali theatre became a predominant form for the upcoming gentry. This modern form of drama was consciously different from indigenous traditions like the jatra or pala gaan or kheurs, which were considered the entertainment of the subordinate classes. Dinbandu Mitra's play *Nil Darpan* (1860) is exceptional as it brought in an element of protest in this era of conformity and subservience to British colonialists. The play deals with the exploitation of indigo planters by British rulers. This is the only play on the proscenium stage which can be considered as an open protest against colonial rule in Bengal. All other plays took the form of social drama or farce, where indigenous traditions and social mores were questioned in the light of an emerging body of knowledge informed by the European Enlightenment.

Resistance as portrayed in theatre was more visible in the popular culture of the nineteenth century. For example the kheurs, storytelling groups of the Vaishnavite women, use crude, impolite and offensive language to ridicule and criticise the bhadrolok class.[3] Institutionalised political resistance in the theatre became discernible only with the formation of the Indian Peoples Theatre Association (IPTA) in the aftermath of the man-made famine of 1943. This theatre group which became the cultural front of the Communist Party was perhaps the first formal theatre that drew its inspiration from protest against colonisation and oppression.

After the Partition of East Bengal, serious theatre developed, as opposed to commercial theatre—through amateur groups and individual effort. Within East Pakistan, the basis for the politicization of the theatre was laid through the Language Movement of 1952, the autonomy movement of the sixties and the Liberation War of 1971.[4]

The real thrust for theatre came in post-war Bangladesh when artists, invigorated by the memories of the Liberation War, undertook to translate the freedom struggle into reality. Thus the Group Theatre Movement was born and various experiments started in earnest. Some groups sought inspiration in the political plays of Bertolt Brecht, some looked towards verse plays, while others turned their attention to indigenous forms of drama.

The history of Bangladesh was marked by the promulgation of martial law at various times. The populist government which emerged from this history continued to help create a pro-establishment culture characterized by regimentation, fundamentalism and the market economy.

The state-controlled media remain locked, to a great extent within these trends. Theatre artists who believed in the cause of the Liberation War and had alternative messages were forced to seek out other sites for performance. They soon became part of the wider political movement within the country, and worked actively in various movements, especially the movement to topple the autocratic regime of General Ershad. It became imperative for the theatre movement to impart its political messages to a mass audience. The theatre movement, in its search for new sites of performance, took to the streets, and street theatre was born in Bangladesh.

While democracy has now been restored and an elected government is in place, problems for the theatre have not disappeared. Theatre artists are eager to get back 'on stage'; but the truth of the matter is that there are still no permanent stages for theatre in Dhaka. Besides, the theatre movement has had to cope with and confront a growing fundamentalist trend and sharpen its own critique of traditional beliefs in the process. The streets thus remain the preferred site for political contestation, where theatre workers continue to question and challenge orthodoxy and the establishment.

This brief review of evolving trends in contemporary theatre in Bangladesh bears testimony to the fact that theatre in Bangladesh has become intensely political. Although the extent of politicization has often been questioned, it cannot be denied that the number of plays which take up exploitation, revolution and social change as central themes far exceed the number of social dramas. Of course it must remembered that this is true only of plays performed by the Group Theatre Movement. But the question to be asked here is that even with intense politicization of theatre, why is it that apart from some very recent productions, the representation of women and the questioning of gender relations has largely remained conventional and untouched? I shall now turn to this near-absence of a gender awareness and the questioning of established notions of femininity in theatre productions in Bangladesh.

Traditional images of womanhood—woman as mother, as home maker, as shy and subservient, as the sacrificer—remain unquestioned and are in fact reproduced even by the 'progressive' theatre movement in our country. This is true even in the case of plays which have been popularly acclaimed as political or progressive. For example in Aronyok's *Ora Kodom Ali* by the Theatre Group—a play with over a hundred shows to its credit—the two women characters appear almost as props to the central theme of class exploitation and struggle. *Dewan Gazir Kissa,* the Bengali version of Brecht's *Pontila and His Man Matte* by the Nagorik Theatre Group, can also boast of the highest number of shows in Bangladesh. Despite the fact that this play gives more visibility and voice to its women characters, it still relegates them to the role of the social victim. Theatre Group's *Payer Awaj Pawa Jai,* an equally popular play, tells the story of how a woman falls victim to the brutalities of the Pakistan Army and its collaborators in the Liberation War of 1971. Here again, the woman who is the central character, is shown as a victim, someone who is brutalised in the cause of the nation; but the play does not analyse rape or violence against women.

The largely unchanging role and representation of women in theatre is not entirely the fault of producers, directors and script writers. The failure of the women's movement to address issues regarding the politics of representation, and to make a sustained critique and analysis of the media, is also responsible for this shortcoming. Mainstream women's rights activists, even professedly progressive ones, are reluctant to challenge the essential mores of Bengali womanhood. In this they subserve the movement to the discourse which sets up stereotypical notions of what is masculine and feminine. This encourages everyone to revere notions such as motherhood in a woman, shyness in a girl, surrender from a bride or coyness in a lover. These are what are considered to be 'natural' to the female. Any deviations such as boldness or recklessness fall outside the definition of femininity. Women's rights activists who cater to such a view therefore fail to question the standard stereotypes portrayed by the media.

The second factor responsible for the failure of the women's movement to make inroads into the cultural sphere is the orientation of most of the gender debates towards development, which is prevalent in Bangladesh. Issues and problems of gender discrimination and gender exploitation in Bangladesh have been featured and initiated, informed and largely defined by donor-oriented development programmes.[5] It is quite safe to predict that donor oriented programmes on women and development are likely to bring in more resources than seminars and publications on women and the media.

Despite this there have been attempts by some women's groups to influence the projection and perpetuation of the woman's image as positive in the media. For example *Naripokkho*, a women's group had sittings with theatre artists about projecting more positive images of women in the media and made efforts to reinterpret women characters in traditional literary texts such as Tagore's *Chitrangada*. Other groups such as *Nari Shonghoti*, 'Women for Women' and more recently *Mohila Porishod* have held several seminars and workshops, and published materials on these topics.[6] Workshops for women writers are also being held. However such efforts have remained on the sideline of mainstream political activity; and as such the results so far have been minimal. But it is also not too optimistic to claim that the situation may be changing somewhat.

But where the mainstream women's movement has failed to make a substantial impact, one woman writer has had remarkable success—Taslima Nasrin. Sexuality had always been a subject close to Bengali literature. But the sexuality traditionally portrayed in Bengali literature has been dominantly a male one, informed by male notions and ways of seeing. This is where Taslima made her intervention. Not only did she start writing about women's sexuality, but she engaged in topics which have been declared taboo by a political culture steeped in self-censorship: religion, fundamentalism and other forms of chauvinism which had denied women's active sexuality and repressed the feminine . It is little wonder therefore that Taslima and her writings have become controversial. Her writings on the politics of sexuality found admiration, sometimes very secretly, among a constituency of middle-class women (housewives, students, professionals) whom the mainstream women's movement had thus far failed to reach. Her writings and views on religion however have created a furore among women and men of all ages—not the least in dominant political circles.

It is interesting to note here that Taslima Nasrin was writing at about the same time that Dhaka Podatik's production of *Bishad Sindhu* was being staged. Both were statements against a fundamentalist politics which was flourishing at that time. Both were seeking reinterpretation of texts where religion and sexuality were construed in such a way as to silence and marginalise the voices of women.

Bishad Sindhu is set against the backdrop of a theatre movement that is intensely political; but a political discourse in which gender analysis has not been made the central issue, and where the womans question is largely ignored. Produced in 1992, *Bishad Sindhu* represents contemporary theatre in Bangladesh in every sense of the word. Originally an epic religious novel by Mir Mosharraf Hussain (1848-1914) it tells the story of Karbala and the tragic fate of Hasan and Hossain, the two grandsons of the Prophet Mohammed.

Director Jamil Ahmed and scriptwriter Biplob Bala have sought to interpret this well-known story, and set it against the current political situation in Bangladesh. A production by Dhaka Podatik, the play is presented in two self-contained episodes: *Purbodhani,* the story of Imam Hasan; and *Uttordhani,* the story of Imam Hossain. Each episode is of approximately three hours duration. The story of Imam Hossain and Imam Hasan echoes in the hearts of most Bengalis in diverse forms. The story is revealed in literature as part of an indigenous oral cultural tradition and also in the written form, of which Mir Mosharraf's novel *Bishad Sindhu* stands out as a brilliant piece of literary workmanship. It was written in three parts, each part published consecutively in 1884, 1887 and 1890. Interestingly however, in adapting this novel to the stage both the director and playwright have borrowed liberally from popular oral traditions—using the kathakatha and other indigenous forms of expression while retaining a "common sky"[7] with Mir Mosharraf Hossain's interpretation of the characters and the structure of the story. The production thus became an interesting experiment in the cross-translating and interspersing of the oral and the literary.

Bishad Sindhu was being staged at a time when the political arena in Bangladesh was riven by debates between Bangladeshi and Bangalee nationhood, and between a religious and a language-based nationalism. Dhaka Podatik's *Bishad Sindhu* attempted to bring in a breath of fresh air into this debate.

The play involves a challenging of religious blindness, and a questioning of all the notions that are embedded within our culture and reproduced unquestioningly by all. The space opened up has enabled an exploration of sexuality and gender as well. Religious orthodoxy and conservatism usually go hand in hand with repression of female sexuality. The question is, if Dhaka Podatik's *Bishad Sindhu* has challenged religious orthodoxy through its reinterpretation of a religious epic, has it also then taken the task of releasing notions of female sexuality from their traditional moorings and redefined gender relations in a new context?

Let us first look at how director Jamil Ahmed proceeds towards this counter-interpretation. The events of *Bishad Sindhu* originate in the far-off lands of the Middle-East and at a distant time. Perhaps one of the greatest achievements of Mir Mosharraf Hossain was that through his rich literary style he was able to transcend the constraints of time and space, to create a bond between religious sentiment and social consciousness. On the other hand, Dhaka Podatik's *Bishad Sindhu,* by reinterpreting the story, aims to create a sense of alienation among the viewers. This alienation is meant to detach the viewers from the mere sentimentality of the drama and to begin questioning the nature of the events portrayed.

The play *Bishad Sindhu* can be seen as synthesized into the syncretic tradition of Bengali history. This is why the play starts with a song in the Kathakatha tradition, paying respect to Mother Nature and following thereon to the noted personalities of Bengali literature: Bankim, Rabindranath, Kazi Nazrul Islam and finally Mir Mosharraf Hossain. It is this literary tradition in which the Bengali world view is rooted and through which we can interpret one religion with the help of another. The characters of Karbala can be understood in the light of characters from the Mahabharata, and vice versa.

Within this cultural frame, two questions are posed to the audience. In both cases the distance between blind sentimentality and human reason is emphasized. Most religious story-telling is fatalistic. Jamil Ahmed's direction helps to warn the audience of this. By making liberal use of the kathakatha tradition, and using the *sutradhar* as the interpreter of events, the inevitability of events and the lack of human control over them is questioned time and again. Why is it that even when one knows what is going to happen, one cannot do anything about it?

The other question raised is about the characters themselves. Detachment helps the viewers to dethrone heroes from their positions, and to see that villains are not mere villains. Roles are so intermixed that at times there is hardly any difference between the two. Thus, even while Imam Hasan is portrayed as an astute and benevolent ruler, his attitude towards women is not admirable. Even though he already has two wives, he does not desist from proposing to Joynab, who he knows is sought after by Ejid. Ejid on the other hand is shown as the epitome of cruelty and self-centredness; yet he often takes a righteous stance in his judgement of others. He stoutly defends his right to fight for the land of Medina.

Does this play shed new light on traditional perceptions of gender. Jamil Ahmed has made an effort in this direction as well. Although there are fewer women than men in the play, the representation of women in *Bishad Sindhu* has fared better than in other contemporary productions. Women in the chorus take part in the fighting scenes enacted through the *lathi khela* with men. They also participate in acrobatic displays, which becomes a deviation from the conventional stereotypical presence of women in plays.The three female characters, Joynab, Zahida and Maimuna, also receive special treatment. Despite this, the portrayal remains incomplete. Joynab is powerfully portrayed, and she yet remains helpless in the face of Ejid's greed. Her social position and standing is precarious and due to the whim of one person; she is divorced by her husband, forced to take refuge at her father's feet—her only hope in life being getting married to one of three suitors. Finally when she does exercise her choice, she is fated to live as the third wife of her husband. Is this a future which a girl like her has dreamt of? Or is it a penance she has to play for being born beautiful and attractive? These questions are raised quite effectively in the play, especially by reading out passages describing Joynab's beauty in Mir Mosharraf's novel. In this way the audience is led to evaluate not only the emotions that lead to such possessiveness, but also the texts which unquestioningly portray such emotions.

Zahida, Hasan's second wife, is consumed with jealousy. Together with Maimuna she conspires to poison Hasan. Though they are typically villainous figures, the play initially portrays them in a sympathetic manner. That Zahida should be jealous of Joynab for taking Hasan's affection from her is not unexpected; but what is inexcusable is her plotting to take Hasan's life—the person she loves most. Yet in this play an effort is made to understand such emotion and there is no outright condemnation. Also the will to kill has released emotions within Zahida which maybe paralleled with the release of emotions epitomised by the dance of destruction.

Positive though such images of women may be, and despite the effort to present them in a different light, the main limitations of *Bishad Sindhu* is that such images are not sustained long enough to lead to any decisive conclusion. Joynab, for example becomes the focus of attention for a while; but after her marriage she is relegated to a back seat—not by Hasan, but by the playwright! Even the first wife's personality has been fleshed out more than hers. Instead of Joynab, Zahida and her accomplice Maimuna become the focus of attention. But here too, the desire to understand them or their motives is not followed through and melts into thin air when they fall prey to Ejid's strong sense of right and wrong. Any sympathy they might have evoked is wiped away at one stroke.

There seems very little to say about the representation of women in the second episode of *Bishad Sindhu*, which echoes the sad tale of how Hossain and his army were defeated by Ejid in the sunscorched deserts of Karbala. The predominant image is one of women's bravery against great odds. This is compared to those women who had taken bold steps in their lifetime and fought against social and political injustice and tyranny—Rokeya, Pritilota, and more recently Jahanara Imam. Apart from this tribute to women's contribution in the Bangladesh nationalist struggles, there is very little in the second episode from which the audience can derive any knowledge about the actual conditions in which women live, and the problems with which they are confronted everyday.

No doubt *Bishad Sindhu* is a play which offers immense possibilities and potentialities for interpreting, challenging and redefining traditional mores and conventional images of women. One would hope that future productions such as these would demonstrate more consistency in their image—building and characterization, and pay greater attention to the appropriate analysis of gender based images, so that it is truly the woman's vision which reaches the audience.

The politics of representing women in the arts and literature is much ensconced in the broader politics relating to the struggle for a secular cultural space—for which many of our artistes, writers, performers and film-makers still yearn. The upsurge of fundamentalist politics in the twentieth century, globally and in the subcontinent, have cast a dark shadow over these aspirations. Such developments have confirmed the fact that progressive politics, in order to be effective, need to incorporate within them a feminist agenda. However whilst there has been a kind of consensus on this basic premise (not easily arrived at), feminists themselves have differed over the strategies to combat fundamentalism.

In Bangladesh too, this has taken different forms. The first strategy opposes fundamentalism by advocating separation between religion and politics. The other emphasizes the rereading and reappropriating of religious texts from a woman's perspective. Although both forms are evident in the Bangladesh scene, they have not generally attained any extreme dimensions. The majority seem to agree on opposing the more institutional manifestations of fundamentalism; but they differ in their suggested alternatives. Whereas one stream of thought wishes to rediscover women in indigenous folk-religious culture as opposed to institutionalised religion, the other tries to locate women's struggle in the more secular tradition of their resistance politics. Needless to say, neither alternatives are unproblematic. Just as one needs to rediscover a woman's perspective in folk-religious culture, one also needs to reread resistance politics in the light of women's experience. A feminist agenda of representation is therefore the need of the hour.

Notes

1. M. Eagleton (ed), *Feminist Literary Theory: A Reader*, Oxford: Basil Blackwell, 1988, p. 34.
2. S. Mitra, *Shakespear O Banglar Natok*, Calcutta: Shahityo Prokashona, 1978.
3. S. Banerjee, "Marginalisation of Women's Popular Culture in Nineteenth Century Bengal" in K. Sangari and S. Vaid (ed) *Recasting Women: Essays in Colonial History*, New Delhi: Kali for Women, 1989.
4. M. Guhathakurta and C. Rozario *Prantikota, Protirodh O Prishtoposhokota: Bangladesh Natyo Andoloner Shorup* (Marginality, Resistance and Patronage: The Nature of the Theatre Movement in Bangladesh) in *Shomaj Nirikkhon*, 46, Dec. 1992.
5. M Guhathakurta, "The Women's Agenda and the Role of Political Parties" National Seminar on *Nari O Rajniti* (Women and Politics), Dhaka, Women for Women, May 30-31, 1992.
6. See Jahanara Huq, *Nari O Gonomadhyam* (Women and the Media) Dhaka, Women for Women, 1988 and Nari Shonghoti, *Gonomadhyam O Nari* (Media and Women), Dhaka, Nari Shonghoti, 1987.
7. The phrase was used by the Director Jamil Ahmed himself.

MADEEHA GAUHAR

Crossing Frontiers: Shared Concerns in Alternative Theatre

In Pakistan, frontiers are all important. The geographical frontiers, are under threat all the time, especially from the East. The ideological frontiers, are being invaded from the East and West and from the skies, converting the 'Land of the Pure' into the 'Land of the Polluted.' The cultural frontiers are also very vulnerable and the Pakistani cultural identity has to be protected vigilantly (it is immaterial whether this identity has ever been clearly defined). Then there are psychological frontiers beyond which people are not allowed to think, imagine or explore. This applies to education, philosophy, media and politics. Even today when the world has become a global village and the communications revolution is breaking all frontiers, the Pakistani Establishment is still determined to blindly protect whatever it has defined as Pakistan's ideological and national interest.

Pakistan has always been a rather unwelcoming place for art and culture, mainly because of the particular circumstances relating to its creation. Since the *raison d'être* of the new state was the two-nation theory, the Pakistani Muslims had to consistently prove that they were a distinct community from the rest. Any manifestation of common history or culture had to be forcefully rejected to prove the point. Continued hostility between independent India and the overwhelmingly Muslim Pakistan strengthened these attitudes. The Pakistani Establishment found an excuse for imposing authoritarian rule in the country and rejecting any expression of cultural or artistic activity which was common between the people of the two countries. Hence the growth of art and culture was most suppressed or at best ignored. This cultural genocide reached its culmination during the military dictatorship of General Zia-ul-Haq.

When Ajoka was formed by a group of young cultural activists in Lahore in 1983, Martial Law was at its oppressive peak. The frontiers had shrunk to such a claustrophobic level that the whole nation was suffocating. Thousands of political workers were behind bars, the Press was totally gagged, and fundamentalist "reforms" were trampling the rights of women, minorities and working classes. Journalists, TV professionals and intellectuals were in prison, accused of serious crimes such as sedition, anti-state activities and occupation of defence installations.

It was not a coincidence that the first order instruction given by General Zia to Pakistan Television was about the banning of a classical dance programme, "Payal" by the Kathak dancer Naheed Siddiqui. This was part of the considered policy of the military government to replace dance, music, sculpture and theatre with religious music, calligraphy, *Qirat* recitation and *naat* singing contests. The emergence of Ajoka and other such theatre groups was an inevitable response to this attempt to stifle the creativity and silence the voices of the Pakistani people. Ajoka's first production was Badal Sircar's *Jaloos*. A play about the political exploitation and betrayal of the masses by political and religious leaders, written in the context of West Bengal, it appeared to be as relevant to the Pakistan of the early eighties. I had met Badal Sircar in Delhi in 1982 and attended rehearsals of a play of his—*Bhoma*. This was my first encounter with the "Third Theatre". This experience gave me an insight into the work being done in India and proved to be a major inspiration to set up a similar group in Pakistan. I brought back with me to Lahore a Hindi translation of *Jaloos* and when Ajoka started looking for its first script, *Jaloos* was the obvious choice.

It was not easy to find a cast, a venue, and of course an audience for such a subversive piece of theatre. We had to settle for my mother's house lawn as no theatre hall, government-owned or private, was available because of stringent censorship laws. Performing in an open space was also not possible as the city was mostly in the grip of section 144, which banned congregations of more than four people. The performance could not be advertised, hence we had to depend on word-of-mouth publicity. We got a sizeable but more importantly an enthusiastic audience. As soon as the agencies got wind of this private activity, they appeared on the scene and started questioning the visitors and noting down the registration numbers of their vehicles. But the barrier had been broken. The audience had got a taste of subversive, meaningful but entertaining theatre and the actors had realised that doing theatre without a stage, set, lights, costumes, sound system, props and most importantly the censorship certificate, was possible. That was the beginning of the alternative theatre movement in Pakistan.

The fact that the first Ajoka script was an Urdu adaptation of an Indian play was no coincidence. It was obvious for us to look East for inspiration. India had a vast and vibrant theatre movement and the issues confronting Indian playrights and directors were very similar to ours. The similarities of history, language, culture, socio-economic problems and the world-view, and most importantly the common heritage of theatre and other performing arts, made it much easier for us to adapt and produce Indian scripts.

Selecting a script by a radical left-wing Indian playwright, motivated by a desire to cross the frontiers, could have led to serious charges of sedition and anti-Islamic activities. There were some left-wing journalists facing such charges for similar activities. But for some reason, the military regime did not overreact, perhaps we were not considered a major threat at a time when the regime was busy crushing the political opposition which by now had resurfaced.

Ajoka continued theatre with a radical social and political content. Its work was a blend of modern and folk forms. Its most frequent themes were human rights, women's struggle for emancipation, persecution of religious minorities, exploitation of workers and projection of the values of humanism, secularism and social justice. Ajoka thus became a part of the democratic movement.

At the same time the bonds established with the production of *Jaloos* were strengthened. This was inevitable because there wasn't much theatre activity within Pakistan and one had to look around for inspiration. Although Pakistan had been exposed to theatre movements in the West, the South Asian experience was more relevant and beneficial, for obvious reasons.

Ajoka's relations with South Asian groups were at two levels: (a) personal contacts and interaction through workshops and festivals, and (b) working on each other's scripts or joint productions. Personal contacts with those involved in the Indian theatre movement inspired us to start an alternative theatre group in Pakistan. This process has continued since then. There has been regular interaction between us and the South Asian theatre groups in spite of problems of visas, governmental permissions and difficulties in communications. Theatre workshops in Pakistan have been attended by Badal Sircar, the late Safdar Hashmi, Anuradha Kapur, Maya Rao and Rati Bartholomew.

There was an attempt to institutionalise this interaction through a South Asian Theatre Committee (SATCO), established in Lahore in 1992 when the Asian Cultural Forum for Development (ACFOD) organised a South Asian Theatre Festival. This festival enabled Pakistani audiences and theatre workers to see theatre from Nepal, Sri Lanka, India and Bangladesh, and also provided theatre activists to have interaction with the visiting actors/directors. SATCO decided to organise festivals in the region and facilitate contacts between theatre groups.

Another successful festival was organised in Dhaka in 1993, where theatre participants and discussants also met to discuss issues of mutual concern. The participants were able to see productions of major Bangladesh theatre groups during their stay, which was particularly useful for Pakistani visitors. The third SATCO festival took place in Kathmandu in 1995, with a focus on street theatre. Once again this was a rare opportunity for Pakistani theatre activists: to see the work of groups from other countries and share experiences.

The next festival was to be held in Colombo; it could not be organised because ACFOD withdrew support and the host group could not raise funds. At present the fate of SATCO is uncertain because of lack of resources; but contacts between the member groups continue.

Although SATCO could not hold any festival in India Ajoka got two opportunities to visit India. First in 1989, when Jan Natya Manch of India organised a solidarity festival after the murder of Safdar Hashmi. Ajoka members travelled to Delhi and performed their play *Itt*, on the theme of bonded brick kiln labour. They watched plays by street theatre groups from all over-India and participated in seminars and discussions. In 1996, Ajoka members were invited as part of a Pakistani delegation to the Nehru Centenary Theatre Festival, and were fortunate to see the best of Indian theatre over the past 50 years. During this festival we were able to meet and interact with the leading theatre figures of India.

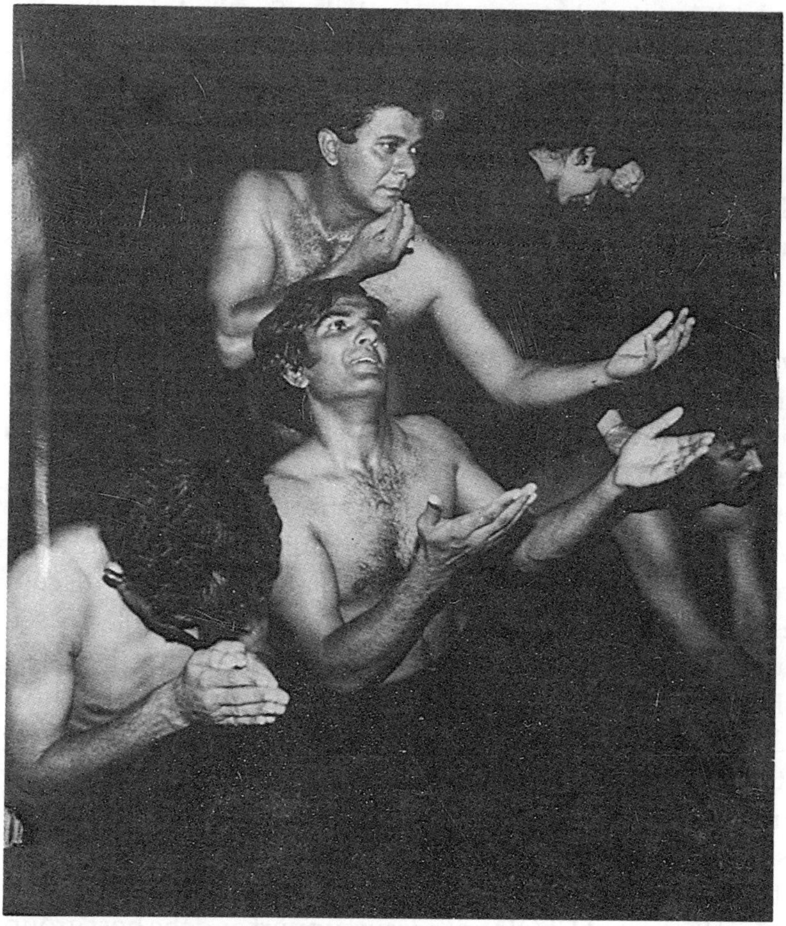

ITT, a play on bonded labour, 1989

Luckily Jan Natya Munch's street theatre festival was also held around the same time, and we saw some excellent street theatre.

There have been other occasions for meeting and sharing with South Asian theatre friends. For example there has been the South Asian Dialogue organised by Centre for Policy Dialogue in Dhaka in February 1997, when fruitful discussions took place between theatre people and intellectuals from the region. Such interaction has resulted in heightened awareness of the work being done in similar cultural milieus. For example its *Chulha* (The Stove) in 1980 by Ajoka was the result of greater awareness of the issue of bride-burning due to the work of Indian NGOs and theatre groups working on similar issues. The script of Ajoka's *Chaak Chakkar* (The Caucasian Chalk Circle), was initially based on a Hindi version of Badal Sircar's Bengali adaptation. Ajoka also used a script by Imtiaz Khan of India on apartheid.

Ajoka invited Indian theatre director/activist Rati Bartholomew to direct Shahid Nadeem's *Jhalli Kithay Javay* in 1990. Ajoka arranged for her travel and stay; she did not charge any fee. She did a workshop with the team first, and familiarised them with theatre techniques and skills being used by Indian theatre groups.

In 1993, Ajoka produced *Aik Thee Naani* (Once there was a Grandmother) by Shahid Nadeem. The play was a tribute to the grand old dames of Indian theatre: Zohra Segal, the acclaimed Indian actress and Uzra Butt, who migrated to Pakistan in the late 50s and, now in her 80th year, is still an active member of Ajoka. Both sisters were prominent figures of the Indian theatre, working with Prithvi Raj Kapoor's theatre and Uday Shankar's dance company. The theme of the story was the hypocritical attitude of Pakistani middle classes towards performing arts, and the denial of cultural freedom by an increasingly retrogressive Establishment. The story was a mixture of fact and fiction, revolving around the reunion of two sisters, separated by Partition. They had both been acclaimed actresses of their time. The elder sister, played by Zohra Segal, stayed back in India and continued her career and was now a revered figure in the theatre world. The other sister, Uzra Butt migrated to Pakistan with her husband, and was living a mundane life as a conventional middle class house-wife, having being forced to suppress her past as an actress. The sister from India comes for a visit. The house in Lahore, where status quo had reigned supreme, is thrown into turmoil and a "cultural revolution" unfolds.

Working with Zohra was a tremendous experience. Her commitment to her work, her discipline and her presences on stage were a great inspiration for everyone involved. It was an emotional experience for the two sisters who were working together after a lapse of over 40 years—another crossing of frontiers.

An interesting experiment for Ajoka was *The Sixth River.* The play was written by Shahid Nadeem of Ajoka and directed by Indian theatre director Anuradha Kapoor. The cast included Govind Singh Rawat of the Sarwanam group from Nepal, and Vidya from India, the rest coming from Ajoka. The play's theme was communal harmony and it castigated the insane violence committed in the name of religion or nations. The play was performed in Urdu, Hindi and Nepali, and effectively linked the spiritual and cultural bonds of the three countries and their religions. The play was performed at the People's Plan for Twenty First Century assembly in Bangkok. The collaborative production and the theme of the play became more significant as the Babri Mosque demolition took place only a few days before the performance, and led to destruction of mosques and temples all over South Asia.

While the *Sixth River* was about communal harmony, Ajoka's hard-hitting play *Dekh Tamasha Chalta Ban* dealt with the impact of the blasphemy laws in Pakistani society. These laws, introduced by the Zia regime and strengthened by an "elected" Government, made the death sentence mandatory for any one found guilty of blasphemy. The fundamentalists used this law to persecute the minorities. *Dekh Tamasha* was not an easy play to perform in Pakistan. Even when this play was performed in the Dhaka festival in 1993, Ajoka had to suffer harassment at the hands of Pakistani intelligence agencies for "defaming" the country abroad.

Since its inception, Ajoka has shared the vision of a secular and democratic society with its counterparts in other South Asian countries. Traditionally the status of women in all South Asian countries is determined by similar patriarchal norms and values. But in Pakistan, the women's struggle against so-called "Islamic" legislation, relegating women to a second class status, has become a focal point of the democratic movement. Ajoka's land-mark play, *Barri* (The Acquittal), first performed on International Women's Day 1987, was a scathing critique of these laws. *Barri* is about four women who come together in a prison cell, accused of a variety of crimes, but all are victims of unjust traditional practices and discriminatory laws. The prison becomes a metaphor of the society at large. This play had a powerful impact on women activists and was later converted into a popular TV serial, *Neelay Hath* during Benazir Bhutto's first government.

Besides being a director, I have also been active in the women's movement, which has enabled me to keep Ajoka close to the issues concerning the women's movement. Shahid's collection of original scripts on Punjabi feminist plays, *Khasman Khanian, The Husband Eaters* is the only play of its kind in Pakistan.

Plays like *Jhalli Kithay Javay, Chulha, Lappar, Sharam di Gal* and *Dhee Raani* deal with issues as varied as bride-burning, rape and the attitude towards the girl-child.

The latest of Ajoka's projects is also a play about women. But *Dukhini* reaches out beyond national frontiers. It is about the trafficking of Bangladeshi women to Pakistan and is a collaboration between Ajoka and a Chittagong-based group, Bangladesh Institute of Theatre Arts (BITA). Shahid Nadeem has written the script based on research material collected from both countries, and it is being directed by Sara Zakir of a Dhaka- based group *Nagorik.* The play narrates the story of four Bangladeshi women who are brought to Pakistan, lured by the prospect of a prosperous future. Their harrowing journey through Bangladesh, India and finally Pakistan highlights the plight of these poor women and stresses the need for a concerted effort on the part of all three countries to fight this repellent trade.

This project has been particularly significant and sensitive not only because of the cultural and language barriers but also because of the history of relations between the two countries.

It was conceived as a result of personal contacts established between us and Bangladeshi theatre activists during theatre festivals and seminars in the region. The plan was to collaborate on an issue of commonality, with creative input from both countries. In early 1997, a group of six actors went to Dhaka and along with Bangladeshi actors started work on the play. These performances are scheduled to be held towards the end of this year in Lahore, Karachi, Dhaka and Chittagong.

A project of this kind could not be free of problems. There were problems caused by geographical distance, weather, visa restrictions and performance permissions. The main challenge was to translate parts of the script into Bengali and make the rest of it simple enough to be generally understandable for Bangladeshi and Pakistani audiences. Then the Pakistani actors had to learn a little Bengali and the Bangladeshi actors had to learn some Urdu.

Most importantly the *Dukhini* experience has been a crossing of a major frontier for most of us. We as a nation have chosen to suffer from collective amnesia, erasing from our memories any reference to the atrocities committed in the then East Pakistan, during the 1971 army action. Even a few years ago it was not really possible in Pakistan to talk about what really happened and why it happened. When Ajoka first visited Dhaka in 1993, we were hesitant and unsure for we carried with us the burden of a quarter century's denial. Among our hosts were many young Bangladeshis who had never seen a Pakistani. They had only heard of the terrible crimes committed by Pakistanis during the Liberation struggle. Nervously we stepped upon the Shilpa Kala Academy stage for our first performance. Before the play started, one of us stepped forward and, expressed our deep anguish at the crimes committed in the name of the Pakistani people. This was perhaps the first public apology to the Bangladeshi people by Pakistanis. Once this barrier was transcended, the barriers of language or culture were easy to cross. The realisation that theatre activists in both countries were fighting against similar forces of exploitation and retrogression brought us closer together. Now that we have worked together in this bilingual collaborative production of *Dukhini*, we feel that no river is unbridgeable.

Through the years, these regional and bilateral contacts have enabled Ajoka to enrich its work both in content and in form. Through its work, Ajoka has also projected a message of communal harmony, humanism and peace in Pakistan and across the borders. It has attempted to counter the fundamentalist propaganda against minorities in neighbouring countries in the region. Like similar theatre groups in India, Nepal, Bangladesh and Sri Lanka, Ajoka has been fighting the retrogressive forces of intolerance, prejudice and violence. Ajoka and its counterparts in the region are voices of sanity, love and progress and they need to build bridges across the barriers erected by the short-sighted and suicidal policies of the religio-political establishments in all these countries.

The next frontier Ajoka plans to cross is literally the one at the Wagah Border. We have been invited to tour East Punjab later this year with our Punjabi plays, the first such tour since 1947. With great anticipation, we are looking forward to crossing over a frontier, so close to Lahore and yet so far. Crossing the final frontier—would be like coming home.

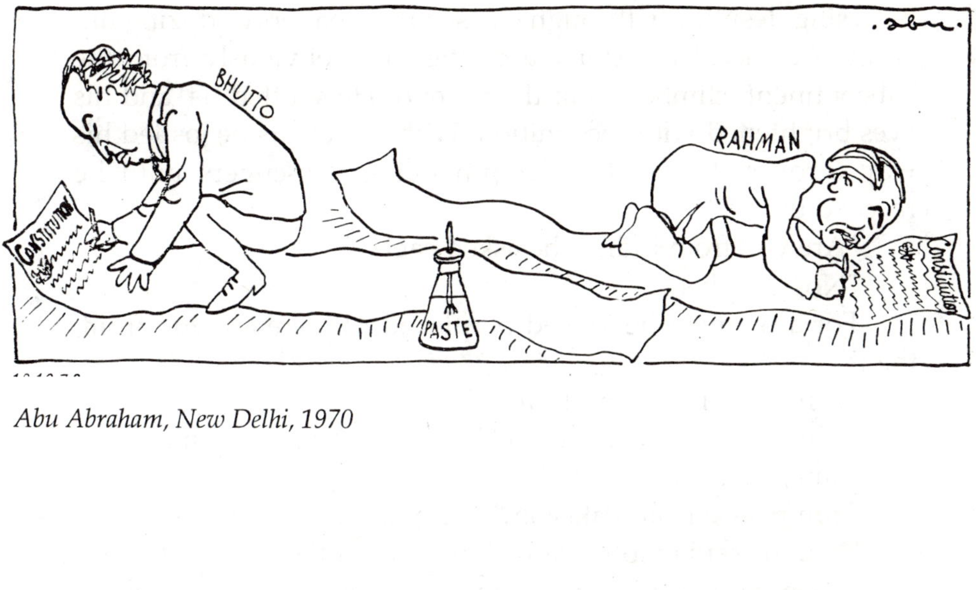

Abu Abraham, New Delhi, 1970

V
IDENTITY: SELF AND THE OTHER

*Same to Same**

We met in Paris of all places. It was an unlikely location for such an encounter. My wife and I had spent the day at the small château which had belonged to Napoleon's empress Josephine, at Reuilly-Malmaison outside Paris, and were travelling back by public bus to our hotel in the centre of the city. The bus was crowded with tired commuters, browsing desultorily through creased newspapers or dozing uneasily. At one of the stops, a young man, obviously from the subcontinent, climbed in at the far end. He spotted us, and his eyes brightened with recognition. Within seconds he jostled his way through the packed strap-hanging passengers until he reached us.

"Are you from India?" he asked eagerly.

"No," I replied.

For a moment he looked perplexed. "Where are you from, then?"

"I am from Pakistan," I said.

"Oh!" he exclaimed, with relief. "India-Pakistan, same to same, yaar!"

"You're also from Pakistan?" I enquired.

"No," he said emphatically, "I'm from India."

"Then why didn't you say that you were from Pakistan—if they're both same-to-same, yaar!"

His ingratiating smile vanished at this unexpected rebuff. He moved sulkily away from us.

This brief exchange, in the neutrality of a Paris public bus, represented in its own pithy way the attitude—essentially a patronising one—the average Indian has towards a Pakistani. The instinctive reaction of an average Pakistani is, as was mine, one of brusque defensiveness.

---

*Excerpted from *The Armless Queen and Other Essays* by F.S. Aijazzuddin, Ferozesons, Lahore

To the Indians, being identified as anything other than an Indian is a come down. They are understandably proud of their nationality, but by including Pakistanis in their own expansive community, they try in this subtle way to turn the clock of history back to a pre-1947 setting, when everyone in the subcontinent—from the western Khyber hills to the eastern borders of Bengal—was known as an Indian. It is almost as if they are striving belatedly to rectify that unfortunate political mishap, the aberration that occurred on 14th August 1947.

Even Sardar Khushwant Singh, whose strong feelings for Pakistan have made him more enemies in India than friends in Pakistan, succumbs on occasions to this transparent condescension. When speaking in Lahore at the Manzur Qadir Memorial lecture in 1989, for instance, he made a taunting reference to Quaid-e-Azam Mohammed Ali Jinnah as having been the son of India before he became the father of Pakistan. He was technically quite correct, of course, Jinnah was the son of India. So was everyone else born in the continent before the 14th of August 1947. Had Jinnah been in the audience that evening, though, he might have been tempted to retort: "A son of India, no doubt, but a son mature enough to know when to leave home."

The divide between the two major communities of Hindus and Muslims in the subcontinent which led to the traumatic two-way exodus in the autumn of 1947 was not of Jinnah's sole making. That schism had already been taking place over the centuries following the gradual dissemination of Buddhism, Christianity, Islam and Sikhism. A genetic split occurred whenever any indigenous Hindu converted and declared his new faith. From that critical moment on, he stood apart from his blood-brothers and became at best a half-brother.

Jinnah recognised the volatile implications of such a division and the political opportunity they offered. He strove forcefully to supply Muslim aspirations with an identity, initially within the framework of a multicommunal society governed by the British, but when it became clear to him that they, after centuries of a policy of divide and rule, intended to rule only long enough to divide, he pressed his advantage until he had successfully negotiated a separate nationhood for Muslims.

The story of the events that led up to the formation of Pakistan is too complicated to be summarised in one essay. Its very complexity forces one to look for apt symbols which can somehow represent, within the limitation of such an abbreviation, the widening chasm which separated one community of Muslims from another community of Hindus until they became the nations of Pakistan and India, adjacent yet 'distant neighbours' as the Indian columnist Kuldip Nayar has described them.

Let one sample of the correspondence between Jinnah and Pandit Jawaharlal Nehru suffice as a telling example. In his book *Distant Neighbours* (1972), Kuldip Nayar mentions:

> In reply to Nehru's letter of 16 April 1938, saying that "the Muslim League is an important communal organisation ... but the other organisations, even though they might be younger and smaller, cannot be ignored," Jinnah said: "Your tone and language display the same arrogance and militant spirit, as if the Congress is the sovereign power(.) Unless the Congress recognises the Muslim League on a footing of complete equality and is prepared as such to negotiate for a Hindu-Muslim settlement, we shall have to wait and depend upon our inherent strength.

By forcing Congress to talk to him at a level of 'complete equality', Jinnah raised himself as the spokesman of his party to a position where he was now eye-level with his Congress opposites. Jinnah alone of all the leaders of the minority communities of India had the stature to do that. It was also the only way he could prevent himself being trodden under by the relentless hostility of the Congress leadership and being browbeaten by the undeniable partiality of the Viceroy Lord Mountbatten.

Historians of this period have been dazzled by the personality of Mountbatten. Few have been able to circumnavigate this remarkable all-rounder—this semi-royal, half-German naval officer, at ease with kings and at home with commoners, whose ambitions were like the oceans he loved, vast and bottomless, and who loved the sea almost as deeply as he loved himself. Who except for Mountbatten would have commented, when he heard of a young seaman having fallen overboard on H.M.S. *Warspite* and drowning: 'What an opportunity for anyone to earn an Albert Medal. Wish I'd been on deck.'

From the work of authors such as Philip Ziegler who wrote Mountbatten's official biography,[1] Mountbatten emerges as the singularly blessed person to whom Fortune never dared to say no. His many superiors in the Navy did not; Winston Churchill as his wartime Prime Minister did not; Clement Attlee when despatching him to India as the last Viceroy did not; and the rich heiress Edwina whom he wooed and whose wealth he pursued did not.

The only person to refuse him anything he coveted was Jinnah, and what Jinnah refused him was what Mountbatten saw as the final consummation of his viceroyalty. Mountbatten wanted to be a wonder of the modern world, the Colossus of India, a singular post-Independence Governor-General straddling both the new Dominions of India and of Pakistan.

It is ironical that it should have been Jinnah who first proposed such an idea to Mountbatten, in May 1947, later dropping it when he reconsidered it and found it constitutionally unworkable. Mountbatten, though having been approached by Nehru (whom he liked and his wife Edwina loved) to be India's first Governor-General, waited for Jinnah to make a similar offer on behalf of Pakistan. On 1 July, Jinnah called on the expectant Viceroy, and then 'suggested himself as G-G Pakistan.' Mountbatten was incensed. Jinnah, he reported back to London, is 'suffering from megalomania in its worst form.'

In an effort to make him change his mind, Mountbatten 'belaboured Jinnah with arguments and appeals and bluster', all of which, according to Chaudhri Muhammad Ali who witnessed the unseemly episode, Jinnah bore with 'great dignity and patience'. Angrily, Mountbatten queried Jinnah: ' "Do you realise what this will cost you?" He replied sadly, "It may cost me several crores of rupees in assets," to which I replied somewhat acidly, "It may well cost you the whole of your assets and the future of Pakistan." I then got up and left the room.'

Recovering his temper later, Mountbatten admitted to his daughter Patricia how he had 'finally and irretrievably "boobed"'. He had fallen into a pit of his own making: 'Either I accept to stay with the Dominion of India and be forever accused of taking sides ... or I let down the Congress leaders (.) Mummy feels I should preserve my reputation for impartiality and go on 15th August.'[2]

Mountbatten decided to remain and serve India. And when there was the inevitable argument over the allocation of assets between the two countries, it is significant that the person who finally coerced the new Indian Government into releasing fifty-five crores of rupees due to the Pakistan Government was not the ex-Viceroy, but Jinnah's adversary, Mahatma Gandhi, who undertook to fast until the money was paid over.

Mountbatten's espousal of the Indian cause was wholly beneficial for India. The damage his partisanship caused to the fledgling Pakistan was immeasurable. As he had predicted, his decision to remain in India as its constitutional head rendered all his actions—past, present and future—suspect to those like Jinnah who already had reservations about him and who had suffered his vainglorious prejudices. Working closely with Nehru, Mountbatten acted as an experienced pilot and guided him and his Congress government through many a storm in those turbulent first years of India's statehood. At a personal level, whenever he had the chance, he presented India in the right quarters and in the circles that matter, as he would later introduce his great-nephew Charles, Prince of Wales, in an avuncular supportive way.

Mountbatten treated India as a twenty-one year old with the mind and immaturity of a juvenile teenager. The Congress leaders viewed India more sentimentally as a beneficent cow, benign and placid bovine, which had been brutally vivisected to carve out a haunch of Pakistan.

Was India really vivisected, one might ask? Was it ever partitioned in the legal sense of the word? Look at the piebald map of the subcontinent as it was on 13 August 1947. India, bounded in the north by the Himalayan mountains and in the south-west by the Arabian Sea and the south-eastern Bay of Bengal, was in fact an assortment of territories owned or managed by Britain. It comprised those areas conquered or annexed by the British, those ceded or leased to them, and some tribal reserves. All of these were known collectively as British India.

Scattered between them like currants in a rich tea-cake were 567 Princely States, of varying size and questionable importance, which in 1947 were formally offered the option to join either India or Pakistan. Privately, Mountbatten advised the vacillating rulers to recognise 'geographical compulsions', and those who did not heed his advice, like landlocked Hyderabad, did so at their peril.

Apart from Kashmir, the final borders of both India and Pakistan followed in the main natural contours and boundaries, except in the case of the provinces of Bengal in the east and Punjab in the west, which became the only two provinces of British India to be partitioned as such.

The word Partition, whether legally correct or applicable, did however have an emotive effect on the minds of the Indians, for it caused them to regard the departing Pakistanis led by Jinnah not simply as former sons of India, not even as half-brothers who had agreed to disagree and decided to live apart (if possible amicably), but as errant prodigal sons who had to make it in time to return to the fold, to rejoin an Indian joint family system.

Are the present generations of post-1947 Indians and Pakistanis still 'same-to-same'? Is there any possibility, despite whatever has transpired during the intervening forty-five years, of a voluntary German-style reunification of the subcontinent? There are realists on both sides of the prickly border, who would consider this now impossible. The only occasion perhaps upon which the clock could have turned back—in 1971, when Pakistan was actually partitioned and its east wing stood available to India for re-integration into a larger Bengal—Mrs Gandhi decided against it. She cannily let sleeping Bengali provincialism lie. She needed the political capital accruing from a punitive military victory over Pakistan, and gained that. She did not need an addition to the already overcrowded Indian Bengal.

This is not to suggest that India has no further designs against what remains of the Pakistan Jinnah fought for, and Nehru and Gandhi fought against. Pakistan still represents an unresolved threat to India. It is in the eyes of many well-placed Indians a volatile, unpredictable and raucous neighbour who refuses to settle down for the night. The Indians think it is too noisy, it creates disturbances, it draws the unwelcome interference of outsiders in what are essentially domestic squabbles, and it has an irritating habit of picking fights which it loses. For any or all of these reasons, India may well try to discipline Pakistan again as it did in 1971, to dissect it into an even smaller and more manageable size.

Jinnah's earlier demand to have his Muslim League treated at par with Congress provided both a precedent and an excuse for the eyeball-to-eyeball confrontation which Pakistanis now regard as the proper height of contact between themselves and the Indians. India, being the bigger and taller of the two, naturally resents this assertion of equality by Pakistan as an impudent affront. Jinnah had been able to carry off this bluff because of his enormous political stature. Modern Pakistani governments though have managed to look the Indians in the eye, only when perched on the shoulders of friendly superpowers.

How secure has such a vantage point been for Pakistan? During the 1965 War, Pakistan invoked the defence pacts it thought it had with the United States and was given a polite brush-off. It should have known what to expect. Kuldip Nayar notes that in 1961, President Ayub Khan returned from a visit to Kennedy's White House 'convinced that now Nehru was Kennedy's favourite and that Washington would not 'alienate 360 million Indians in order to please 80 million Pakistanis''.

During the 1971 War, it interpreted (mistakenly) the sympathetic tilt in its direction by the Nixon administration as the prelude to an overt involvement by the Americans on its behalf. And today, if Pakistan looks to the post-Mao Chinese for help, it needs to remember the reaction of the Chinese dragon in 1971; it growled, it flicked its tail, but it did not bite. (The French writer and philosopher Andre Malraux once cautioned President Nixon before his historic trip to China: 'But China has never helped anyone! Not Pakistan. Not Vietnam. China's foreign policy is a brilliant lie! The Chinese themselves do not believe in it; they believe only in China. Only China!')[3].

Against such a stark backdrop, can Pakistan afford to be a continuously unfriendly neighbour? Should it take pride in being known as an international irritant? Does it have any stature of its own or if not, is it safe tottering on borrowed stilts? Is it strong enough, resilient enough, resourceful enough to resist a concerted attack by a larger nation? Can it stand up to a determined bully?

More important, perhaps, than Pakistan's own capability to defend itself, how long will it be before India decides to enforce an undisguised perception of itself as the Colossus of the South-Asian continent? Will it continue to persist in dominating its 'younger and smaller' neighbours, instead of acting as it can do the responsible elder half-brother?

In 1947, when introducing his plans for the creation of India and Pakistan at a press conference in Delhi, Mountbatten was asked whether he foresaw any continuity of relations between the two new dominions after their independence. He could see no reason why not. He cited the example of a Protestant northern and a Catholic southern Ireland. Both, he said, lived on amiable terms with each other. 'The world is really a sensible place once you get the anger out of it', he explained, 'and unless I have a completely wrong estimate of the Indian character, India will be sensible too.'

Thirty-two years later, on 27 August 1979, Mountbatten was blown up while sailing off the Irish coast by a bomb planted by the Irish Republican Army. The Irish proved him cruelly wrong. Mountbatten's birth centenary will be celebrated in the year 2000. Will his beloved Indians also have proven him wrong before then?

Notes

1. Ziegler, Philip. Mountbatten: *The Official Biography* London: 1985.
2. Ibid., pp. 396-398.
3. Richard Nixon, *The Memoirs of Richard Nixon*, New York, 1978, p.557.

ABU ABRAHAM

The Big and the Small

In May 1971, I visited the Refugee Camps in Tripura—it was an appalling experience. I could hear the shelling and destruction from across the Padma river. The scale of genocide was so great that I became a hawk and I wanted military intervention and was supported in this by both Jayaprakash Narayan and Khan Abdul Gaffar Khan who also wanted intervention.

The idealists were in fact the ones who wanted intervention; the pragmatists were not so sure and sat on the fence. Finally the idealists won the day and proved to be better pragmatists. It would have been cowardice on India's part not to have intervened.

The sheer horror of the events inspired me to draw so many cartoons. These first appeared in the Indian Express, and were subsequently published by Vikas.

Without being unduly modest, I should take some credit for the creation of Bangladesh, don't you think?

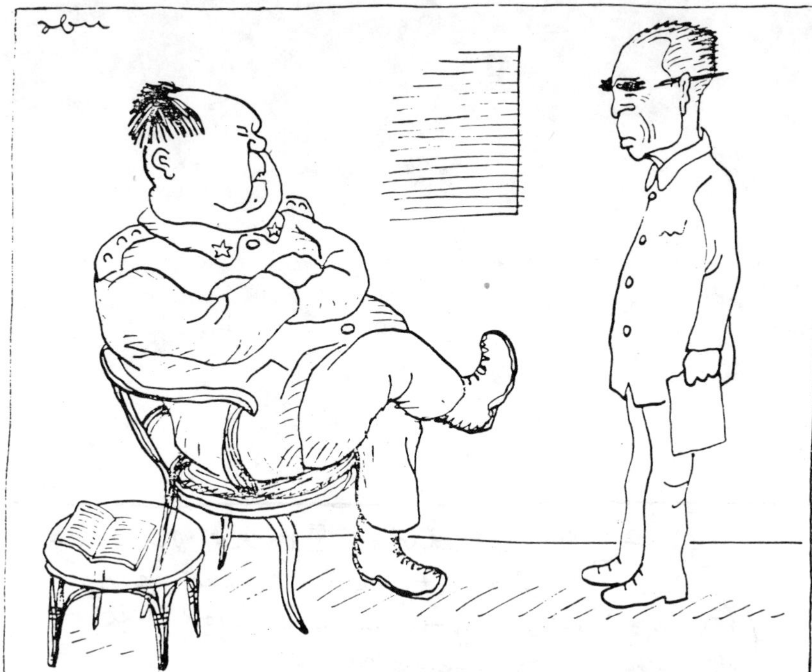

Do you have to ask me? If the social imperialists and the expansionists are for Mujib, we're against, that's all.

Take my advice, Ershad Old Boy -
Never put off till next year
what you can put off till
the year after
ELECTIONS
18.12.83

HOW COULD YOU SAY WE IN PAKISTAN HAVE BEEN TRAINING YOUR TERRORISTS? WHERE'S THE EVIDENCE?
I HAVE NO EVIDENCE- AT LEAST NO **HARD** EVIDENCE.
BUT ON THE OTHER HAND, HAS IT OCCURRED TO YOU THAT BY HOLDING ELECTIONS IN THE FACE OF TERRORISM...
...RIGHT ACROSS OUR BORDER, YOU'RE INCITING OUR PEOPLE...
...TO DEMOCRACY?

Kanjiwala, *water colour by Ajaz Anwar*

AJAZ ANWAR

Lahore and Delhi
Two Sides of a Mirror

Delhi appears in the literature and folklore of Lahore as if it were another extension. "Anwar brought this mirror from Delhi", my grandmother used to say. That was in Ludhiana and before I was born. Each time I see the Delhi gate of Lahore, it reminds me of my grandmother. And when I saw Lahori gate in Delhi Fort this year, she was already dead long ago. Cultural similarities are reflected with both the gates facing each other, and both people looking towards a new era of greater cooperation and friendship.

Lahore has its history of invaders who having captured, plundered and looted it, marched towards Delhi with fresh supplies. For this reason Sher Shah Suri had remarked "Such a city should not be located on the very route of an invader" and ordered it to be razed to the ground. But then, Sher Shah himself died in a gunpowder blast.

The debate as to how old Lahore is may continue, but with one starting point. For strategic and climatic reasons it was always located on the left bank of the Iravati, later the Ravi. This smallest of the five rivers of the Punjab formed, since pre-history, a natural defence barrier against invaders from the north. Its inhabitants built over it, and the subsequent rebuilding of houses provided debris for still higher plinths. A breeze from the north was further cooled and filtered as it passed over the river before hitting the multi-storeyed houses. Timber was abundantly used in balconies, roofs, windows, ventilators and huge doorways in a style reminiscent of Kashmir and Punjab. The alluvial clay and forest around the city provided good fire-burnt bricks. Sand in neat layers facilitated glazed tile and glass industries. Virtually no trees are found inside the old city because of its being built over debris; yet, the city was always surrounded by gardens.

Every city evolves its culture from the local climate and geology. Economic and historical factors only further facilitate the process. Lahore is at the junction of the mountain ranges of the north and the fertile plains of the Punjab, and the Sindh desert. While it is very hot from the middle of April to the end of September, dust storms and monsoons provide relief. The river swells to spread a thick layer of fertile clay and fills in the natural ponds.

Lahore was basically a market for agricultural produce. Artisans from different parts of South Asia settled here for patronage, resulting in a cosmopolitan culture. The indigenous people of Lahore mixed with the immigrating stock, enriching its language and traditions. This process was accelerated with the coming of the railways, when people from as far as Bengal, U.P. and from the Deccan began visiting more frequently. Many of them settled here, all under the same climate and geology. Excavations inside Lahore Fort indicate the sixth century B.C. for the earliest remains of settlement in Lahore, but it may be older. The present Lahore was relaid or rebuilt during the times of Mahmud Ghaznavi and hence, being over a thousand years old, it is on the World Heritage list of Unesco. This heritage is contributed to by the Hindus, Muslims, Sikhs, as well as the British. Lahore has continued growing since partition as the cultural capital of Pakistan. A cultural capital it always had been, second only to Delhi, of a vast region.

Lahore achieved its glory during Akbar's long sojourn here during 1584 to 1598. The city walls and the fort were rebuilt with a moat around it. Some buildings of the Fatehpur Sikri style in red sandstone date from this period, including the *Diwan-e-Aam*. The courtiers and officials too, built havelis inside the walled city during the emperors, prolonged stay. Akbar's *Fiil Khana* or elephant stables have now been usurped by squatters, but the size of the royal retinue can be well imagined.

On his way to Kashmir, Jahangir stayed in Lahore every year. Though there were many gardens in Lahore, he always camped in the Dilkusha gardens owned by Nur Jahan Begum where, according to his wish, he was finally buried. Lahore gained the status of a city for retired ladies of the royal harem who had to be kept away from Delhi lest they should play a part in the court intrigues. But the latter-day ladies were expert at pulling the strings. Hence developed the royal palaces of Naulakha and the royal necropolis of Baghbanpura. Delhi, with the Red Fort facing Jamia Masjid along the Jumna, inspired in Lahore the building of Badshahi Mosque facing Lahore Fort, along the river Ravi. Both these forts survive now as archaeological sites, bringing in tourists.

It must be said, Lahore always had two facets: it was influenced both by Imperial Delhi, and also locally influenced by the Punjab. The imperial influence was superfluous; the local or Punjab influence was and remains a reality. This is graphically illustrated in Moghul period monuments in Lahore. They appear to have been built in red sandstone and white marble; but they are not. The actual core of the structure is in brick, with only a cladding of stone given for the facade. These monuments look foreign to the local geology where no stone is to be found. The red and white facades do not blend with the local environment. But it is a reality that Delhi exercised influence over Lahore. Badshahi Mosque looks like a neat, clean model—artifically transplanted from Delhi.

This red and white colour scheme was imposed over Lahore by traditions set by Delhi, the imperial capital. Hence it did not survive after the weakening of the Moghuls in Lahore. In 1751 Bhikari Khan, one time governor of Lahore, built the Sonehri Masjid in bricks with stucco mouldings. The two mosques with the same name in Delhi and Lahore date from about the same period of 1722 and 1751.

With the Satluj forming a boundary between the Sikhs and the British, and each suspicious of the other, stone was no longer available in Lahore. Hence the Sikh monuments here do not have the red and white garb. The use of white plaster and stucco mouldings over brick arches and domes, and terracotta mouldings were a logical and local medium. Terracotta or burnt clay whether in brick form or perforated slab, is more porous and hence suitable to the hot climate. Incidentally this is also the material used in houses. Vaults, half domes and arches were also used in secular constructions, as distinct from the trabeate system. This system of construction has possibly been influenced by cross cultural links with Afghanistan and Persia.

A clearer clue can be provided by the date-palms lining and dotting the Grand Trunk road to Lahore and beyond. Dates were

Paan Mandi, *Anarkali, water colour by Ajaz Anwar*

the conserve food before the advent of the railways. Caravans brought in and carried out cultural influences. Uncertainty prevailing in Iran and western Anatolia may have brought some influence from the Seljuk lands; but Indian stone carving traditions are much older and indigenous.

More important perhaps are cultural commonalities in the secular life of these twin cities. Even though earlier Calcutta was the capital of British India, Delhi did not lose its cultural identity. Being administered from Lahore, Delhi developed a greater cultural link with that city; and the same was true for Lahore. The partition of Bengal, as first put forward by Lord Curzon, brought in a shift in the equilibrium. It transferred the capital to Delhi in 1911, with Peshawar becoming capital of the North-West Frontier Provinces. Yet the cultural connections remained independent of state control. There was an Association of Merchants of Delhi in Lahore (Anjuman-e-Tajiraan-e-Delhi). Lahore had the largest number of educational institutes, newspapers and publishing houses. All this facilitated the vibrant culture that was capable of assimilating modern-day techniques of survival. Here, away from the centre, yet in the heart of the cultural capital, political movements were launched in mammoth meetings.

To a distant traveller, the skyline of an approaching city is the first signal. Delhi and Lahore, both being walled cities built over high topography, have multi-storeyed houses with towering churches, temples and minarets projecting into the skyline as symbols of human presence and tolerance. But the fauve-coloured paper kites, white pigeons fluttering over high bamboo stands and the colourful laundry spread over the parapets constitute the living culture. Down below in the narrow streets vendors selling seasonal vegetables and fruits or local cookies are live actors in the large theatre of human life.

The walled city is a monument by itself, having a tightly-knit atmosphere constituted by the multi-storeyed houses built over smaller areas, the monotony of which is so frequently broken by large havelis belonging to old families; virtually no trees exist there, the lanes are narrow and sometimes only five feet wide and present a more complicated *cul-de-sac* and flow into wider streets which terminate into open areas with some sort of specialised market. The city is located over mild slopes formed by its own debris shed during the course of centuries. Originally it had twelve gates, many being named after the cities towards which they opened. The planning seems to conform to the recommendations for a city laid down in the ancient *Artha Shastras.* This most picturesque part of Lahore is unfortunately missed by most visitors and the city lords.

The old city as always is thronged with children, old men and women. Equally it is shared by buffaloes, horses, oxen and sacrificial goats, occasional camels, and encaged birds singing musically coded messages to the ones in the trees. The large zoo housing a fine collection is supplemented by snake charmers with big serpents and the tiniest of snakes, and the jugglers with monkeys and bears and trained goats—chased from locality to locality by piedogs who seem to have divided the city amongst themselves. Musical gangs hurry to the house into which a son has just been born, and the hawkers with fauve-paper toys and balloons and musical instruments entice the children and provoke the parents; while a youth listens attentively to a palmist who is more concerned about his own fortune—all these are a common sight. The goods displayed and dumped outside the shops attract the most reluctant of customers. The sweetmeat shops are nicely displayed with silver leaves, but watch out for a sudden sprinkling of water—they are more concerned about settling the dust and cooling the air rather than your clothes. This is Lahore.

Lahore is best seen by the pedestrians. Each street, each corner, each turn offers surprises in art, architecture, in decoration and crafts. Many cottage industries provide an opportunity to see the artefacts being styled on the spot. The artisans work laboriously, and yet can always give time to the inquisitive visitors, proudly pose for them, and even help them to the rooftops to get some of the most prized snaps. It is possible to go around the whole city along the circular road, entering from one gate, and leave by the other. The most inspiring point to start from would be through Delhi gate. The spectacular view of the streets in vivid colours and textures is really rewarding. After going through the grain market with its thousands of pigeons, one enters the cloth market where all sorts of hand-woven clothes and embroidered silks can be had.

Muslim Masjid, *water colour by Ajaz Anwar*

The shimmering minarets of the Wazir Khan Mosque with the world-famous tile mosaics depicting floral patterns are of course an important landmark that guide travellers through all those lanes. The street ends into an open area with three huge, bulbous, ribbed, gilt domes of the Sonehri Mosque. Behind these are more narrow lanes having numerous shops where some of the most interesting copper and brass utensils can be seen with the workmen etching and hammering detailed motifs on them.

The adjoining streets accommodate jewellers and goldsmiths; another winding lane terminates into a view of the colossal walls of the Fort and the largest mosque in the world, the Badshahi Mosque. A ticket to one of its minarets pays to get a panoramic view of the entire city tinted green by the trees through which roofs, minarets and domes project out, giving an unbelievable skyline. Here one can see the neighbouring Minar-i-Pakistan, and to further north is the Arcadia of Lahore where the Ravi is seen with boats and the picnicking parties and the lone angler; and still further are the four white marble minarets of the tomb of the Emperor Jahangir standing amidst countless date-palms.

Lahore offers such variety that a tourist, businessman or a scholar would all find ample places of interest. Once visited on the flying-carpets, it now forms the largest carpet centre in the world. Yet it is a city of museums and educational institutes. At the end of the Mall are located the offices of the Mayor, the Punjab University, the Museum housing some most important heritages in the history of art. Next is the 120 years old National College of Arts which endeavours to preserve the ancient skills of the region and produces artists of the twentieth century. A giant gun, two hundred years old has been placed in the chowk in front. Equally impressive is the Tollinton Market, the venue of the internationally acclaimed Punjab Industrial Exhibition of 1864, and later the first museum in Lahore.

Local fairs are the venue where the most spectacular and hair-raising feats are ventured. The only serious people at the carnivals are the volunteers of the lost-and-found camps where the children and the old are reunited with their kin, to be lost again. The exhausted people return with souvenirs like wheel-turned pottery, balloons, toys and musical instruments for the children to rehearse more of it in their neighbourhood. Bosch or Bruegel would feel no strangers; but the pickpockets are also vigilant on these occasions.

Haveli Mian Khan, *water colour by Ajaz Anwar*

INTERVIEW

Issues and Censorship in Indian Cinema

SHYAM BENEGAL
In conversation with Geeti Sen

Geeti Sen: *Mr Benegal, your involvement with films goes back at least twenty-five years. The films directed by you have a wide range, but several of them have focused on the question of nationalism or addressed themselves to issues about identity. Our interview today is really about this question of identity: what it means to be an Indian, and yet have relations across the border; and what it means to be a Muslim or Hindu in this country, and elsewhere. I would like to begin with your film* Mammo, *which is an endearing study of an old woman who comes back from Pakistan to visit her sister in India. Is this based on a true story?*

Shyam Benegal: Yes, it is based on a true story, although fictionalised in its treatment. Khalid Mohammad had written up a little piece about his grand aunt in the Sunday edition of the Times of India, under a section called "the Personal Eye." I was very moved by the piece and asked him whether he would like to do a screenplay—because I was keen to make a film based on it.

GS: *Khalid Mohammad is renowned as one of our eminent film critics—I didn't realise he was a script writer!*

SB: The original screenplay was by him. Later, Shama Zaidi and Javed Siddique made further inputs. The film was set in Bombay, where the incidents took place.

His grand aunt, who used to live in Pakistan, came to live with her sister in India, after her husband's death. Her sister was her only next of kin. She had a temporary visa, and had to go back. The only way she could continue to live in India was to lose her passport—to become stateless, and melt into the multitudes of India.

GS: *I recall that very vivid scene of a whole trainload of people being shunted back to Pakistan! The pivotal point of this story seems to be that the old aunt comes back, she wants to live in India and tries by various means such as a doctor's certificate. But finally nothing works, and she goes back. Was that the main issue that you were addressing—the need for improvement of human relations between the two countries?*

SB: That is one of the issues I was addressing; but another issue emerged since the story hadn't really ended there! The piece that was written by Khalid ended there; but in reality she did return once again, and some means had to be found to make her stay here. And they resolved it in a fashion—the way it was solved in the film was by getting her a death certificate. And getting that death certificate meant that she became invisible— a non person. This way she could stay because there was no record of her anywhere. Now, this is really a big problem because it happens to a lot of people—whether in India or Pakistan or Bangladesh: you have people who suddenly become non-persons. To me the irony is that she is accepted only when she becomes invisible.

GS: *She is not invisible at all, she is absolutely vibrantly alive in the film! I thought the part was played very well by Farida, as also the role of the elder sister by Surekha Sikri.*

SB: That was the point being made in the film! We can accept people as dead, but cannot accept them as living. The real tragedy is the manner in which relations between our neighbours and ourselves have deteriorated over the years.

GS: *Shyam, I am curious whether you have faced any flak from the censor board about this film. Since you have been in-*

volved in censorship yourself, I am curious how they dealt with this story. Censorship in India is usually on problems of eroticism. Does censorship address itself to these delicate questions of identity?

SB: Actually, no. I had no problems with the Indian censors as far as this film was concerned. My problem with censorship is that it does not work. The guidelines have not been effective in creating an intelligent system.

GS: *Would you go so far as to say that censorship should be thrown out?*

SB: Frankly, I think so , because in a democracy it has no place. What is more, film censorship is pre-censorship which is even worse.

GS: *We have an audience that is really quite open to all issues. I believe that sensuality and eroticism is something that we live with in India. Would you agree?*

SB: It is such a minor issue. We make so much of eroticism, we make so much of pornography as though this is something that is predominant in the audience's minds. I don't believe this to be true at all. We are the same kind of people as most people all over the world. There is a certain amount of interest in pornography and eroticism, but it does not mean that it has overtaken our lives. I don't understand at all why the censor board should concern itself with trivialities of this kind.

Veena Das has made a very interesting statement about the way the censors have territorialised the human body; certain parts can be shown, and other parts cannot. This is a very warped kind of thinking that takes over when you apply guidelines in a literal way. Funnily enough, our censor board is not so strict on political issues, nor is it terribly concerned about social attitudes, superstitions or even violence. The board is predominantly concerned with sex. I have never understood this.

GS: *The censorship board has changed its attitudes on marriage alliances. The fact is that in the early films of the '50s and '60s, you could never really have a marriage alliance sanctified between a Muslim and a Hindu. Something like this was absolutely taboo, and therefore all the more delicious because it was forbidden—but it could never be sanctioned by society. Has that changed in say, Mani Ratnam's film on* Bombay?

SB: Well obviously a lot of things have changed. The world has changed too, if you look at Hollywood films... The only reason I take the example of Hollywood is because the United States and India are the only two countries in the world producing films in such large numbers—and essentially for a mass audience. There was an unwritten code in American film-making, particularly in the '30s and '40s. If you compare American films of the '30s with the Indian films of the '50s or '60s, you will find that they are very similar in their attitude to sex. Now of course, the social attitudes of urban people to sex has changed all over the world. All that does get reflected to some extent is the manner in which the censor board operates. For instance you can have young couples very much in love with each other kissing on the Indian screen today. This wasn't allowed earlier, but the odd part is that these films automatically get an adult rating.

GS: *What about the censorship on* Bandit Queen *by Shekhar Kapoor? How did you feel about the tremendous controversy this provoked? It is a film which people either like or dislike—there are no two ways about it.*

SB: Well, one of the interesting things about *Bandit Queen* is that the censors didn't cut too much of the film. They cut some parts of the film, particularly the rape scene, which was snipped off a little here and there. But there was one scene that entirely escaped their attention.... when Phoolan beats up her husband. This went on and on... Even for an audience hardened to film violence the sadistic nature of the scene was enough to brutalise any kind of audience. I think a little bit of cutting that down would not have harmed the film. But I feel the Director himself should have done that. Where the censors really went to town was the love scene in the Kanpur Hotel. I was told it was really hacked. I have only heard about this since I haven't seen the film after it was cut.

GS: *So you think that the censor board did a sensible thing?*

SB: Overall, it was the tribunal and not the Censor Board which dealt intelligently with the film.

GS: *The question of Phoolan Devi as a woman brings up an ancillary question in my mind, about how films have changed. You will find many more films today focus on the anti-hero—beginning with* Sholay *which was made quite some 20 years ago. This has been a growing trend in that heroes and villains are no longer rendered black and white. In films such as* Is Raat Ki Subha Nahin *there is sympathy now for the anti-hero. Do you think that this affects the social mores of the audience?*

SB: It isn't quite like that. If you look at the Indian film industry, you will find that one of the interesting things that has happened on a popular level is that the mainstream Indian film does reflect the attitudes of the cinema audiences. If you take the film heroes of Indian cinema of the 1950s or early '60s, you will find that they were driven by ideology, their moral attitudes were all very correct and they were very virtuous. In many ways this represented the idealism of a young nation. Raj Kapoor's films for instance, like *Shri 420, Awara* and so on, projected heroes who were essentially honest people who meant to do good. That whole pattern has changed because, a great deal of cynicism has seeped into urban society—particularly when things didn't seem to work as well as they should or at least as far as expectations were concerned—this got reflected in films.

GS: *A very powerful film like* Ardh Satya *for example, shows the vulnerability of the police and criminalisation.*

SB: Then you have the angry young man of the early '70s, best represented by Amitabh Bachchan. Now that kind of character did not mind using any means to achieve the right ends. There is a further change from that position in the '90s. At first there was a stress on the right means to achieve just ends. By the 1970's this had changed to any means as long as the ends could be justified. Today, it appears that you can use any means to achieve your personal ends.

GS: *In a sense you are saying that acting today is a reflection of how people are actually thinking. Do you think it is the role of the film director or the film script writer to change attitudes in films? Or should they reflect attitudes as they exist? Are we dealing with realism here, or can we deal with other dimensions? For instance a film like* Khamoshi *is such a beautiful, light, wonderful film—but it does engender tremendous sympathy for Christians, for the deaf and dumb—it does something.*

SB: It would be presumptuous on the part of a film maker to imagine that he can change the world, or change attitudes. What he can do, what he does do, is to make films where his own attitudes get expressed... not always directly. His/her own sensibility comes into it, and all these things tend to leave some kind of impression.

GS: Khamoshi *is a musical film, set in Goa—like your film* Trikaal. *Both engender a kind of nostalgia. I feel there is place for this now.*

SB: *Trikaal* really dealt with a certain kind of a world; of a culture that developed differently from the rest of India for the last five hundred years. This is obviously changing now.

GS: *Shyam, I believe that art is a reflection of social mores! All your earlier films such as* Nishant *and* Mandi *are about changing values, about society in transition—which of-course is the most fascinating aspect about India.* Trikaal *is about that particular juncture of time when there is a change in governance which will necessarily change the whole culture and sensibility—beautifully personified in the old lady played by Leela Naidu.*

Earlier we had talked about films that are steeped in ideology, films that are about the early patriotism. Isn't it strange that there are no films that are dealing with this today? It is something that we do not even discuss or consider. Would you have any comments on this?

Just take for instance, the lampooning in the film English August—*which is really a lampooning of the whole bureaucracy, really a question of "us" and "them."*

SB: I think, we have yet to rid ourselves totally from our colonial past. Even today we call the government, 'Sarkar' in Hindi. It is a hierarchical relationship between us and the government which sets the tone, and defines the relationship. That definition has not changed from the time we were a colony, and now 50 years after independence we still have the same kind of an attitude towards people who occupy positions in the government.

GS: *The whole structure of society was perhaps more nebulous, and there was not this kind of division into Hindu, Muslim, Parsi, Christian. Do you think that this is a leftover of the colonial mind?*

SB: I am not too sure.... I think we have always been identified by caste and religion. Among Hindus, we have always had brahmins, baniyas, land-owning communities, farming communities; people identified by the work they did or were forced to do-menial chores so on. Our communities were always classified in a hierarchical way, quite separate one from the other—although we all lived together. We always knew, despite the vertical hierarchies of the Indian system, that we would never overstep these social arrangements. Overstepping these social arrangements started to cause all sorts of problems.

When I was a child in Nizam's Hyderabad, we used to live in an area where there were almost an equal number of Muslim families; and there never was any kind of problem of living together. If there was a Hindu festival being celebrated in our home, it wasn't as though we didn't invite our Muslim friends—they all came and partook of everything. But having done that, we also did something else when the guests left; the plates from which the Muslims ate were separately washed. Similarly, we always participated in Id dinners, and never had any kind of problems. These were very intricate social arrangements that Indian society formulated for itself—so that it functioned as a totality. I do not agree with it, nor am I am apologist for it. What we need to develop are now social arrangements that will replace these social hierarchies which persisted through the colonial period.

GS: *I wonder if I could go back to* Mammo, *and ask about the reaction to your film in India.*

SB: The film didn't have too much of a cinema release in India; but it did reach a large number of people through television. The general response to it was good. A lot of people were moved by the film. Many were concerned about the predicament of people like *Mammo.* It did bring into focus problems of borders, and how they affect the lives of people where families have been separated arbitrarily—when movement between the countries (India and Pakistan) became increasingly difficult.

GS: *Now if one were to compare* Mammo *to* Garam Hawa, *made much earlier and set in the aftermath of the Partition, the earlier film is much more nostalgic. In yours, there is a perceptible shift in perspective.*

SB: *Garam Hawa* dealt with an issue that was very specific for a particular time. It dealt with the choice that the Muslim community had to make since a nation was carved out in the name of Islam. It dealt with those problems on a very human level. Today, you accept the fact that the subcontinent is broken up into three different nations, and that is a fact of life. Pakistan, Bangladesh and India are realities.

People of these three different parts in many ways share a common past. This incredibly rich heritage that we all possess in the subcontinent belongs to all three of us; and to reject this heritage is tragic.

GS: *And was the film* Mammo *shown in Pakistan?*

SB: Well, it was shown on Indian television and obviously a lot of people must have seen it in Pakistan and Bangladesh. I do believe that there were cassettes in circulation in Pakistan, I wouldn't really know. I did visit Lahore but it was before I made this film.

GS: *Was the visit to Lahore an exploratory trip for you?*

SB: My wife was born in Lahore and her mother's family was from Lahore, and they lived on a street named after her grandfather. So for her, going back was an emotional thing. It was my first visit to Pakistan. I enjoyed being there. People were warm and welcoming. It was like meeting long lost friends. It is obvious that we can live with each other cordially.

GS: *Yes, this is the amazing dichotomy that exists. On one level the political concord/discord continues, and on the other, there is a question of cordial relationships and human bonds.*

I also wanted to ask you about films that you may have

seen from Pakistan. Do they address the same issues? We know that the theatre is outstanding.

SB: I am not very familiar with films made in Pakistan. I have seen a few films, but they really have been made by expatriates like Jameel Dehlvi. But I haven't seen what one might call popular films made in Pakistan, because they hardly ever come here.

GS: *Shyam, I think you might have something to say about the demolition of Babri Masjid. The fact is that apart from the excellent documentary made by Anand Patwardhan (which stops before the demolition) and the film made by Saeed Mirza (a very lyrical and gentle protest), very little has been done.*

SB: I was absolutely shattered. I never believed that we Indians were capable of something like that. These things have happened before in History. Temples have been destroyed, so have mosques at other times. But for a mosque to be destroyed as a clearly well-thought-out political action—something like that had never happened. And therefore the experience, when it happened, was one of utter shock.

GS: *You were living in Bombay, so you felt the aftermath of it...*

SB: I was in Tokyo at the time. However, when I reached Bombay, a couple of days later, the road from this airport was littered with stoves, burnt vehicles, groups of people hurling rocks at one another, and the car in which I was running a gauntlet through them.

I am still very confused about how and why something like this could have happened. We have always taken our secularism for granted, and I think this shook us out of that complacency. I tend to agree with Akeel Bilgrami who has said somewhere that secularism is something that needs to be constantly negotiated—it is not something that automatically exists.

GS: *I would now like to discuss your major epic film,* The Making of the Mahatma. *Inevitably, people have compared this to the other film on the Mahatma by Richard Attenborough, and commented that in a sense this is a "non-patriotic film"—after everything that Shyam Benegal has done! I see it differently. I see that it is important to realise that this man was not a Mahatma; he was a man initially, and it is the vulnerability of the man that is brought out. Would you have any comments?*

SB: First of all the vulnerability of Gandhi was the vulnerability of a human being. The film was really about him evolving into a Mahatma. A man of extra ordinary will and commitment and also utter selflessness.

GS: *And utter selfishness?*

SB: Well obviously, because both of them are two sides of the same coin. A man of tremendous commitment and compassion, and with the will to carry it out. Now these qualities which were in him—are also somewhere in every human being. And there were contradictions too. Here was a man of conscience, a very high moral sensibility combined with a deep sense of commitment. When you put these things together, you have a personality who at times seems terribly self righteous—it is not always easy to deal with him. His eldest son had great difficulty in dealing with him. But Gandhi was extraordinary in a way that is different for a lot of us to understand. He was fair to the point of seeming insensitive. He would inflict on himself the sins of others. Taking over somebody else's burden, as it were, is an aspect that makes him seem even more self-righteous. These are some of the qualities that I was very interested in exploring.

GS: *Did you get any insights into Gandhi by visiting Africa?*

SB: Absolutely. The impact of South Africa on him was the first thing that stuck me. Without his South African experience, Gandhi would never have become the Mahatma. The late nineteenth and early twentieth century is an interesting period for India. The Indians who went to study in England came back with ideas of liberal democracy, nationalism—all European ideas, really.

GS: *Gandhi was also there influenced deeply by the Vegetarian Society in London. I mean he started his writings actually by writing for them...*

SB: ... He returns to his own country which is very much a colony—but he is not affected by this as deeply as when he goes to South Africa. Here he experiences the naked force of colonial imperialism. This was what struck me when I went to South Africa soon after the release of Nelson Mandela when apartheid was being dismantled but the effects of it were still evident.

GS: *Were you already interested in making this film when you went there and was this a commissioned film?*

SB: I went primarily to explore the possibility of shooting the film there. The decision to make the film was taken earlier. Prof. Fatima Meer was here in India to participate in the Indira Gandhi International Seminar when she gave me her books, *Apprenticeship of a Mahatma* and the biography of Nelson Mandela that she had written. She wanted to know if I would be interested in making a film based on either of the books. After having read both, I was very excited by the book on Gandhi, mainly because it dealt with a period of Gandhi's life that very few people in India knew anything about. He had lived twenty one years of his life there—I was sure I wanted to make a film based on the book. Fatima and I eventually succeeded in getting the funds together for the film. The Government of India put in two-thirds of the budget, the remaining part coming from South Africa.

GS: *The one weakness in this film which I see is that you don't have moments which show him at any point lacking confidence, or lacking courage. You know, he had a great fear of violence which comes through in books such as* The Good Boatman. *You also see this vulnerability in Gandhiji's own writings, written in the manner of a confessional. But in your film, he is a heroic figure all the way through!*

SB: I don't necessarily think that is true. You see, Gandhi did have an introspective quality—but his own anguish he kept completely hidden. I read many of the letters and petitions he wrote, in the Archives at Pretoria and in Durban. You don't ever get to see his personal anguish. He wrote a lot about his personal life with great honesty but with considerable detachment. Interesting sources for me were written accounts by people who knew him then. Henry Pollack's wife's account of her life in Phoenix. Although her account is coloured by her own eventual dislike of the life in the Phoenix settlement, it does give some insights into Gandhi of that time.

GS: *My concluding statement about this film returns to what I said earlier. We are looking at the Mahatma and you have fleshed him out; he is not a cardboard figure. But ultimately is your concern in this film with that old fashioned term, moral upliftment?*

SB: The film I think, *is* morally uplifting in many ways—although I didn't choose to make it that way. It is Gandhi himself who makes it so. Many people have responded to the film in the way you mention. But if you say it is not a patriotic film, I don't understand what you mean. Here is Gandhi, the Father of our Nation; the holiest of icons of independent India. That is already there. I am really interested in seeing him as a human being to see whether we can connect with him or not.

GS: *Before he became an icon?*

SB: If we cannot or could not connect with him, is it possible that he would have had this country following him? It was Gandhi, the human being that the masses of India made a connection with..

GS: *What films are you planning now, Shyam Babu?*

SB: I am planning to make a film called *Zubeida. Zubeida* is also written by Khalid Mohammad. In a sense it is the last part of the triology; *Mammo, Sardari Begum* and *Zubeida.* In all three, the central figure is a woman. This is also a very personal kind of film, as were *Sardari Begum*, and *Mammo.*

GS: *And all three are about the Muslim community, if you want to call it a separate community—or is it about the meshing and interaction of communities?*

SB: Yes it is really about us.

To me one of the more important things is to recognize that all of us have *several* identities: there are larger and smaller identities, there are general and specific identities.

I do not think of muslims as the 'other'. To me 'us' represents the Muslim, the Hindu, the Christian, the Parsi and all other communities of India. That to me is the definition of 'us'. To me this all inclusive definition is a necessary part of being an Indian. It is the qualities in human beings that either bring you closer to one another or even distance you from each other. What has religion got to do with it?

INTIZAR HUSAIN is one of the subcontinent's finest Urdu writers. Born in Dibai near Bulandsahar in Uttar Pradesh, he spent his early childhood and did his schooling in Hapur and his college education at Meerut. After the Partition of 1947, he migrated to Lahore in Pakistan where he continues to live and write. He has published three novels, several travelogues and literary essays and a number of short stories.

NIRMAL SEN GUPTA, a former officer of the British Indian Army, was posted to Karachi soon after Independence where he was assigned to the newly established Indian High Commission. Between 1947 and 1950 he was the administrator in the Food Department attached to the High Commission. He now lives in Calcutta and Narendrapur, devoting much of his time to informal education for children in the villages around Narendrapur.

ZOHRA SEGAL, born in Sahranpur, Uttar Pradesh, completed her college from Lahore in 1929. Between 1930 and 1935 she went to Dresden, Germany, to study modern dance, and on her return to India, joined the Uday Shankar Dance Company where she met her husband. In 1945 she made her big move into acting by joining Prithvi Theatres, where she was the leading lady till 1949. Subsequently she went to the UK where she did a stint at the Old Vic, the British Drama League and made a number of BBC films. Among her many awards are the Sangeet Natak Akademi Award in 1967 and the Norman Beaton Award for her significant contribution to multicultural film and television drama in the UK.

PRAKASH TANDON, educated at the Universities of Punjab, Manchester and Harvard, has served in the multinational and public enterprises. He has also been associated with academic institutions in management and technology, and has served both as a teacher and on the governing bodies of these institutions. He has written a number of books on social history, management and banking. Among his publications are notably, *The Punjabi Saga* and *History of Banking*.

N.N. VOHRA. After a two year tenure as Lecturer at Punjab University, Mr Vohra joined the IAS in 1959. He was assigned to the Punjab Cadre which he served in various capacities for over two decades. Before retiring from the IAS in 1994, he held tenure as Secretary Defence Production, Defence Secretary and Home Secretary at the Centre.

KRISHNA SOBTI was born in Gujarat in West Punjab and educated at Lahore. After partition she lived with her family in Shimla and Delhi. She has so far published seven novels, many short stories, and a collection of essays. Her novel *Zindaginama* won the Sahitya Akademi Award in 1980. A sequel to this is planned and to be published.

ALOK BHALLA teaches at the Central Institute of English and Foreign Languages, Hyderabad. Educated at St. Stephen's College in Delhi, and Kent State University in Ohio, USA, he has also been a Fellow at the Institute of Advanced Study in Shimla, and at the Rockefeller Centre in Bellagio, Italy. Alok Bhalla is a critic and translator, and is Editor of the Journal *Yatra: Writings from the Indian Subcontinent.* Currently, he is working on a book about novels of the partition era.

SUKRITA PAUL KUMAR teaches English Literature at the University of Delhi. Formerly a Fellow at the Indian Institute of Advanced Study, Shimla, she has published two collections of poems entitled *Oscillations* and *Aparna.* Her other publications include *Conversations on Modernism, The New Story Breakthrough, and Man, Woman and Androgyny.*

SUBHAS MUKHOPADHYAY joined the Communist Party of India and worked as a journalist until 1948. During this period, he was active in trade union work. He was a member of the executive board of the Sahitya Akademi and edited a literary monthly, *Parichay* and a children's magazine, *Sandosh*. His publications include several books of poems, letters and essays. He received the Sahitya Akademi Award for *Jatao Durel Jai*, a collection of poems.

KABIR CHOWDHURY is a well-known essayist, critic and translator. He was educated at the Universities of Dhaka, Minnesota and Southern California, and is currently professor of English Literature at Dhaka University. Previously he has been head of the Bengali Academy of Bangladesh, and has served as Education Secretary in the Government. He is the author of over hundred books, and recipient of several national and international awards. Among his forthcoming publications are a book in Bengali on Picasso, and a Bengali translation of the works of German playwright Heiner Muller.

SHAMSUR RAHMAN is today one of Bangladesh's most widely read poets. He has published over 30 volumes of poetry, received many awards, and been honoured at home and abroad by institutes, universities and various cultural bodies.

SYED SHAMSUL HAQ is a poet, essayist, novelist, playwright and short story writer. Since 1954, he has published 16 volumes of poetry, 11 plays, 8 novels, 37 novellas, 5 collection of short stories, and 2 books of essays and impressions. A major voice in Bangladesh, he was conferred the *Ekishay Padak*, the country's highest national award.

KISHWAR NAHEED is a prominent Pakistani feminist, and has been for several years the editor of a prestigious monthly *Maah-i-Naau*. A prolific poet and writer, her works include *Lips that Speak, Unnamed Journey, The Colour Pink*, and *A Black Border*. Her work *Women twixt Dreams and Dust* deals with women's issues in Pakistan.

FAHIM AZMI is a retired Wing Commander of the Pakistani Air Force. He is well known as a novelist, short story writer and poet; in particular for his experimental work in Urdu fiction. His best known published work is *Janam Kundali.*

RAKSHAT PURI has been a journalist by profession and a poet by vocation since the early 1950s. He covered the China-India border hostilities of 1962-63, the Vietnam War, and the Indonesia-Malaysia confrontation upto 1968. He was a newspaper correspondent based in London from 1978 through 1987. As a writer, his work has been published both in Indian and foreign journals including the *Sahitya Akademi Indian Literature, The Delhi-London Poetry Quarterly, Orbis* and *New Poetry from Oxford.* His published works include *Love is His Own Power, The Slokas of Baba Farid, the Hallucination of Words, and Blossoms of the Apricot.*

MUCHKUND DUBEY is at present President of the Council for Social Development in New Delhi and Chairman of the Asian Development Research Institute in Patna. He is also Professor of South Asian Studies in the School of International Relations at the Jawaharlal Nehru University. Before retiring as Foreign Secretary in the Ministry of External Affairs in 1991, Professor Dubey served *inter alia* as India's High Commissioner to Bangladesh, and as its Permanent Representative to the United Nations in Geneva.

SUMANTA BANERJEE Born and educated in Calcutta, Sumanta Banerjee was formerly with *The Statesman* in Calcutta and Delhi, and is now a freelance journalist based in Delhi. He is also associated with the Indian Council of Historical Research as a Senior Research Fellow. He is the author of *India's Simmering Revolution (1984)*, and *The Parlour and the Street—Elite and Popular Culture in 19th Century Calcutta* (1989).

NABANEETA DEV SEN is a leading poet, fiction writer and travel writer in Bengali. Educated in Calcutta, Cambridge, Harvard, Indiana and Berkeley, she is Professor of Comparative Literature at Jadavpur University, Calcutta.

BINDU CHAWLA has written extensively on Hindustani music for a number of Indian newspapers and journals including the Hindustan Times and presented talks on AIR. Daughter of Pandit Amarnath, the great maestro of the Indore Gharana, she studied and practiced Hindustani music for over two decades. She is the recipient of the 1995 Times of India Fellowship Award for her project 'The Musical Idea in Hindustani Music.'

AMEENA AHMAD AHUJA combines a varied educational background in Urdu, Persian and Russian literary classics. She has a doctorate in philology and art. She takes a line or a passage of memorized poetry and transmutes the inner sound, the meaning and spirit of the text into a calligraphic design. Through her art form she is able to vivify the works of poets such as Ghalib, Mir Taqi Mir, Zouk, Firdausi, Rumi, Atbar and Iqbal.

ENAMUL HAQUE was educated at Dhaka, London and Oxford and is currently working as Professor of National Culture and Heritage in the Independent University of Bangladesh. He was the founder Director-General of the Bangladesh National Museum. Previously he taught art history at Dhaka University, and at the Bangladesh University of Engineering and Techology.

His notable publications include *Treasures in the Dacca Museum (1963) Nawab Bahadur Abdul Latif: His Writings and Related Documents* (1968) *Islamic Art Heritage of Bangladesh* (1985) and *Bengal Sculptures: Hindu Iconography upto 1250 AD* (1992)

KAZI KHALEED ASHRAF is at the doctoral programme in architecture at the University of Pennsylvania following his master's degree from the Massachuetts Institute of Technology. He has worked as an architect, taught at New York's Pratt Institute, and has written for International journals. His recent work incudes the essay for the the GA (Global Architecture) monograph on Louis Kahn's National Capital Complex.

JAMES BELLUARDO practices architecture in New York city after graduating from Harvard University's Graduate School of Design. He has travelled extensively in South Asia including India, Bangladesh, Sri Lanka and Pakistan, and has taught at the Architecture School, New Delhi. His special area of research has been the work of the Sri Lankan architect Geoffrey Bawa.

RANABIR SAMADDAR is a Senior Fellow in South Asian Studies at Calcutta University where he is currently working on a study of nationalism in Bangladesh. He is also author of a book on Asian nationalism titled *Whose Asia is it Anyway? Region and the Nation in South Asia.*

SALIMA HASHMI is the Principal of the National College of Arts in Lahore.

MEGHNA GUHATHAKURTA is Associate Professor at Dhaka University. Her field of interest lies in international development, including South Asian development and gender studies. She has translated many works in these areas from Bengali to English, and has written herself extensively on these subjects.

MADEEHA GAUHAR, is an actress and theatre director who studied at Lahore and at London University from where she has a Master of Arts. She is the founder of *Ajoka,* a theatre group committed to socially meaningful theatre, which pioneered the alternative theatre movement in Pakistan. Madeeha has also conducted theatre workshops for theatre activists and women's groups in various parts of Pakistan. She is currently representing Pakistan on the South Asian Committee. She is married to playwright Shahid Nadeem.

F.S. AIJAZUDDIN was educated in Lahore and England. He is a Chartered Accountant by qualification, an art historian by reputation, and a writer by inclination. His published works have included a catalogue of the Pahari and Sikh miniature paintings in the Lahore Fort Collection. He is currently the Honorary Consul for the United Kingdom in Lahore, and the Managing Director of the first International Investment Bank Ltd.

ABU ABRAHAM is a well-known political cartoonist and writer who now lives and works in his home-town, Trivandrum. He started his career as a journalist with the *Weekly* in New Delhi, before joining the *Observer* in England as its staff cartoonist in 1955. Subsequently he did a three year stint with the *Guardian.* He was a Rajya Sabha member between 1972-78.

AJAZ ANWAR is currently working as Assistant Professor at the National College of Arts in Lahore. A gold medalist from Punjab University, Ajaz has subsequently worked as a scholar in Turkey and Italy, and taught art in Uganda. Founder and executive member of the Lahore Conservation Society, he has written many articles on the cultural environment of Lahore. As artist he has participated in many major exhibitions including holding ten solo shows.

SHYAM BENEGAL, among the leading film makers of the country, was one of the pioneers of the New Cinema in India. The subjects of his films are mainly centred on the contemporary Indian experience. Problems of development and social change appear on many levels as a continuing thread in practically all his films. His notable films include *Mammo, Junoon, Nishant, Mandi, Trikaal, Making of the Mahatma,* and his more recent *Sardari Begum* . Apart from feature films and documentaries, he has also done considerable work on Television.

GEETI SEN is one of India's leading art historians and critic, and is the Editor of the IIC Quarterly, and Head of Publications at the India International Centre. She has held teaching appointments in Art History at the Delhi School of Architecture, the J.J. School of Art, the National Gallery of Modern Art and Jawaharlal Nehru University, and has lectured widely in the USA, Canada and Germany. Her published books include *an Illustrated History of India for Chidren* (1974), *Paintings from the Akbar Nama* (1984) and *Image and Imagination: Five Contemporary Artists in India* (1996), and *Bindu: Space and Time in Raza's Vision*, (1997).